Russia in World History

Russia in World History

Selected Essays by

M. N. Pokrovskii

Edited, with an Introduction, by
Roman Szporluk
Translated by Roman and Mary Ann Szporluk

Ann Arbor   The University of Michigan Press

ISBN 0–472–08737–1
Library of Congress Catalog Card No. 75–107981
Published in the United States of America by
The University of Michigan Press and simultaneously
in Don Mills, Canada, by Longmans Canada Limited
Manufactured in the United States of America

Acknowledgments

The editor is pleased to express his gratitude to some of those who helped in the preparation of this book. The idea for such a volume first took shape in discussions with John W. Eadie and Elisabeth Case. Nancy Sandweiss was a precise and stimulating editor. My former teacher, Wayne S. Vucinich, supported this undertaking with friendly advice and criticism. For a number of years now, and against her better judgment I am afraid, my fellow translator has maintained an interest in Pokrovskii, and her share in the translation is only the more visible sign of her involvement with her husband's work.

Horace W. Dewey kindly helped to identify the sources of several quotations and advised on the translation of a particularly troublesome passage. Vartan Gregorian brought to my attention a source I might have otherwise missed. The anonymous consultants of the Press made valuable suggestions. To the University of Michigan Center for Russian and East European Studies and its immediate past director, Morris Bornstein, I am much indebted for the support of my research.

Ann Arbor, Michigan   R. S.

Translators' Note

The essays included in this volume originally were lectures, occasional pieces of journalism, or encyclopedia entries. It is unlikely that Pokrovskii spent very much time writing any of them. At his best, Pokrovskii was brilliant, witty, sarcastic; his argument was clear and logical; he could be both erudite and informal. At times, however, he was a careless stylist, and one finds passages in these essays which are awkward and difficult to render without rewriting. We have resisted interference with the texts and have tried to produce exact English versions which are faithful to Pokrovskii's meaning and form. We hoped that a more literal translation might introduce the reader who does not know Russian to the peculiarities of the manner in which Pokrovskii and many of his contemporaries thought and argued.

To our best knowledge we have translated Pokrovskii's texts in full, without any omissions; in only one case was an irrelevant point—clearly a digression—transferred to a footnote in order to preserve the flow of argument. Insofar as we know, none of the essays included here has previously appeared in English. Pokrovskii frequently quoted Lenin, Marx, and others. Wherever English translations of the quoted material were available, we have used them. In particular, we should like to acknowledge our use of passages from the translations of Lenin and Marx published by International Publishers, New York, and Progress Publishers, Moscow. In transliterating Russian names we have followed the practice of *Slavic Review*.

R. S.
M. A. S.

Contents

Introduction

M. N. Pokrovskii (1868–1932) is the best-known and most controversial Soviet historian. Although his reputation is primarily that of a militant—perhaps ruthless—polemicist, Pokrovskii was also a conscientious scholar who would not sacrifice intellectual honesty to the demands of propaganda. Even before the 1917 Revolution he had written a survey of Russian history from the Marxist point of view. Although there were other Marxist or Marxist-inspired writers in Russia in Pokrovskii's generation and he benefited from their works, his *History of Russia from the Earliest Times* was unquestionably an original achievement.

Marx's historical studies had concentrated on Western Europe, and Marx had warned his followers not to apply the West European scheme mechanically to other historical settings. Pokrovskii paid heed to Marx's warning. If the central problem of his work—Russia's transition from feudalism to capitalism—bore clear marks of Marxian inspiration, Pokrovskii's solution to this problem showed him to be a disciple with an original approach. Pokrovskii was particularly interested in recent and contemporary history, and in covering the last decades of the nineteenth century (after Marx had died) and the first ones of the twentieth, he had to be even more on his own.

After the October Revolution Pokrovskii continued to be preoccupied with the problem of transition, but he extended the scope of his inquiry by examining the origins and importance of the revolution in Russia. Despite his frequently expressed determination, Pokrovskii never completed his great work: neither of his histories of Russia (he wrote a second, popular work after the revolution) covered the immediate antecedents or the course of the October Revolution. In many of his articles, however, Pokrovskii discussed this subject as well as revised his old views on the more distant periods of Russian history. Some of these articles have been collected in this volume.

Although Pokrovskii's books on Russian history were first published in English over thirty years ago, this is the first English-language collection of his historical essays and the first book in English to present Pokrovskii's interpretation of Russian history up to and including the October Revolution of 1917. Pokrovskii locates Russia in world history, shows in what respects it was similar to other countries, and identifies the main forces and events that gave Russia its unique character. Two problems stand out as the leading themes of the book: *Russia's transition from feudalism to capitalism* and the *origins and historical importance of the revolution in Russia.*

Pokrovskii did not have a uniform view of the revolution and its meaning in Russian and world history. After 1917 there were antinomies in his historical views (they are noted in this introduction) which Pokrovskii never resolved. This volume, it is hoped, will demonstrate the continuity in Pokrovskii's outlook as well as record the new and sometimes contradictory elements which appeared in his thought after 1917.

Following the October Revolution (in which he had actively participated) Pokrovskii enjoyed a singular position as "the leader of the historical front," but his views were a subject of controversy among Communist scholars and ideologists. This was a time when there was still much discussion in Russia, and when scholars and artists were trying to reach the uneducated, often illiterate, peasants and workers through posters, theatrical plays on historical subjects with mass audience participation, cinema, and educational experiments. In Pokrovskii one may find over-simplified generalizations of a popularizer side by side with erudite insights of a scholar.

In the mid-1930's, Pokrovskii was summarily pronounced an "anti-Marxist," and all his works were suppressed. Stalin's death has brought a slow and limited rehabilitation of Pokrovskii: even now many of his articles, including most of those assembled here, remain unavailable in the U.S.S.R. This volume, then, besides presenting an original interpretation of Russian history, is also a document on the intellectual climate of Russia in the 1920's and early 1930's before Stalin established his new ideological orthodoxy.

Biographical Sketch

The Early Years
Mikhail Nikolaevich Pokrovskii was born on August 29, 1868, in Moscow. He was the son of an official and belonged legally to the estate of the nobility. Pokrovskii attended a classical *gimnaziia* (high school in which Greek and Latin were the main subjects), from which he was graduated with a gold medal, and then studied history at Moscow University (1887–91). Pokrovskii's most important university teachers were the distinguished historian of Russia, Vasilii Kliuchevskii, and the authority on West-European feudalism, Paul Vinogradov.

Little is known about Pokrovskii's political beliefs before 1905 other than what he himself has disclosed. As he recalled many years later, he "stood quite far" from the working-class movement; rather, he participated in the "Union of Liberation," a liberal group with a constitutionalist program. (The Union of Liberation was the immediate predecessor of the Constitutional-Democratic party, the *kadety*.) Lenin's emigré revolutionary journal, *The Spark (Iskra)*, was not reaching him in the early 1900's, Pokrovskii further recalled, but the bourgeois-democratic and reformist *Liberation (Osvobozhdenie)*, also published abroad, "was arriving regularly."[1] Many years later Pokrovskii described his pre-1905 period as one of "democratic illusions and economic materialism." He said that it had been perfectly compatible for one who held an economic interpretation of history to have collaborated with the bourgeois democrats in politics.[2] Pokrovskii thought that his early inclination toward economic materialism had resulted from his upbringing in "the petty bourgeois milieu, the burgher milieu"; for "nowhere else are the economic motives of human activity so clear." He attributed his radical democratic opinions to an early hatred of bourgeois liberalism. As a high school student, Pokrovskii could not understand how a person (his father?) could censure autocracy in private and then on state holidays don a uniform "with a ribbon and star."[3]

At the university, Pokrovskii wrote in an unpublished autobiography, "besides history I studied philosophy a great deal and very little political economy; I knew Marx only from hearsay. Nonetheless, while still an undergraduate I developed independently my own view of history which was largely materialistic though nondialectical—that is, without revolution and class struggle."[4]

Pokrovskii's interest in philosophy was reflected in his earliest writings, which focused on broad historical interpretation. He contributed eight chapters to Vinogradov's edition of readings on the history of the Middle Ages[5] and a chapter to a book of readings designed for study at home. Two important essays from this period appeared in symposia dealing with subjects of wide public interest; in both volumes Pokrovskii's name stood next to some of the most distinguished names in Russian scholarship and liberal public opinion.[6]

After graduation Pokrovskii did not hold a regular university appointment. He taught in secondary schools, extension courses, and at the "Higher Pedagogical Courses for Women." Later, during the revolution of 1905–7, he also taught industrial workers in evening classes. On the basis of his lectures for workers he wrote a pamphlet *Economic Materialism* in which he advocated revolutionary historical materialism and criticized passive reliance on the "objective" economic-historical forces, an outlook commonly identified with economic materialism. In those years Pokrovskii became a regular contributor to both legal and illegal revolutionary periodicals. In 1905 he joined the Bolshevik faction of the Russian Social-Democratic Workers party. On behalf of the latter he participated in the London party congress of 1907.

During and under the impact of the revolutionary events of 1905, Pokrovskii's political outlook changed. Before the revolution he had been a "bourgeois democrat"; when it was over, he had become a Bolshevik. The class struggle was transformed from theory to a fact of life: Pokrovskii met proletarians; he lectured at secret or semilegal gatherings; he wrote articles on current topics in the social democratic papers. "My convictions, sincere and scientific, but sharply democratic, drove me into the revolution. I joined the only revolutionary party there was—the Bolsheviks." [7]

Even before the revolutionary outbreak, in the summer of 1905, Pokrovskii had visited Lenin in Geneva. "Lenin spoke almost exclusively on the subject of armed uprising. . . . I had just come from Russia, immediately after the attempt . . . to organize a general strike in Moscow had failed. What utopians these leaders abroad are, I kept saying on my way from the meeting. . . . You can't even stir a worker to strike, and here he is saying something about—an armed uprising." Yet back in Moscow, by September, Pokrovskii found himself in the midst of a street clash between a crowd and a group of Cossacks. "And a month later, in October, I was concluding my 'criminal lectures' . . . with the cry: Long live an armed uprising! . . . two months later . . . came the December barricades." [8]

Pokrovskii in Exile
The reaction following the defeat of the revolution forced Pokrovskii to flee, first to Finland and then to France. He lived in France from 1908 until the summer of 1917, except for short periods spent in Italy. While in exile, Pokrovskii continued writing both on historical topics and on current issues. A major Moscow publisher commissioned Pokrovskii to write an interpretative history of Russia in several volumes. The royalty was high enough to secure comfortable living conditions for Pokrovskii and his family in Paris. Pokrovskii fulfilled

his obligations by sending to Moscow at regular intervals chapters of what was appearing in installments as the *History of Russia from the Earliest Times* (ten parts in five volumes, 1910–13).[9] The work was a cooperative effort to some extent: N. M. Nikolskii wrote the chapters on religion and church, and V. N. Storozhev provided "documentary supplements" and numerous illustrations. (In its definitive form, from the 1920 edition on, the *History* was exclusively the work of Pokrovskii and consisted of four volumes instead of the original five.)

The reading public of tsarist Russia never received the full text of the *History of Russia*. The copies of volume V (part 9 and 10) were seized by the police and then, following a court order, destroyed. The Moscow Court found it to contain many "tendentious descriptions of historical events" and to give a "negative interpretation" to the activities of the late rulers of Russia. (It displayed "insolent lack of respect for the supreme authority" and insulted in particular "the memory of the late reigning grandfather of the reigning Emperor [i.e., Alexander II].") Book 10 (part 2 of volume V), in the Court's opinion, expressed "sympathy for the revolutionaries" and contained a "summons to terror to overthrow the state system existing in Russia."[10]

The Moscow Court exaggerated when it saw a "summons to terror" in Pokrovskii's book. But it was unquestionably right when it recognized the revolutionary challenge which the work posed. The failure of the revolution in 1905 had prompted Pokrovskii to abandon his expectations that Russia would follow the West politically and socially; he concluded (as he recalled later in 1924) that "the world has passed from the period of bourgeois revolutions—the future revolution can only be socialist." This belief was reinforced by his experience in France, "the first democracy of Europe," where he completely lost his "democratic illusions." The pettiness of the political ideals of the bourgeoisie even led him to an "anti-democratic reaction."[11]

During his period of exile Pokrovskii's views about the prospects for a social revolution in Russia were in opposition to Lenin's belief that Russia had yet to complete the bourgeois democratic revolution. Lenin rejected Pokrovskii's idea that "every social class makes its own revolution." Lenin thought that the proletariat ought to participate in the bourgeois revolution as fully as possible, thereby establishing preconditions for the transition to the next, socialist revolution.

Pokrovskii also disagreed with Lenin about the immediate prospects of the revolutionary movement. Lenin expected that the defeat of the revolution would be followed by a fairly long period of reaction and relative peace; he therefore urged his followers to take full advantage of the limited opportunities that were available for carrying out revolutionary work legally. For example, he recommended Bolshevik participation in the Russian quasi-parliament (*Duma*), in activities in workers' educational, cultural, and insurance societies, and in publishing. (All this was to be done without giving up the conspiratorial party work.) Pokrovskii was one of those who expected a new revolution to come very soon and viewed Lenin's "Dumizm" with scorn. In a talk with Lenin (he later recalled), he expressed fear that Lenin's tactic "would drive the Russian workers away from revolution, to Bernsteinism."[12] Lenin's assurances that Russian history "absolutely guaranteed" that the Russian worker would remain revolutionary did not satisfy Pokrovskii, and he broke with Lenin for several years. He joined the *Vpered* Group, whose members largely shared his own views on the strategy and tactic of the proletarian revolution, and participated in their various undertakings (he wrote for the collection of articles published by the *Vpered* Group and taught in its "party schools" at Capri and Bologna).

Whatever Lenin may have thought about Pokrovskii's scholarship, he was unflattering about Pokrovskii's politics. When Lenin's associate, A. I. Rykov, wrote to Lenin about Pokrovskii's expected break with the *Vperedists,* Lenin warned Rykov not to take the matter too seriously: after all, Pokrovskii was "a high school teacher, a philistine, an old woman (*baba*)— but not a politician."[13] Lenin's judgment may have been too harsh, but the fact remains that Pokrovskii's important work in the years before the revolution was not in politics but in writing history.

After the 1917 Revolution

Pokrovskii returned to Russia in August, 1917, and in the following month was formally readmitted to the Bolshevik party. He wrote for and edited the newspaper of the Moscow Soviet and on November 8 was appointed Commissar for Foreign Affairs of the Moscow Soviet. A week later he became its chairman. In the elections to the Constituent Assembly which took place after the Bolshevik takeover Pokrovskii ran as a Bolshevik candidate and was elected a deputy. In March, 1918, Pokrovskii was appointed chairman of the Moscow regional *Sovnarkom* (and remained in this post until the *Sovnarkom* was dissolved in May). He was a member of the Russian delegation at the Brest Litovsk peace negotiations with the Central Powers. Like the chief delegate Trotsky, he was against concluding peace and joined the "Left Opposition," whose leaders included Bukharin. After the Central Committee had voted to accept the German ultimatum, he later recalled, "I was exasperated to such an extent that I lacked the spirit to go up to Lenin . . . and greet him." Pokrovskii felt that something "morally horrible beyond the limits of belief" had happened. Later he understood that Lenin had been right: the masses did not and would not fight.

> I often quarrelled with him about practical matters, got into a mess each time, and after this operation was repeated about seven times, I stopped arguing and submitted to Il'ich even when logic was telling me you must not act that way—but, I thought, he understands better. He sees three *arshin* deep in the ground and I cannot.[14]

From May, 1918, until his death, Pokrovskii was a deputy People's Commissar of Education of the RSFSR and helped to prepare many of the education reforms of those years. He presided over the Learned Council under the Commissariat of Education. In 1921, when he was appointed chairman of the "Academic Center," Pokrovskii was placed at the head of an organ that administered all academic institutions in the Republic, and his leadership and advice were highly valued by Lenin.[15]

Pokrovskii was instrumental in the establishment of several distinctly Soviet educational and academic bodies. He organized the "workers' faculties" (*rabfaki*), the preparatory courses which enabled proletarians to enter college without having passed regular secondary school. (The *rabfak* attached to First Moscow State University was named after Pokrovskii.) The Institute of Red Professors (IKP) was something like a graduate school; it trained historians, philosophers, economists, jurists, and natural scientists. Pokrovskii became its first *rektor* (1921) and stayed in that position for several years. Finally, Pokrovskii was one of the founders and first president of the Socialist Academy, soon renamed Communist Academy, a rival to the old Russian Academy of Sciences. Pokrovskii also helped to establish, and for a time was the president of, the Russian Association of Social Science Research Institutes (RANION) which provided a working place for the non-Marxist scholars. He conducted seminars at the IKP and RANION, held a chair at the Sverdlov "Communist University" (for party agitators and propagandists), was a visiting lecturer at many other establishments, and—very typically—lectured at various training courses for provincial party functionaries. A. L. Sidorov, who had been a student and lecturer at the IKP, recalled that Pokrovskii highly valued independence of judgment and "never edited his disciples in the way that became common later." "He gave everyone an opportunity to express his own point of view and noted his own agreement or disagreement in the preface." [16]

In 1925 Pokrovskii became the first president of the Society of Marxist Historians and later also editor of its journal *Istorik-marksist*. Pokrovskii achieved his highest party position in 1930 when he was elected a member of the presidium of the Central Control Commission. (By that time he was already greatly incapacitated by cancer which had been first diagnosed in 1925.) He was also a member of the All-Union and the All-Russian Central Executive Committees. In 1928 Pokrovskii traveled with a group of Soviet scholars to Berlin for the Soviet-German Historical Week and to the International Historical Congress in Oslo. On each occasion he presented a paper on

Russian absolutism. In 1929, Pokrovskii was elected to the U.S.S.R. Academy of Sciences.

Pokrovskii organized and headed the Central State Archives (*Tsentrarkhiv*) of the RSFSR and edited its official publication, *Krasnyi Arkhiv*. This work was highly praised by many "bourgeois" historians abroad (e.g., Professor Otto Hoetzsch).[17] The material made known by *Krasnyi Arkhiv* included documents on the foreign policies of the tsarist and Provisional government and on the revolutionary movements and political parties in Russia. Pokrovskii also organized the publication of collections of documents devoted to problems such as the Pugachev rebellion, the Decembrists, the revolution of 1905, and others. (Many of these documents were uncovered only after 1917, and they led Pokrovskii to revise some of his opinions.) He presided over the special committee for the publication of documents on "International Relations in the Age of Imperialism." Professor Bernadotte E. Schmitt, in a review of the first five volumes of its German edition, noted that the Soviet editors did not allow "their political sentiments to affect their historical scholarship," and concluded that the Soviet commission deserved "high praise for issuing so scientific a publication."[18]

In the 1920's Pokrovskii wrote many articles and edited collections of essays on various non-Marxist historians: Karamzin, Kavelin, Chicherin, Solov'ev, Shchapov, Kostomarov, Kliuchevskii, Hrushevs'kyi, and Miliukov; he tried to demonstrate the reflection of their political views in scholarly writings. Pokrovskii argued that some Marxist writers, such as Plekhanov and Trotsky, had not escaped the ideological influence of bourgeois theories.[19] During this period—a decade marked by much public debate—Pokrovskii's historical interpretation was the subject of lively controversy. Pokrovskii engaged in numerous polemics, the most famous of which was with Trotsky.

Because he occupied so many official posts and because his language in polemical articles was sharp and bitter, Pokrovskii has often been held responsible for the persecution of non-Bolshevik scholars, historians in particular, immediately after the revolution and also during the purges of 1929–31. But obviously more needs to be known before one can safely pass judgment. It was Pokrovskii who had initiated and directed RANION, an organization specifically designed for the bourgeois scholars. In 1921 he proposed to Lenin that a number of prominent Mensheviks, including Martov and Sukhanov, be given academic posts at Moscow University. (The text of Pokrovskii's proposal is not available, but Lenin's reply gently turning it down and suggesting that the matter had better be left to the Politbureau has been included in Lenin's *Complete Works*.)[20] In an article published in 1928 Pokrovskii credited the bourgeois scholars writing in the U.S.S.R. after 1917 with some successes. He said he was in favor of allowing them to write and publish in the U.S.S.R., although he opposed their ideology. It would be harmful to give Marxist literature a monopoly; "being a reflection of the class struggle, a social science becomes stronger precisely in the struggle."[21]

Some of the bourgeois historians against whom Pokrovskii had written (for example, Tarle and Platonov) were arrested in 1929–31. But his critical articles alone are hardly sufficient for holding Pokrovskii responsible. Violent tone in debate was an old revolutionary tradition, not a unique feature of Pokrovskii's writing. It is doubtful whether Pokrovskii's critical reviews or speeches were needed to inspire Stalin or the secret police in their actions.

Pokrovskii himself was not very safe at that time. By 1929 or so, as Professor Shteppa has written, "the crisis of orthodox Marxism and the omens of the downfall of Pokrovskii personally and of his school had already appeared."[22]

The arrests of bourgeois historians had hardly ended when a new wave of the purge came late in 1931 and included many persons associated with Pokrovskii. O. D. Sokolov, Soviet author of many valuable articles on Pokrovskii, noted that Stalin showed particular hostility toward scholars who did not speak about his allegedly "exceptional role in the development of the social sciences"; and Pokrovskii was one such scholar. Clearly suggesting that Stalin began an anti-Pokrovskii campaign about two years before the latter's death, Sokolov claimed that Kaganovich, a Central Committee secretary and Stalin's close associate, had himself appointed to the presidium of the

Communist Academy and used his position there to create "an atmosphere of slander, duplicity, and intrigues . . . against Pokrovskii." Pokrovskii tried to fight back, and sent a memorandum in his defense to the "Secretaries of the Central Committee and to the Chairman of the *Sovnarkom*." But "Pokrovskii's memorandum changed nothing. It was not published. The baiting continued."[23]

Toward the end of his life some politically inspired attacks on Pokrovskii appeared in a party history book edited by E. Iaroslavskii. Pokrovskii refuted the charges made against him, claiming the volume's anonymous collaborators had distorted his views and created imaginary differences between him and Lenin. Pokrovskii also defended his practice of quoting non-Bolsheviks when they expressed opinions similar to his own.

"So we, the Old Bolsheviks of those days, considered ourselves obliged to do . . . . If our opponent was right about anything, we stressed the fact." Pokrovskii recalled that at times Lenin had expressed preference for the views held by non-Marxists rather than those of Marxists. With sorrow, he noted that "the mores and rules of the Old Bolsheviks" were being disregarded by his anonymous critics, to whom Pokrovskii was simply a "heretic" who did not deserve to be talked to.[24] Pokrovskii's reply to his detractors reached the office of *Istorik-marksist* in November, 1931. He did not live to see it in print; on April 10, 1932, he died in the Kremlin hospital.

Although he had found himself in political difficulties in the early 1930's, Pokrovskii remained to the end a publicly recognized leader of the "historical front." He was given a state funeral attended by high party and state leaders including Stalin. However, as later events would bear out, Pokrovskii's posthumous status was far from secure.

What Is History?

Before reviewing Pokrovskii's interpretation of Russian history as res gestae, it may be useful to summarize briefly what he thought about history as an *intellectual activity*. Was it a *science* or a form of *ideology*? The question of "what is history?"

should be clearly separated from another question with which Pokrovskii was also much concerned: "What kind of history should be taught to children in school, and how?"

Since much of the criticism of Pokrovskii arose from a confusion of these two questions, one should note that Pokrovskii did not regard his own histories of Russia as suitable for children. If Pokrovskii did not give a satisfactory answer to the latter question, he was very emphatic as to what should be avoided. In 1927 he noted that "some educators" were "rejoicing" that in history textbooks "there will once again be ministers, reformers, etc." Pokrovskii was sure that "this kind of history will never be taught again."[25] He had serious doubts whether any kind of "descriptive history" would do. Even if one changed the content of such a course, it would still remain very similar to the old.

> . . . Formerly there were holy tsars, ministers and philan-thropists. Today we have great rebels, revolutionaries and socialists. . . . In a sense this is progress. It is better that children learn to understand the Pugachev rebellion than the terrible *Nakaz* of Catherine II. That is better, of course. But it was not necessary to spill so much blood to achieve such petty results.[26]

What Pokrovskii wanted was a new *kind* of history; it was not enough merely to recast the old heroes into villains (the tsars and generals) and the old villains into heroes (rebels and revolutionaries). What was to be done? One of the ways toward a new history was to make the subject more sociological and less a story of great men. Another, to show that one's own country was not the center of world history. If Russia influenced the lives of other countries, so other countries (and forces transcending the limits of individual countries) influenced the course of events in Russia. Besides noting the causal interrelation of Russia and the outside world, Pokrovskii also showed that even those traits or events in Russia that seemed quite unique or "national" were explainable scientifically: other countries had analogous events or traits when they were in comparable stages of *their* history.

But it would be quite misleading to think that Pokrovskii's own writings completely lacked "human touch." About Peter the Great—"the most active, most gifted and altogether the most remarkable of the Romanovs"—Pokrovskii wrote:

> Peter, whom fawning historians have called the Great, locked his wife up in a convent so as to be able to marry Catherine, the former servant of a Lutheran pastor in Esthonia. He personally supervised the torturing of his son Alexis, and after that ordered him to be secretly killed in a cell of the fortress of St. Petersburg. We have already spoken of the way in which he suppressed a mutiny. He died (1725) from the consequences of syphilis, after having transmitted it to his wife. . . . [27]

Pokrovskii did not think that Peter was an exception. "Nowhere, except perhaps in the criminal division of a convict prison, is one likely to find people burdened with so many sins as were the 'most pious and autocratic' Emperors and Empresses of Russia."[28] However, in writing about individuals Pokrovskii did not limit himself simply to exposing their crimes.

The reader of Pokrovskii's articles on Lenin (chapters XI and XII) will see that Pokrovskii did not think only "economic forces" mattered in history. Lenin, Pokrovskii wrote, took responsibility for "steps on which hung the fate not only of his own person or of his party, but that of the whole country and to some extent of the world revolution." Pokrovskii compared Lenin's genius—which he did not explain away "sociologically" —with great leaders of the past (Calvin, Cromwell, Robespierre, Napoleon) and concluded that Lenin was superior.

Pokrovskii's view of the role of the individual in history may be elucidated by reference to his distinction between historical studies and sociology. He thought that "in sociology we may proceed more or less directly from economics" because sociology "covers vast periods in the history of large nations." In history, on the other hand, "every particular moment is important." Economics or sociology might be decisive in the "ultimate resort," but there were important elements that sociology (and even less economics) could not unveil. Accidents did, in fact, play a role in history; among these accidents Pokrovskii included the character of individual leaders.[29]

If the science of history was not reducible to that of sociology, it was because man's political and intellectual life was not a mere by-product of his economic-social relations. Pokrovskii did not believe that the individual's political attitude was to be attributed exclusively to his class origin; nor did he believe that the holders of power were necessarily *motivated* in their actions by the interest of one or another social class. It was enough for him that every political action, however subjectively motivated, inevitably favored one or another of the conflicting classes.

Pokrovskii thought that history was not only a science, but also an ideology. One of the tasks of the Marxist historians, he wrote, was to picture "the development of historical ideology as a part of the development of ideology in general." Both before and particularly after 1917 Pokrovskii made many efforts to discover ideology and politics behind the cover of "objective scholarship." At the same time he recognized the achievements of non-Marxist scholars. "He who would throw Solov'ev or Kliuchevskii under the table because they are not Marxists would only prove himself to be an extraordinary fool." Pokrovskii went even so far as to say that when a non-Marxist historian "conscientiously collects the facts, 'historical dialectic' appears in his work independently of his will and consciousness." Any historian who worked seriously enough on a historical topic would reach historical materialism. Even Machiavelli had made it: "read 'History of Florence'—that's a Marxist book; class struggle runs through the whole book. It almost does not require a translation into Marxist language; it already is Marxist."

Pokrovskii claimed that the establishment of a "scientific history" of nineteenth-century Russia was primarily due to the "Marxist historians in the broadest meaning of the term." He included among them Peter Struve for his study of serfdom and Michael Tugan-Baranovskii for his history of the Russian factory. (Both were Pokrovskii's contemporaries and in their youth shared his ideas in many respects.) But he also recognized as important the contributions by the populists Semevskii and Bogucharskii, the military historian Shil'der, and the Berlin professor Schiemann who gave "fair" and "fresh" material on Nicholas I "in the worst Black-Hundred light one can imagine."

Thus, good history was *not only* ideology, and Pokrovskii appealed to his proletarian students at the Institute of Red Professors to learn what every historian needed to know: "to work on documents, to approach critically the sources, to analyze, etc." The young Marxist scholars had to master "the technique" and only *after* they did it would they be "stronger than the old bourgeois generations" of scholars. A superiority in the theory of history alone did not suffice.

Pokrovskii noted that "the most political of all existing sciences" had been also regarded, by Marx and Engels, as "the only" science. "History is the politics of the past without which it is impossible to understand the politics of the present"; the existing conditions could not be understood unless one examined their historical roots. In historical analysis, a form of "uniting theory with practice," peculiar to history, was achieved.[30]

Pokrovskii believed that Marxism was "an objective scientific theory," and not "a simple reflection of reality through the prism of guild-interests of the working class." He explained that he was using the term "Marxist ideology" only because "we have got accustomed to this senseless expression." "Marx and Engels understood by ideology that more or less false and illusory picture which one or another social class was elaborating for itself exclusively under the influence of its class interest."[31] Thus, Pokrovskii distinguished between the "more or less false" ideologies of various classes, including the proletariat, and the real science of history and society.

The Scheme of Russian History

There is no room here to summarize Pokrovskii's *History of Russia from the Earliest Times*.[32] It is important, however, to identify the *types of society* which he used as a foundation for judging progress or retrogression in concrete historical situations and for locating Russia's standing in the context of world history. His typology did not employ the economic element only: it combined social and political features as well. What were, then, the types of society Russia had known in its thousand-year history?

Chronologically the first social type known in Russia, according to Pokrovskii, was the *clan* or *large family*. Its primitive collective system of production was combined with communal property and patriarchal authority. (Pokrovskii thought that elements of that system, predominant in the ninth century, survived in the more backward areas of Russia up to modern times.) The second type, *feudalism*, was characterized by small-scale, individual agricultural production combined with the "extra-economic" coercion of the peasantry by the military class of landlords (that is, peasants were coerced physically and legally to deliver goods to their masters without receiving reciprocal payments by the latter). Unlike the clan, where there was no class differentiation, feudalism divided men into the exploited producers and the ruling and exploiting lords. Both economic systems were "natural," however; they produced for their own subsistence and not for sale. When the subsistence economy broke down and commerce appeared, the feudal system began to disintegrate. Its disintegration was marked by the rise of towns and of new social classes (merchants and artisans) and eventually by the appearance of international trade. This development was conditioned by the emancipation of the peasants from their subjection to lords. In the transition from feudalism to *modern (or industrial) capitalism* there was a period when some capitalist forms such as large-scale trade and production of commodities intended for sale coexisted with the surviving elements of feudal peasant bondage. Pokrovskii called this *merchant* or *commercial capitalism*, which he regarded as a lower stage of capitalism. This socioeconomic transitional system had a corresponding form of government, *absolute monarchy*, which was itself an active participant in and organizer of *primitive capitalist accumulation*. The "transition period" from feudalism to capitalism in Russia, as Pokrovskii understood it, lasted from Ivan IV to 1861, and in some respects to 1905–17. It ended when it was no longer necessary for the state to employ coercion in economic activities and when economic necessity sufficed to compel the legally free but propertyless workers to sell their labor for wages. A state based on the rule of law, a *Rechtsstaat,* was the typical political form that corresponded to the economic and social system of industrial capitalism.

Of course, Pokrovskii did not write history as a succession of "social types." He distinguished major historical periods or epochs—but in analyzing them he employed the concept of social types. Any period of Russian—or another country's—history could be "located" on the scale of social types. However, Pokrovskii did not regard history as simply a movement of constant advance to higher and higher forms. History was a result of many counteracting forces, and it knew periods of retrogression as well as progress.

Pokrovskii thought that until the later part of the sixteenth century Russia was undergoing a process of historical evolution analogous to that of Western Europe. In his *History* he tried to explain why in the sixteenth century Russia had switched from the European path: while the peasants in the West had become free in the late Middle Ages, in Russia their subjection to landlords became even stronger after the sixteenth century. According to Pokrovskii, both internal and external factors contributed to this turn of events, among them the success of capitalism in the West. The West, for whom Russia became a supplier of agricultural produce and raw materials, contributed, paradoxically, to preserving the socioeconomic system of Russia on the pre-"industrial-capitalist" stage. The Russian landlords, who were forcing the peasants to give them part of their produce and to work on their lands without pay, were able to sell grain and other agricultural products *abroad* and thus did not need to be concerned with the establishment of a domestic market. Instead of a modern society, a partially capitalist and partially feudal system was retained in Russia for a long time.

To the extent that it protected the traditional landlord rule over the peasants, Russian absolutism was "feudal." Inasmuch as it promoted industries and capitalism, the Russian absolutist state was "capitalist."

Russia, the West and the East

According to Pokrovskii, the tsarist state also had a dual nature in respect to foreign affairs. In relation to Western Europe (and even the Balkans) Russia was a backward, "feudal" state, but to the East it was a force which brought capitalism, albeit a primitive variety. In its latter role modern Russia could be compared to the Western powers at an earlier stage of their history. Pokrovskii first formulated this view in his articles written for the Granat *History of Russia in the Nineteenth Century;*[33] he restated his position more clearly after 1917.

Pokrovskii admitted that "primitive accumulation" in Muscovy did not reach the level of Western nations; there had been "no Fuggers or Medici." He insisted, however, that in Muscovy there had been "analogous phenomena," even if more primitive. For this reason, the rise of autocracy in Russia should be attributed to these economic phenomena rather than, as Trotsky thought, to the allegedly primitive and backward character of the Russian economy. Pokrovskii admitted that it was the contact with Western Europe that had strongly stimulated the development of Russian commercial capitalism. Nevertheless, he said Russia would have become a purely colonial country (not even similar to India, for India did have an accumulation of her own, but to "central Africa") had there been no native accumulation before the contacts with the West began. Pokrovskii believed—indeed he said this was one of his "heresies"—that the development of Russia was, "in its type, one of a colonial country," but he had to refrain from going too far in that direction. "After all, Russia did not become a downright colony," while if it had been as backward as Trotsky claimed, it should have become one.[34]

Pokrovskii quoted certain passages from *Capital* and argued that what Marx had to say about Spain, Portugal, Holland, and England was applicable to Russia:

The discovery of gold and silver in America [Marx wrote], the extirpation, enslavement and entombment in mines of the aboriginal population, the beginning of the conquest and looting of the East Indies, the turning of Africa into a warren for the commercial hunting of black-skins, signalized the rosy dawn of the era of capitalist production. These idyllic proceedings are the chief momenta of primitive accumulation . . . .

The different momenta of primitive accumulation distribute themselves now more or less in chronological order, particularly over Spain, Portugal, Holland, France, and England. In England at the end of the 17th century, they arrive at a systematical combination, embracing the colonies, the national debt, the modern mode of taxation, and the protectionist system. These methods depend in part on brute force, e.g., the colonial system. *But they all employ the power of the State, the concentrated and organised force of society,* to hasten, hot-house fashion, the process of transformation of the feudal mode of production into the capitalist mode, and to shorten the transition. Force is the midwife of every old society pregnant with a new one. It is itself an economic power.[35]

Following Marx's general thesis, Pokrovskii concluded that one could speak of Russia's colonies (which included her "Siberian taiga and North-Russian marshes") just as one did of the countries with a hot climate and colored populations.[36] Pokrovskii argued, then, that although Russia resembled a semicolony in relation to the West, it acted as a colonial power in relation to its Eastern neighbors.

This interpretation underlies the two essays in this collection that were written before 1917: "Russian Imperialism in the Past and Present" (1914), and "Historic Mission" (1915). Pokrovskii did not conclude his review of Russia's "Historic Mission" by claiming that Russian policies were an inevitable consequence of economic causes (which might have been expected had he been an "economic materialist"). On the contrary, Pokrovskii argued that Russia lacked sufficient economic potential to accomplish her goal of establishing herself politically on the shores of the Bosphorus. "Political conquests last only when they consolidate an economic supremacy" which has been established earlier. But the Russians could sell their goods to their potential customer in Asia only "by driving him with a bayonet behind the Russian customs border." As in the postrevolutionary articles, so in these two earlier ones, Pokrovskii saw in Russian foreign expansion an attempt to avoid economic reforms and political liberalization at home. Mr. Struve, Pokrovskii said in 1914, would have liked Russia to act like a great power in world affairs and to be liberal at home: Pokrovskii thought that to demand both these things at the same time was as realistic as to expect of a plant that it would both "bloom with roses and bear tasty pears."

Pokrovskii also thought that the Russian rule in the European parts of the Empire (acquired in the eighteenth and nineteenth centuries) was of a colonial type, though it completely lacked those elements of progress that could be found in Central Asia. (This was because Russia's Western borderlands were more advanced than Russia proper.) The oppression of Poles, Latvians, Ukrainians, and worst of all, Jews, represented a colonial policy of the ruling landowners. He believed that the Russian government exported backwardness to the "borderlands" to preserve a reactionary and outdated system in Russia itself.

Capitalism in Russian History

In *Russian History in the Briefest Outline*,[37] the popular history which Pokrovskii wrote immediately after the 1917 Revolution, he attempted to prove that the real tsar who had ruled from Ivan the Terrible to Nicholas "the Last" was "Tsar Capital," first, merchant capital and then, industrial capital.[38] In the brief history Pokrovskii focused on the modern period of Russian history, beginning with the accession of the Romanov dynasty (1613). The Romanovs laid the foundations of a political order based on serfdom, officialdom, and a standing army. The machinery of the Romanov state, which took its final shape during the reign of Peter I, had been "created by a combination of two social forces, whose basic units were respectively the *squire's estate* and the *merchant's capital*." The state machine forced the peasant to part with his produce for the benefit of the squire and the large-scale merchant. Peter's fiscal and administrative reforms served the aims of primary accumulation in Russia, for "primary accumulation was the object served by the whole system, just as it was the one object of all Western Europe in the period from the sixteenth to the eighteenth century." In Russia this order survived much longer than in the West. Even after the so-called peasant emancipation of 1861:

> the machinery for extracting "surplus product" from the peasant was retained, only in a perfected form. Formerly, each landlord had to squeeze it out of the peasant by means of *barshchina* or *obrok* [labor rent or money rent]; now the task was taken over by the landlords' government who did it by means of taxation. . . . This is the real meaning of the famous "emancipation of the peasants together with the land."[39]

Pokrovskii stressed that many precapitalist social and economic institutions survived the reform of 1861. The peasants continued to be discriminated against in various ways. They were subject to special police and courts, they could not leave the village without permission, and so on. Only the agrarian reforms of Stolypin (1906–10) gave the "medieval forms of land tenure . . . a blow the like of which they had never received." Stolypin's aim was "to destroy the commune, to create in its place a solid class of kulak farmers and to transform the remaining mass of peasants into a reserve army of labor."[40] These reforms of Stolypin were in Pokrovskii's opinion extremely important: they removed the last obstacle that was blocking the growth of industrial capitalism in Russia.[41]

In the final volume of his *History of Russia*, Pokrovskii had questioned why Russian "large capital," a revolutionary force in the economy, was conservative in politics throughout the nineteenth century. He argued that the Russian urban bourgeoisie found it quite convenient to manage without a parliamentary or constitutional regime because the tsar's Ministry of Finance protected the industries very effectively. Also, Russian economic development depended to a very great extent on foreign credits and investments, and these were safe only if the government was stable. Had they become part of the opposition, the Russian merchants would have been cutting the bough on which they were seated. At the same time, however, foreign credits made the government more independent of the native bourgeoisie. Therein lay a profound difference between the West (where, for example in England, "the bourgeoisie held the government's purse") and Russia (where the government "held the purse of the bourgeoisie").

Moreover, the tsarist government, which was a feudal government of the nobles in its origin and class character, pursued protectionist policies which were detrimental to the economic interests of the nobles who wanted to buy industrial goods from abroad. (Foreign goods were lower priced and of better quality than those produced at home.) Accordingly, some of the nobles were economic liberals who favored free trade, and if *they* came to power, Russian industry would lose its protection. For this reason, too, Russian industrialists opposed the liberals and supported the tsar. As for the petty bourgeoisie (artisans, small shopkeepers, etc.), they were being swallowed up by the large industries. Thus this group, that "most reliable bulwark of the democratic revolution in the pre-capitalist West," was ineffective in Russia.

Another potential source of opposition to the tsar's government was the populist and socialist revolutionaries who spoke for the peasantry; however, they were primarily anti-capitalist and believed that Russia should go directly to socialism without passing through capitalism. Of course the capitalists opposed this position, which gave them yet another reason to continue their support of the tsar.

The peasantry itself was not a revolutionary force, Pokrovskii believed. This was because the 1861 reform had failed to emancipate the peasants fully, preserving many obsolete feudal institutions as well as a primitive and reactionary outlook. Thus, the peasant revolt against the landlords in 1905 did not

have a revolutionary character; it was reactionary or restora-
tional. Rather than seeking progressive social change, the peasants were looking back to an idealized, mythic past.

It followed that the proletariat was the only truly progressive class.[42]

Antinomies of Revolution

Pokrovskii's historical prophecy came true in 1917 when first
tsarism and then the bourgeoisie were overthrown. But this
prophecy was fulfilled only partially: Pokrovskii, like the other
Bolsheviks, had expected that the Russian revolution would be
a link in the international revolutionary upheaval. In his
writings after 1917 he attempted to explain the origins and
nature of the revolution both in the context of world history
and as a Russian phenomenon. One may distinguish several
conflicting themes in his reflections on the revolution. He saw
it as a proletarian revolution—and as a peasant revolt; as an
episode in the worldwide struggle of the workers—and as an
assertion of the national independence of Russia; as evidence
that Russia had reached the level of the advanced West—and
as the first successful rebellion of the non-Western world (comprising Russia as well as China and India). He recognized
Lenin's historical role as a leader of the world proletariat—and
compared him with Peter the Great, as a man who also tried
to modernize Russia in order to meet the challenge from
abroad. Finally, in his reflections on the Russian revolutionary
movement, Pokrovskii extended the concepts of "Bolshevism"
and "Menshevism"—a product of twentieth-century Russian
politics—far back into the nineteenth century. Rather than
denoting the two factions in Russian Marxian socialism, they
became for Pokrovskii synonyms of reformist and revolutionary
methods.

The Proletarian Revolution

In an essay written in 1921 (chapter X of this collection), Pokrovskii spoke of the Russian revolution as a part of the inter-

national proletarian revolution. The French railroad strike of 1910 and the strikes of the pre-1914 years in Germany, Britain, and Russia were all part of the general struggle of the proletariat. "World Bolshevism" was born in the half-decade before 1917. Against the united front of the proletariat there stood the united forces of the bourgeoisie (although war had divided the bourgeoisie into two groups: "the English-French-American" and the "Austrian-German"). A revolutionary outbreak could occur anywhere: why did it begin in Russia?

Pokrovskii suggested two specifically Russian circumstances to explain why the world revolution started in Russia. First, the bourgeoisie was internally split; and the issue of war and peace still further deepened the antagonism between "commercial capital" and "industrial capital." Second, the Russian proletariat was in a different position from that in the West. Pokrovskii thought that the Russian workers had nothing to gain from a victory of "their" side in war: the conquest of the Dardanelles (or of other places) by the tsar would not have improved the lot of the Russian worker. On the contrary, a radical domestic change, the extension of the home market, promised such an improvement. It could be achieved, for example, by increasing the peasant's share of land. In contrast, the workers of Western Europe could rightly expect that a victory by their side would bring benefits to them, too, and not only to "their" capitalists. Only a defeat on their own side, with the accompanying threat of a decline in wages, "raised the question of socialism." In other words, the Russian workers were actually revolutionary under any circumstance, the Western—only when threatened with a decline of their standard of living in consequence of a military defeat. Pokrovskii did not explain whether this conclusion was compatible with his argument on the international community of the workers' class interests and on "World Bolshevism."

Curiously enough, writing four years later (1925) on the revolution of 1905 (chapter IX) Pokrovskii stressed the historical originality of Russia and made no references, however general, to any wider "proletarian front." On the contrary, Pokrovskii noted those particular aspects of Russian history which suggested that Russia might have been superior to the West. In his pre-1914 writings Pokrovskii had argued that the Russian intelligentsia exhibited "excessive modesty" when it compared Russia of the 1900's with Central Europe of 1848 or even France of 1789. This "modesty," he said, ignored the presence of a class-conscious proletariat in Russia and its absence in the West in 1848 or 1789, and also Russia's progress in technology since 1848. After 1917 Pokrovskii went even further and suggested that the only Western revolution the Russians could learn anything from was the "Paris Commune" of 1871. He asserted that the Paris revolt of 1871 was "the single case where a revolution in Europe arose on roughly the same level of economic development as that at which Russia stood in the beginning of the twentieth century" (chapter IX). Since by the twentieth century Western Europe obviously had moved beyond the economic level it had been at in 1871, was Pokrovskii suggesting that the West had passed the stage at which "Russian-style" revolutions were possible? What conclusions was one to draw about the future of socialism in Western Europe? Alas, Pokrovskii did not elaborate on this idea and limited himself to a passing remark.

The presence of a proletariat in Russia made it possible, Pokrovskii also wrote, to prevent a repetition of the "Austrian tragicomedy" of 1848 in which nationality conflicts tore the revolutionary forces apart. Nationalist aspirations expressed themselves to some extent also in Russia during 1905–21, but in the end the Ukraine and Transcaucasia combined with Russia in forming a single Soviet Union. Pokrovskii argued that the existence of a network of railroads covering and binding all Russia made the preservation of the state unity possible. He did not explain why Austria-Hungary disintegrated in 1918, though the proletariat of Vienna or Budapest presumably was no less advanced than that of Moscow or St. Petersburg and the railroad network in Austria was surely denser than in Russia.

Perhaps Pokrovskii's next point does explain the Austrian "failure." Making a virtue of what before 1914 would have been regarded as a shortcoming, he said that Russia had an advantage over the West in that the Russians "were weak with

regard . . . to political concepts." Pokrovskii explained his
meaning with an example from 1907, when the workers, he
said, could not understand why the Constituent Assembly was
needed. The proletariat did not require "artificial expressions
of popular will" like parliament: that was a petty-bourgeois
idea, its origin explainable by the fact that the petty bourgeois
were isolated from each other in work and needed a symbol of
unity (parliament, king, or emperor). Pokrovskii took pride in
the neglect of this "formal aspect" which the Russian revolution displayed: the Bolsheviks did not care to think about a
constitution until after they had held power for some time, and
when they finally adopted one, it was because "some kind of
order" had to be established. He thought that their lack of
concern with the ways to implement the Bolshevik program
proved that the Russians were superior to the West. The
workers' lack of opposition to the Bolshevik dispersal of the
Constituent Assembly (1918) was another proof of their "realism." Pokrovskii thought that the Soviets of Workers Deputies
were a universally applicable contribution of the Russian revolution. (The obverse of this concept, automatic disenfranchise-
ment of those not engaged in productive work, was only subsequently formalized in the Soviet Constitution of 1918.) "Our
revolution has for the first time linked modern economy and
politics, ruthlessly shattering all those fetishes . . . of the old
petty-bourgeois democracy."

Pokrovskii concluded that peasants of India and China
were entering on the revolutionary course which Russia had
traversed. Their enemy was "the Western European bourgeoisie" that had earlier been "lending money to Nicholas II."

It seems that in this article Pokrovskii was moving toward
a "two-blocs" concept of revolution, in which the class conflict
of workers and capitalists within a single society is transferred
to the international plane, to be treated as a conflict between
"capitalist countries" or "the West," on the one hand, and
"socialist countries," or "the East," on the other.

The Peasant Revolution

The reference to the peasants of China and India following in
the steps of the Russian revolution was not accidental: in Po-

krovskii's view the October Revolution was not only a part of
the international proletarian revolution but also the final act
of the peasant revolution which he called the Russian "national revolution." The latter was completed when the peasants were given land. There existed, Pokrovskii said, a direct
link between "the sixteenth century" (the imposition of serfdom on the peasants) and 1917, when the Soviet government
confiscated landlords' property and gave land to the peasant.
Before 1917 Pokrovskii regarded the transformation of serfs
into legally free men (who were forced only by "economic
coercion" to work for large estate owners) as a part of the
process of transition from feudalism to capitalism, and thereby
a progressive step. He retained this view after 1917, but also
paid greater attention to the problem he had previously
neglected: how did the peasants react to the change in their
status?

Of course, Pokrovskii always knew that the peasants,
whether serfs or free men, hated their masters. However, as
noted earlier, before 1917 he wrote that the peasants opposed
their subjugation to the lords from the standpoint of an
idealized feudal order. After October, 1917, Pokrovskii gave
a new explanation to the peasant rebelliousness in Russia:
from the sixteenth century until 1917, he argued, Russian
peasants were struggling for the freedom to exist as independent producers. They had fought against enserfment (in the
sixteenth and seventeenth centuries) and the eventual "emancipation" that had deprived them of land (in the nineteenth
and twentieth centuries). They finally triumphed in 1917 when
"the parasite-landowner was crushed, the landlords' lands came
into the possession of the peasants, and a basis was finally found
for the native, natural peasant capitalism in Russia, about
which Lenin had spoken in 1905–1906."[43]

Tsarism and the Roots of Revolution

There is a certain suggestion of inevitability in Pokrovskii's
presentation of the history of absolutism, bureaucracy, and
bourgeoisie in Russia (the subject of the first three essays in this
anthology). They are shown as the forces that were moving

history forward. The two following essays ("The Revolutionary Movements of the Past" and "Tsarism and the Roots of the 1917 Revolution") cover the same ground from another vantage point. When Pokrovskii wrote about those who actively resisted and opposed the Establishment, he went back several centuries: the Russian revolution seems to have been truly permanent, having started virtually in 1605 during the "Time of Troubles." Thus, Russia was the most revolutionary country in Europe.

While the first three essays stress absolutism's role as a promoter of capitalism, the essay on tsarism and the roots of the Russian revolution treats it as the organized embodiment of the *dictatorship of feudal nobility*. ("Feudal" in this context means that the nobility retained control over the peasantry owing not only to its economic power as employer, but also to its *legally* privileged position.) Pokrovskii did not think that the nineteenth-century nobility had been homogeneous. It was split between the "planters," for whom the serfs were the equivalent of Negro slaves in America, and the "Manchesterists," who favored peasant emancipation (not for altruistic reasons of course: being "progressive," they needed *capital* for land improvements and wanted the peasants to provide it by paying for their land and liberty).[44]

Because of its feudal ancestry and nature, the tsarist regime was ultimately incompatible with "industrial capitalism," its active support of capitalist industry notwithstanding. It must be stressed that Pokrovskii used the term "industrial capitalism" broadly, to designate modern society, with its representative institutions, legal equality of all citizens, and rights of the individual. (For example, a highly industrialized state which discriminated against the Jews did not qualify as "industrial capitalist.") Legal discrimination and inequality of any sort were to Pokrovskii characteristic of a lower stage of development.

The growth of industrial capitalism, Pokrovskii further argued, gave rise to a social stratum that was its peculiar product and was uncompromisingly hostile to absolutism: the intelligentsia. Thus, there appeared to be three social groups in opposition to feudal absolutism: the peasantry, the intelligentsia, and the proletariat. Tsarism was successful in terrorizing the revolutionary intelligentsia (in the 1860's and 1880's), but the agrarian crisis—whose causes were international—accomplished what revolutionary propaganda had failed to achieve: it "stirred the peasant masses." The "proletarianization of the peasantry" at the end of the nineteenth century cleared the ground for the proletarian revolution. Eventually the two revolutionary currents, the urban working class and the peasantry, combined in a joint struggle that resulted in the overthrow both of the tsar's regime and of the bourgeoisie.

This "dual" interpretation of the revolution (proletarian-international and peasant-national) is open to some questions. Were the two revolutions compatible, and if not, how were the contradictions between their aims to be resolved? Did the Bolsheviks win power because they led the proletariat or chiefly because they managed to use the peasant revolt to their benefit? Was Russia unique in this combination of favorable circumstances—Pokrovskii clearly suggested that the West lacked at least some essential prerequisites—or was it the first revolutionary country, to be followed later by others in a like condition?

Lenin's Role

Perhaps Pokrovskii's reflections on the historical role of Lenin can help to answer some of these questions. According to Pokrovskii (see Chapter XI), besides being a great leader of the world proletariat Lenin was also a *Russian* revolutionary who brought the "Russian revolutionary movement" to its conclusion. As a Marxist, Pokrovskii had to attribute some *class* character to this revolutionary movement, and he described it as petty bourgeois. Did Pokrovskii believe Lenin had both "concluded" a petty-bourgeois revolution for the establishment of a free capitalist order (see above, his reference to October, 1917, as the conclusion of the peasant revolution) and led a proletarian revolution which could, of course, aim only at overthrowing capitalism?

Perhaps it will be possible to explain the seeming contradiction between these two roles of Lenin by making a comparison with yet another revolutionary. As early as 1919, Pokrovskii compared Lenin with Peter the Great. In an article entitled "History Is Repeating Itself," he claimed that it was legitimate to compare the two men, because "then as now the issue at stake was the fundamental transformation of the whole economic system of Russia." Two hundred years earlier, Pokrovskii continued, the question was raised whether Russia would manage to pass from a natural (self-sufficient) medieval economy to merchant capitalism. England, the Netherlands, France, and to some extent Germany and the Scandinavian countries had become merchant capitalist by then.

> In Russia this was not yet the case, and this accounted for her lagging behind the West. The question whether she could catch up with the West was the question of life and death for the economic independence of Russia. For merchant capital, having established itself firmly at home [in the West], was capturing underdeveloped countries and transforming them into its colonies.[45]

India and America had become the prey of the most powerful plunderers, while a relatively weaker power like Sweden engaged in wars of conquest with Muscovy. The struggle against Sweden for economic independence was "the pivot" of Muscovy's foreign policy in its last decades and that of Russia in the early imperial period (i.e., after 1721, when Peter assumed the title of Emperor of Russia). Peter's policies imposed a heavy burden on the people; his aim was merely to replace old exploiters with new ones who were more "European." Peter was also in conflict with the nobility, whom he controlled through his creation of a "bourgeois administration," and with the intelligentsia. The latter was hostile to Peter, as was the modern Russian intelligentsia to the Bolsheviks. Lenin and Trotsky were being called "anti-Christ" after 1917, as had been Peter in his time. But both Peter and Lenin were in the long run victorious: "The tale of the anti-Christ tsar was the funeral bell for pre-capitalist Russia. The tale about the Bolsheviks and 'devil disguised as Christ' is the funeral bell for pre-socialist Russia. History is repeating itself. . . ."[46]

Pokrovskii's article about Lenin and Peter is interesting for several reasons. First of all, nowhere in the article did he say that Lenin's revolution was part of an international proletarian revolution. On the contrary, Pokrovskii claimed that the Bolsheviks, like Peter in his time, were upholding Russia's national independence. Since in his books Pokrovskii had argued that Peter's reform had failed because Peter aimed to achieve more than was possible, one wonders if Pokrovskii expected the Bolsheviks to fail too. Some of his statements indicate that after October he thought so: "I do not know if anyone besides Il'ich expected we would survive for years. There were few men like him. Il'ich did count; in general he was going ten *verst* ahead of us." Pokrovskii also wrote that immediately after 1917 the Bolsheviks acted in a doctrinaire manner, disregarding historical traditions and overestimating the material capacities of their country[47]—and in this respect, too, they resembled Peter.

Bolshevism and Menshevism: Two Responses

In an article published in 1923, "The Roots of Bolshevism in Russian Soil," Pokrovskii argued that Russia was not the only country to defend its "economic independence" against the more advanced powers. Japan, China, India, and other countries of Asia belonged to the "huge complex of countries subject to the same law of historical development as Russia—the countries sentenced to Bolshevism by fate." At this time he did not speak about West European Bolshevism: West European socialism, which Pokrovskii called "Menshevik," would one day appear to have been a historical "episode," while the "Bolshevik type" would be the rule.[48]

Pokrovskii argued that those who interpreted "Bolshevik" to mean "maximalist" did so with some justification, inasmuch as Bolshevism "did not recognize compromises." One such "maximalist" (or "Bolshevik") program appeared in Russia as early as the 1820's when Colonel Pestel' postulated the abolition of autocracy and the nationalization of land. "This petty bourgeois in a colonel's uniform" was a Marxist "long before . . . Marx himself." Among those who were Bolsheviks before the appearance of Bolshevism (in the usual sense), Pokrovskii included radical, "maximalist" figures like Pestel', Karakozov, Tkachev, and Zaichnevskii. "Menshevism," on the other hand, was synonymous with moderate reform policies and "minimalist" projects.[49]

Pokrovskii spoke about Marxists before Marx and Bolsheviks before Lenin, thus disregarding the strict historical meaning of these terms. Perhaps this method may help to solve the apparent contradiction in Pokrovskii's thought between Lenin as both the concluder of the Russian (peasant) revolution and leader of the proletarian revolution. Pokrovskii's reference to Peter's historical role gives additional support to this interpretation.

One may infer that Lenin, the pre-Marxian revolutionaries of the nineteenth century, and Peter the Great, all shared a desire to reorganize Russia in a revolutionary way to make her capable of meeting the challenge from without. "Revolution" should be understood here as a radical attempt to rearrange a country's internal structure in order to "catch up" with the most advanced nations. If one looks at the matter in this way, the class identification of revolutionaries in different periods becomes less important, and even Peter might be seen as a "Bolshevik" of sorts (perhaps a "Bolshevik of the age of merchant capital"). And with "Menshevism" being synonymous with "reforms," perhaps Alexander II or even the Supreme Privy Council (the effective rulers under Catherine I and Peter II, 1726–30) could be called distant precursors of Lenin's moderate rivals in the socialist movement, the Mensheviks. In its historical importance Lenin's Bolshevik revolution did not contradict or oppose the petty-bourgeois revolution—it "transcended" it—which in the language of Marxism means reaching a higher level of development while retaining the contribution of the by-passed stage.

National Emancipation

Pokrovskii never drew such conclusions himself. But his reflections in "The Historical Importance of the October Revolution" (Chapter XIII of this collection), in particular his reasons

why the revolution would not be followed by "reaction," show
that he began to recognize the national factor as distinct from,
and independent of, class aspects of the 1917 revolution. He
claimed that even before 1914 Russia had been increasingly
dependent on the Entente powers. During the war the "English
ambassador in St. Petersburg was the second emperor." Because of Allied pressure, Russia stayed on in the war even
though the war had become obviously harmful to her. The
peace which the Bolsheviks concluded with Germany and
Austria-Hungary (Brest-Litovsk, 1918) was "important and
necessary . . . not for the Bolsheviks . . . but for the *country*,
the whole country, all Russia." A "reaction" did not take place
in Russia because reaction would have meant Russia's return
to war. What mattered most about the peace of Brest, Pokrovskii continued, was not the peace with Germany but the break
with the Entente. Brest freed Russia from "the most despicable
condition that one can imagine," when a "foreign ambassador
becomes the uncrowned emperor of a country." The Soviet
regime's repudiation of all war and prewar debts signified an
end to "the Entente's yoke upon Russia." Because a "reaction"
(i.e., overthrow of the Communist rule) would force Russia to
repay these debts ("a tribute in the hundreds of millions"),
"reaction" was impossible in Russia except as a result of a
foreign intervention.

These comments do not of course suggest that Pokrovskii
became a professed "nationalist." He continued to oppose
nationalism, Russian patriotism, and "national defense." He
argued that besides international considerations there were
also domestic factors that made reaction impossible in Russia.
First of all, the October Revolution was a proletarian revolution while the revolutions of the past that inevitably ended in
a "reaction" had been ideologically influenced by the petty
bourgeoisie. Though petty-bourgeois attitudes and ideas were
also expressed in the Russian revolution, they were eventually
overcome. "Objectively," the revolution dealt a severe blow
to the petty-bourgeois outlook; by concluding peace it destroyed the bourgeois illusion of a "national war" and "the
defense of the native home." The proletariat had no wish to

defend the "geographic 'fatherland,' that true product of feudal conquests sanctified by antiquity." The defense of the revolution took precedence over "any nationalistic geography." Moreover, when they dispersed the Constituent Assembly, the Bolsheviks destroyed another myth, the "faith in the absolute rightness of an unorganized, atomized arithmetical majority."

Clearly, Pokrovskii was not consistent in his comments on the revolution. There were contradictions in his views, and perhaps the concluding essay in this anthology (Chapter XIII) demonstrates this most vividly. There Pokrovskii interpreted the Brest peace *both* as an instrument of Russia's *national* liberation *and* as an event that sacrificed "Russia" to "the revolution" and rejected the petty-bourgeois "myth" of a geographic fatherland.

After Pokrovskii

The official attack against Pokrovskii began in 1934 when a joint decree of the Soviet government and the Central Committee of the Communist party accused the Soviet teachers of using "abstract and schematic" textbooks and methods and presenting "abstract definitions of social-economic formations" instead of teaching history in "a lively manner." The decree ordered that the students should learn the most important facts chronologically and should be acquainted with important historical figures. The material studied would become accessible, clear, and concrete only if one taught history in chronological sequence, "fixing" dates firmly in the students' memories. This would enable students to grasp the Marxist interpretation of history.[50] Although Pokrovskii was not named in the decree, it was clear he was being repudiated.[51] The decree ordered the preparation of new textbooks; however, after the deadline had passed, it was announced in 1936 that the submitted drafts were all unsatisfactory. The textbook authors (some of the best-known Marxist-Leninist historians) were accused of continuing "to adhere to the obviously unfounded historical definitions and interpretations which have already been uncovered many times by the Party and which have their root in the well-known errors of Pokrovskii." In the refusal to abandon these errors, the Party saw "a proof that among a part of our historians, and particularly historians of the U.S.S.R., there have taken root anti-Marxist, anti-Leninist, in point of fact, liquidationist, and anti-scientific views on history as a science."[52]

Thus, the next step was reached in the criticism of Pokrovskii. His history was not only inaccessible to the understanding of schoolchildren; but also anti-Marxist, anti-Leninist, and liquidationist. The Soviet newspapers and journals started an anti-Pokrovskii campaign. It was said that he denied (and lacked) objectivity in historical studies; that his concept of commercial capitalism was anti-Marxist and anti-Leninist; that in his history there was a "scheme of social formations" but no class struggle; that the state was not being recognized as an active historical force; and that in general Pokrovskii was quite alien to Leninism.[53]

The struggle against Pokrovskii and his school continued throughout the 1930's and was intensified after the publication in 1938 of the *Short Course of the History of the C.P.S.U.(B.)*, that model of Stalinist falsification. (Its authorship first was attributed to an anonymous "committee"; later, however, Stalin was extolled as the author of this "work of genius.") The importance of the new *History* was stressed in the November 14, 1938, decree of the Central Committee, which recalled the harmful influence exerted in the past by Pokrovskii and his "school." In response to the decree, the Institute of History of the Soviet Academy of Sciences issued a two-volume collection of articles entitled *Against M. N. Pokrovskii's Historical Conception* (volume I) and *Against M. N. Pokrovskii's Anti-Marxist Conception* (volume II).[54] In her introduction to volume I, Anna Pankratova added new themes to the usual charges. Pokrovskii and his school were "the basis" for the acts of sabotage committed by the enemies of the people whom the N.K.V.D. subsequently unmasked. These enemies included "Trotskyite-Bukharinite hirelings of Fascism, wreckers, spies, and terrorists," who had "cleverly disguised themselves with the help of Pokrovskii's anti-Leninist historical ideas." Only "unforgivable and idiotic carelessness and lack of vigilance" on the part of historians could explain how it was possible for this "gang of enemies" to carry on their activities with impunity.[55]

It was difficult to go further in this "critique" of Pokrovskii, and in the following years his name came to be mentioned only in passing. An official publication of the Soviet Academy of Sciences, issued on the twenty-fifth anniversary of the October Revolution, managed to ignore Pokrovskii almost completely, except for noting the harm he had done to the study of history. These remarks were accompanied by appreciative statements about the old historians such as Solov'ev and Kliuchevskii.[56] Pokrovskii and his followers in the meantime were found guilty by Professor Tarle of "moral disarmament of the Russian people."[57] N. L. Rubinshtein was the only one to discuss Pokrovskii dispassionately (although even he had to repeat some standard charges), and he tried to defend Pokrovskii by making a distinction between Pokrovskii and "Pokrovskii's school," on whom he laid the greater share of blame.[58]

The years following World War II were marked by changes in the interpretations of various historical problems and in the reputations of scholars, but there was no retreat on Pokrovskii. As late as 1955, Professor A. I. Sidorov (his former student and subsequently, after Pokrovskii's rehabilitation, the author of a friendly memoir) claimed that Pokrovskii's writings and activities had caused "considerable harm" to Soviet scholarship, though Pokrovskii had also played a certain "positive role" in the struggle against bourgeois historiography. Pokrovskii had tried, but failed, to become a Marxist.[59]

First indications that the question of Pokrovskii might be reopened appeared shortly before the Twentieth Party Congress at which Khrushchev delivered his famous secret speech on the "cult of Stalin" (1956).[60] The old charges that Pokrovskii and his associates had been ideological saboteurs, traitors, or terrorists were dropped. Eventually Pokrovskii was also acquitted of the charge of "vulgar sociologism," "economic materialism," and "anti-Marxism." A secretary of the Central

Committee of the CPSU, Leonid Il'ichev, declared at the Twenty-second Party Congress (1961) that despite his errors Pokrovskii had been a Marxist and that he had made a major contribution to historical studies.[61] This was an official rehabilitation of Pokrovskii, but it was not accepted unanimously by the Soviet scholars: Pokrovskii remained controversial. Depending on their own academic background, careers under Stalin, or positions they held in the late 1950's and early 1960's, the historians responded to the rehabilitation of Pokrovskii in different ways. The rehabilitation affected the standing and power of the academic Establishment whose members had contributed to the denigration of Pokrovskii. It also touched on several important issues: ideological orthodoxy (what *is* Marxism in history?); party authority (does obedience to the party line really serve historical studies?); and, although only implicitly, the nature of the Soviet society itself (what kind of a society is it where things like the condemnation of Pokrovskii can take place?).[62]

There were some, like M. E. Naidenov, who continued to describe Pokrovskii's historical ideas as basically un-Marxist and un-Leninist. Writing in 1957, Naidenov praised the 1934 decree because it secured a "full triumph of Leninism" within the following five or six years. He conceded that, unfortunately, this triumph had been accompanied by what he called violations of socialist legality. He concluded that Pokrovskii's works were only of "historiographical importance" since Soviet historiography had much advanced after it had overcome Pokrovskii's errors.[63]

It followed from Naidenov's argument that in the early Soviet period the Leninist approach to history was ignored while anti-Leninist and anti-Marxist views, such as those of Pokrovskii, enjoyed dominant position. Not surprisingly this interpretation was resented by other historians, not only those whose personal careers went back to the 1920's. Militsa Nechkina was the most outspoken critic of Naidenov on this count. Nechkina was prepared to recognize Pokrovskii as a Marxist-Leninist, although she, too, thought the stage of Marxist-Leninist historiography which Pokrovskii represented had been passed by his successors. While historians like Nechkina reject the Stalinist distortions of Pokrovskii's ideas, they also make it "clear to everybody that there can be no question of any 'return' to M. N. Pokrovskii. We have gone far ahead by now."[64]

S. M. Dubrovskii, Pokrovskii's younger contemporary, was one of the very few Soviet historians who considered some of Pokrovskii's views to be superior to those of his successors. He praised Pokrovskii for his presentation of Russia as a "prison of nations." Dubrovskii also contrasted favorably Pokrovskii's interpretation of historical personalities with the Stalinist practice of glorifying tsars, princes, and "tsar's servants." This practice had put national interests above class interests. Even Dubrovskii thought, however, that Pokrovskii did not appreciate sufficiently the "cultural heritage" of the Russian nation and that his views contained "elements of national nihilism."[65]

The alleged "national nihilism" of Pokrovskii has been generally condemned by Soviet writers. Pokrovskii's failure to understand the wars against foreign invaders became "intolerable" in the 1930's on the eve of war, when it was necessary to educate the masses in the spirit of Soviet patriotism.[66] The party ideologists in the field of history, Fedoseev and Frantsev, wrote that although Pokrovskii "did not always show the importance of national traditions and in this respect passed incorrect judgments," Pokrovskii's struggle against "tsarist ideology" continued to be topical: "there are still historians calling themselves Marxists who engage in direct apology (*apologiia*) for Genghis Khan and his campaigns of plunder and robbery."[67] In other words, the Soviet ideologists were censuring Pokrovskii for his criticism of Russian conquests and invasions; but they thought that Pokrovskii might still be useful against those who would like to justify the Mongol invasions of Russia. (The Soviet authors had in mind the Communist Chinese historians who prominently celebrated an anniversary of Genghis Khan.)

In 1965, for the first time in thirty years, a volume of Pokrovskii's works appeared in the U.S.S.R.: it was volume II of *Izbrannye proizvedeniia* ["Selected Works"] which was scheduled to appear in four volumes. Volume I came out in 1966, followed by the remaining volumes in 1967.[68] Volume I opened with a long essay by O. D. Sokolov, one of the most "pro-Pokrovskii" writers. Sokolov warned that the publication of Pokrovskii's work did not mean that they were suitable for study by "the unprepared reader." Like the other writers on Pokrovskii, Sokolov stressed the historian's "nihilistic approach" to Russia's past. Thus, among other things, Pokrovskii mistakenly regarded the "Tatar-Mongols" as relatively more advanced than Rus' over which they ruled; Pokrovskii paid little attention to the "national liberation struggle of the Russian people against foreign invaders"; he made similar mistakes in analyzing the war of 1812; and finally, he was not interested in the "rapprochement" that had allegedly been taking place between the Russians and the workers of non-Russian nationalities in their "joint struggle" against exploiters and oppressors.[69]

The reappearance of his writings has to be welcomed, especially because the edition includes his principal works, the two histories of Russia. The texts are complete, and the editors have provided extensive and helpful notes. Pokrovskii's bibliographic references have been checked, quotations verified; we also find important passages from earlier editions which Pokrovskii subsequently omitted or rewrote. However, some serious criticism may be addressed to the selection of articles in volume IV which attempts to omit Pokrovskii's more controversial works.

The revaluation of Pokrovskii was only one element in the post-1956 Soviet historians' review of the past. Those historians who viewed the 1920's with more sympathy than Naidenov were correspondingly less inclined to pass tactfully over the "violations of legality" that occurred in the 1930's. In trying to locate the precise date of transition from the "good" twenties to "bad" thirties the Soviet authors refer to Stalin's celebrated letter to the editors of *Proletarskaia revoliutsiia* as a turning point. The letter ostensibly dealt with some specific questions of party history, but in fact Stalin proclaimed in it the right of the party leaders to intervene directly in scholarly disputes and to resolve them ex cathedra, thus putting an end to that relative freedom which the Marxist historians (and other social scientists) had enjoyed until then.[70] Stalin's letter was important for another reason too: after its publication, dissent in scholarly discussion came to be identified with political unorthodoxy and even treason (Slutskii, whom Stalin attacked in his letter, was found guilty of "Trotskyist contraband"). From the early 1930's on, it was no longer possible to assume that the authors of published works (and this applies to those whose opinions on Pokrovskii were noted in this essay) actually believed what they wrote. For, in the words of A. V. Snegov who survived the Stalin era, Stalin "not only exterminated honest men but also corrupted the living."[71] According to Academician Mints, after the publication of Stalin's "letter" to *Proletarskaia revoliutsiia* many historians were slandered, then subjected to repression; many were forced to admit "errors." The events of those years prompted Mints to speak of a "period of the extermination of the cadres."[72] Another wave of mass reprisals, including arrests and executions of the historians who belonged to Pokrovskii's school, or expressed views similar to his, came in 1934–36. According to M. Nechkina, a "hail" (*grad*) of unjustified repressions and the "destruction" (*gib'el'*) of many talented scholars took place in the 1930's and caused "irreparable harm to historical science." While Pokrovskii was being condemned, Nechkina said, the followers of the "hostile ideology" proclaimed a "return to Kliuchevskii."[73] A. L. Sidorov (who like Mints and Nechkina, but unlike Naidenov, belonged to the generation of the 1920's) recalled that when in 1936 he came back to Moscow after spending several years in the provinces, he found that "there had virtually taken place a complete replacement of the cadres, and many of the talented young scholars had perished."[74] As it is impossible to understand the revolution in historiography that occurred shortly after Pokrovskii's death without taking note of these purges of the 1930's— the "Pokrovskii Affair" was only one aspect in the change of the Soviet culture and society—so the issue of Pokrovskii's "rehabilitation" should be seen within the broader issue of Soviet attitudes to Stalin's legacy. What is the present Soviet line on this matter?

An unsigned *Voprosy istorii* editorial on "The Study of Patriotic History during the Fifty Years of Soviet Power" (November, 1967) provides an authoritative answer on the current historical "line." It reads as if it had been written by Naidenov, repeating a number of (false) charges which had been raised against Pokrovskii under Stalin. It also speaks of the alleged failure of the early Soviet historians to present "correctly" tsarist Russia's foreign policy and the annexation by Russia of other countries: the negative aspects of Russian conquests were being exaggerated in Pokrovskii's time, according to *Voprosy istorii,* and the "progressive" ones neglected. The editorial praises party intervention in the historical science during the 1930's as having had beneficial results. The terror and extermination of the historians are not even mentioned; the only thing that went wrong during that period was apparently the appearance of "dogmatism and quotationism" in *some* works in *some* fields of historical study. The article further deplores the partial revival in the late 1950's and early 1960's of "nihilist" attitudes toward the past (i.e., a more critical view of the past). On the balance of fifty years, it credits Soviet historiography with a successful presentation of the heroic achievements and struggle of "the nations of our country" for "its freedom and independence from foreign invaders."[75]

Conclusion

About sixty years have passed since Pokrovskii wrote his main work, and nearly forty since he died. There is not much point in trying to balance what is "true" and what is "false" in Pokrovskii's statements. Historical research on the many specific issues upon which he reflected has progressed since his time in the U.S.S.R. and abroad; Pokrovskii the historian has long become a fit subject for historical study himself. Also Pokrovskii's diverse and important activities in the Commissariat of Education and other organizations are a matter of history, a topic worth examining separately. It is as an interpreter of

Russian history, of its various components and their interrelation, that Pokrovskii remains of interest. What he regarded as the principal problems of Russian history have not been solved to this day (not in that relative sense in which historical problems are ever "solved"), and in Pokrovskii's own reflections one may still find stimulus and inspiration for thought and study. The central theme of his work, Russia's transition from feudalism to capitalism, continues to engage the attention of Russian historians. They have been finding less and less satisfaction in the periodization of Russian history which was imposed on them after Pokrovskii's death and which puts a thousand years of Russian history under the heading of "feudalism" (tenth to nineteenth centuries) and then assigns fifty-six years (1861–1917) to "capitalism." This periodization, as the Soviet scholars are very well aware, is not perfect. Inevitably, Pokrovskii's solution of the problem ("types of society" and "historical epochs") looks less ridiculous than it was made to appear under Stalin and for some years after.[76]

There is a political side to Pokrovskii's interpretation which may be hindering a fuller discussion of his views. Comparisons have frequently been drawn between the policies of the Soviet state toward the peasantry (as expressed in collectivization), and the capitalist "primary accumulation" described by Marx in *Capital*.[77] A large literature has grown among the unorthodox Marxist or ex-Marxist writers suggesting that the Soviet Union, in its industrialization programs and policies, has continued in the tsarist state's role as exploiter of the peasantry. This and similar analogies had already been made (in the U.S.S.R. and elsewhere) during the 1920's and 1930's by Bukharin, Rykov, Tomskii, Radek, Preobrazhenskii, and Trotsky.[78] One of the difficulties which Soviet authorities are facing in connection with Pokrovskii is that his synthesis *may* be interpreted to support such arguments questioning the unimpeachably socialist nature of the Soviet regime.

The other reason which holds back the full rehabilitation of Pokrovskii is related to the nationality question. Despite all his hesitations and ambiguities—evident in his essays and noted in this introduction—Pokrovskii belonged to the prenationalist phase in the Soviet Union's history, to the age when one still believed in the world revolution and denied the supremacy of one nation over others within the Soviet state. This outlook was and remains profoundly alien to the official ideology prevailing now which demands that the peoples conquered and oppressed by tsarist Russia recognize it as their "fatherland." Little did Pokrovskii know that after his death children (and adults) would be taught to admire not only the "great leaders of the proletariat," Marx, Engels, Lenin, and Stalin—this may have been poor historical materialism but it remained at least a *proletarian* hero worship—but also the conquering tsars and generals. As late as 1963 a high party official (significantly from a non-Russian republic) complained that Soviet history textbooks currently in use were devoting disproportionately much attention to "the biographies of tsars, princes, and military leaders," and that even their chapter headings had "tsarist" names: "Tsar Fedor Alekseevich," "The Reign of Sophia," "Peter II," and "The Beginning of the Reign of Catherine II." Correspondingly, textbooks neglected class struggle and socioeconomic problems, merely mentioning, for example, the peasant uprisings of Bulavin or Pugachev. Nearly fifty years after the revolution, the speaker demanded that the Soviet historians "should at last produce a genuine Marxist-Leninist textbook."[79]

It is reasonable to think that a revision of the Soviet view, and thus a fuller rehabilitation of Pokrovskii, would have to be preceded by domestic *political* changes involving the abandonment of Russian supremacy and an evolution of the Soviet state toward some form of genuine federalism and equality of Soviet nations.

On a more general level, there is a profound difference between the way Pokrovskii (and his contemporaries) looked at Russia and the way in which the later Soviet historians and ideologists have done. In Pokrovskii's "scheme" the development of Russia was not an isolated, self-sufficient process. On the contrary, with the appearance of the early capitalist age of commercial capital in Europe, history became world history—

according to both Pokrovskii and Marx. What happened in Russia was influenced by, and in its own turn influenced, events in other countries. The Soviet ideologists who attacked Pokrovskii, perhaps under the influence of the doctrine of socialism in one country, thought that "internal factors" were the only important ones; in short, they began to view the past in terms of a "history in one country." This was the real meaning of the charge that Pokrovskii, because of his belief in the importance of merchant capital, neglected production relationships and exaggerated the importance of exchange. It is noteworthy that his Soviet critics have consistently ignored the references to the writings of Marx, Engels, and Lenin which, Pokrovskii claimed, gave proof of his adherence to Marxism. This neglect of comparative aspects and limitation to national elements, internal causes, etc., has been evident in Soviet historical thinking throughout. A typical example is an article by Academician Nechkina summarizing the Soviet discussion on the "stages of feudalism"; only as if in an afterthought did she remark, near the end of her essay, that it was important to consider the "world-historical aspect" of the question before deciding whether feudal relationships in sixteenth- through seventeenth-century Russia were progressive or retrograde.[80]

If Pokrovskii's historical outlook may have to wait long for a full "rehabilitation," the more specific questions which he thought important are now gaining increased recognition and attention: the history of the Russian bourgeoisie (Pokrovskii had pushed it far back into the past; the Stalinists tended to limit it chronologically); the origins and history of the Russian absolutist state and its various organs; or the effect of Russia's foreign relations on her domestic conditions (and vice versa). The history of the Russian revolution is among the most controversial and important of these subjects, and Soviet historians will not be able to progress until they recognize the issues Pokrovskii (and his contemporaries of the 1920's) discussed. Whatever their judgment on Pokrovskii's merits as a student and interpreter of 1917 may be, they must admit that Pokrovskii placed the revolution firmly in the mainstream of Russian and world history and boldly sketched the vistas it had opened.

One may wonder if after 1917 Pokrovskii paused at any time to ask himself what he should do next to be most effective and useful to the Communist cause: should he devote himself primarily to academic research and writing, now that the archives so long closed to him had been at last opened, or should he rather concentrate on administrating, reforming, organizing, teaching, and popularizing? If he ever considered the alternative—and it may well be that for a man of his character and temperament the choice was illusory in the first place—he chose to become a leader, an organizer, reformer, and teacher. Perhaps it was not necessary to be a "historical materialist" to believe that the social effectiveness of a high state official and a teacher of hundreds of students and young scholars would prove in the long run weightier than that of a writer of two or three additional books. Could he have foreseen that in the near future his institutes and academies would all be dissolved and the proletarian and Marxist "cadres," the Red professors and Communist academicians, would perish? Could one foresee that ideas would prove to be the most enduring legacy of this materialist?

I

Absolutism

Absolutism (from the Latin *absolutus*—independent, un-limited), an unlimited monarchy, corresponding to the Russian word *samoderzhavie* [autocracy]. The absolute monarchy, as a form of the state system, arose on the basis of *commercial capitalism*. We find it along with the latter everywhere—first in the Eastern states of the Hellenistic period (third to second centuries B.C.), then in the Roman Empire, then in China. The most recent growth of absolutism in the various countries of Europe falls in the period of the fifteenth up to the eighteenth century —during the age of so-called *primary accumulation*. Having described the methods of the latter, Marx said: ". . . they all employ the power of the State, the concentrated and organised force of society, to hasten, hot-house fashion, the process of transformation of the feudal mode of production into the capitalist mode, and to shorten the transition."[1] The coercion of this period must be distinguished from feudal coercion, even though the absolute monarchy was the direct successor to the feudal monarchy. The feudal oppressor could not act alone— the so-called natural, precapitalist economy did not give him the means for that. He had to rule with the help of a whole

First published in *Bol'shaia sovetskaia entsiklopediia* (1st ed., Moscow, 1926–48), vol. I, cols. 87–90.

group of other large landholders who supplied him "in kind" with troops, police, and all other administration. Since he was unable to manage without these helpers ("vassals"), he had to share power with them, give them patents, privileges, summon them to council, and so on. In a word, on the strength of purely economic conditions the feudal monarch could be absolute, could be an autocrat, only in his relations with his servants and peasants, whom he ravished as much as he wanted; but in his relations with his vassals he could be only a limited sovereign, a *suzerain,* and not a *sovereign.* The picture began to change as soon as a commodity economy began to develop and *money* turned up in the hands of the "suzerain," in the form of money taxes, compulsory loans, and so forth. Now he was able to *buy* services instead of having to request them from his vassals. He acquired a *mercenary army, hired officials,* and so on. With their help he was quickly able to cope with the feudal militia and the feudal administration of his vassals, and to transform the latter into his *subjects.* They kept their privileges, but only in relation to their servants and peasants and not versus their suzerain, who became transformed into a sovereign, an autocrat. Power acquired, especially in its first stages, an extraordinarily stern character; at first glance it was even more oppressive than feudal power. All of the early representatives of absolutism appear before us with the classical traits of *tyrants* (Philip "the Fair" [1285–1314] and Louis XI [1461–83] in France, Henry VIII [1509–47] and the Stuarts [seventeenth century] in England, Ivan the Terrible [1533–84] and Peter Romanov [1682–1725] in Russia; the very earliest representative of this type was Frederick II Hohenstauffen, the King of Naples [1215–50]). These are deceptive impressions, however. As a matter of fact, the oppressiveness of the age of primary accumulation originated in the feudal school and operated by its methods; however, it was directed now not only to the common people—the peasants and manor serfs, as before, but also to the great aristocracy, whom the earlier "suzerain" dared not touch. When peasants were hanged, it seemed natural to the nobility, and no one was outraged by it; but when noble heads began to be chopped off and the titled aristocracy was not spared, the nobles began to feel that it was impossible to imagine a more evil tyranny. When coercion had accomplished its immediate goal, breaking the independence of the most important vassals and clearing the ground for the capitalist development, the forms of absolutism became significantly milder: the absolutism of Louis XIV (1643–1715) in France, the "enlightened despotism" of Frederick II of Prussia (1740–86), Joseph II of Austria (1780–90), or Russia's Catherine II (1762–96)—no longer evoked cries of tyranny; for by this time again only common people were being executed, and the aristocracy was left alone.

Appearing as the powerful tool of capitalist development, absolutism had an enormous influence on the *political ideology* of bourgeois society. In its form, absolutism represented purely *personal* power. The colossal power of money, which the new "sovereign" personified politically, compelled everyone to pay it homage. Louis XIV expressed this in the classical phrase: "the State—it is I." In "The Justice of the Monarch's Will," which was compiled on his orders, Peter Romanov assumed the position of the real owner of the state, which he could transfer to whomever he wanted: "He shall bestow succession on whomever he wills," spoke "the Justice." It goes without saying that the doctrines of that period regarded absolutism as the "normal," natural, and indispensable form of the state system. The most prominent theorist of absolutism was the French jurist of the sixteenth century, Bodin (1530–96), noteworthy for being the creator not only of the theory of absolutism but also the theory of *mercantilism,* i.e., the policy of commercial capital. Later, in the seventeenth century, attempts were made to give absolutism a broad "sociological basis," to use a current term (*Hobbes*). In Russia the theory of absolutism was worked out primarily by the contemporaries of Peter I, especially *Tatishchev,* but as early as the sixteenth century the essential idea of absolutism found a remarkable herald who wrote under the pseudonym *Peresvetov* during the days of Ivan the Terrible. The public thought that the personality of the monarch "created the era": it was precisely at this time that such expressions were formed as "the age of Louis XIV," "the age of Peter," "the age of Catherine," and so on, which our present programs and history textbooks manage to remove with such effort. In very fact, of course, even the new "sovereign" could not rule without assistants, without a vast apparatus—of generals, governors, judges, and other officials; and in his dealings with the peasant masses, he could simply not manage without the landlord who, for that very reason, guarded his "privileges."

This apparatus, however, was much more flexible and obedient than the old feudal one. In fact, personal absolutism was itself concealing the absolutism of *commercial capital,* before which even a crowned head bowed when it was necessary. A characteristic anecdote of this sort was the reception which Louis XIV gave in Versailles to the biggest moneylender of the day, Samuel Bernard, whom the Sun King himself guided through the Versailles park and showed how everything was arranged. His distant predecessor in the same line, Louis XI, was the godparent of almost every Parisian merchant.

Ministers from the merchant class were very common phenomena in the absolute monarchies of this period (in Russia the most famous representatives of this type were two from the era of the so-called Troubles—Fedor Andronov, who ruled on behalf of the tsar Vladislav, and Koz'ma Minin, who became the head of those who later enthroned the Romanovs). After Peter, almost all Russian ministers in the middle of the eighteenth century were on the payroll of English commercial capital in whose service was even Catherine II when she was a grand duchess. These persons were thus as much marionettes in the hands of capital, as the bourgeois ministers are today. Power, which was personal in form, was in essence class power. It was natural that it existed as long as the class needed it. When the task of "primary accumulation" was accomplished and commercial capital began to transform itself into industrial capital, the bourgeoisie came to feel that absolutism was a burden—it retained its privileges, but no longer served a useful purpose. The hour of the final liquidation of feudal relations was thus everywhere the beginning of the end of absolutism. First it proved itself superfluous—and thus "harmful" and "intolerable"—in England, where its liquidation came about in the seventeenth century, while under the oligarchy of large land-

holders and big entrepreneurs which replaced it, the same oppressive methods were employed. In France absolutism fell
together with the last traces of "privileges" at the end of the
eighteenth century. In Central and Southern Europe it lived on
until the middle of the following nineteenth century. It held
out longest of all in Russia, where it had a great many foot-
holds owing to the extraordinary speed and at the same time
unevenness of economic development (the rapid capitalization
of the center versus the extreme backwardness of the peripher-
ies), and also owing to the completely undeveloped countries
of the Near and Middle East which for Russian capitalism
were an area of exploitation and partially even of direct conquest (the Caucasus, Central Asia, Manchuria). The attempts
of industrial capital (very weak and indecisive ones) to "euro-
peanize" Russia thus remained unsuccessful, and absolutism
lived on in Russia until the age of imperialism, when capital
again needed a "strong power." Along with the fall of Russian
imperialism, absolutism fell in our country in 1917, having
lived, however, for the preceding twelve years (from 1905) in a
kind of compromise with industrial capital.

II

Bureaucracy

Bureaucracy, a barbarism formed from the French *bureau,* which means a *writing desk* and at the same time *cabinet,* a room where a desk stands, and the Greek *kratos—*"force." Formed by analogy with "aristo-cracy," "demo-cracy," and so on. A literal Russian translation would be: "rule by the desk" or "dominion of the cabinet." The word arose in the beginning of the nineteenth century in France, which until this time has remained the classical land of bureaucracy. This word designated the type of state regime under which the administration was conducted by "privileged persons, divorced from the masses and standing *above* the masses" (Lenin).[1] According to the apt definition of Marx (in "A Critique of the Hegelian Philosophy of Law"),[2] bureaucracy is something like the Jesuit order—the execution of state power by an exclusive corporation, whose essential nature is a secrecy that is protected inside the corporation by the hierarchical structure (the nature of the policy carried out by the government is known only to the upper strata; the lower the rank, the more limited is the knowledge, which becomes increasingly concerned with details) and from the outer world by the inaccessibility of the corporation to out-

First published in *Bol'shaia sovetskaia entsiklopediia* (1st ed., Moscow, (1926–48), vol. VIII, cols. 468–80.

siders. The door with the sign "No admittance without appointment" is the most expressive symbol of bureaucracy and the bureaucratic outlook that one could invent. The other feature of bureaucracy pointed out by Marx was its *formalism*. The form of state (and the governmental rules, the ritual formalities of day-to-day government operation) is transformed by the bureaucracy into an independent entity: the aims of the state are replaced by the aims of the bureaucratic corporation as such. Matters are not decided according to their substance, nor by considering what the government or the people need, but according to what is convenient and beneficial to the bureaucracy. This aspect of bureaucracy was marvelously expressed in our literature by the words of Famusov in "Woe from Wit":

> *"For me, beside the point or not,*
> *I treat them all one way;*
> *Once signed, why let them go, I say."* [3]

All these features of bureaucracy—hierarchy, exclusiveness, formalism—presuppose as a social base a fairly complex social system: neither patriarchical democracy, nor even patriarchical despotism forms the ground for bureaucracy—under these everything is managed directly, without any kind of formality, and authority, whether it is the authority of an assembly (*veche*) or the authority of a patriarchical lord, acts quite openly and directly, not camouflaging itself at all. Bureaucracy presupposes an authority that has already been considerably isolated from the masses; it presupposes—at least, in embryonic form—a *class society*. The serf estate in Russia in the eighteenth century through the first half of the nineteenth century might serve as an example of a rudimentary form of bureaucracy. At the head of such an estate, if it was not large, there usually stood a steward, a literate serf who could read and count, and if the estate was large, there was a whole group of such literate serfs and an office which reminded even one populist historian of bureaucratic government. The serf stewards of one of the Orlovs (the favorites of Catherine II) were, in the words of V. I. Semevskii,[4] "rather state officials in miniature than agronomists. . . . They were presenting reports accompanied by their draft resolutions, which they had signed unanimously, or with opinions and representations. . . ." The real birthplace of bureaucracy was precisely the *commercial-feudal state* which enserfed the masses, though it already had a money economy and the rudiments of an "education" (which above all served to advance exploitation and increase the surplus product that was being squeezed out of the peasantry). It can be said with full justification that bureaucracy, by its origin, was the apparatus of *absolutism*.

As such an apparatus, bureaucracy appeared extremely early in history. According to the famous historian of antiquity, E. Meyer,[5] in Egypt the Old Kingdom was already "not a feudal state, but a bureaucratic state." In Egyptian history the Old Kingdom came into being at the end of the fourth and the beginning of the third millennium B.C. According to this chronology, bureaucracy is no less than five thousand years old. Because we find in ancient Egypt a complex hierarchy of ranks and extensive use of writing by officials, the external resemblance to a bureaucratic state is, in fact, very complete. The enslavement of a large part of the population, firmly established for that epoch, even increases the plausibility of E. Meyer's characteristics. Yet we know too little (mainly the nomenclature of ranks) about this most ancient of bureaucracies in the world, much less than about the authentic, unquestionable bureaucracy at the end of antiquity, the age of the *Roman Empire,* which in many respects is the prototype of later bureaucracy. The Roman Empire both in its center and in the provinces created a very complicated system of chancelleries, with all of the features of a bureaucratic regime—secrecy, hierarchy, and formalism. Along with the institutions of the Roman Republic, which survived formally, these chancelleries formed a truly alien body which little by little drained the blood from the whole organism. This bureaucracy provoked a terrible bitterness on the part of the surviving landed aristocracy, which was insulted primarily by the low origins of the new masters of the situation: a major part of the imperial Roman bureaucrats were freedmen. In historical literature the protest against the Roman bureaucracy has found an outlet in the innumerable ancedotes about the abuses and insolence of the *freedmen*. In point of fact the "freedmen" were the first ministers of the new state that was based on commercial capital. They already formed a kind of permanent corporation, which in fact controlled the entire current administration. The emperor determined the general course of policy only if he was an outstanding man like Trajan or Marcus Aurelius; or he made the life of his courtiers impossible if he was a nonentity: the "freedmen" governed. One of them, Claudius Etruscus, to whom the poet Statius devoted a special poem and who had served ten emperors, according to the findings of a recent historian, simultaneously occupied four ministerial posts: commerce, public works, finance, and the imperial court. Another, Abascantus, whom the same poet had also praised, was the minister of the post. The staff in their chancelleries no longer was made up of freedmen but directly of slaves, for whom making a career meant gaining freedom by long and diligent service and, for the more successful ones, getting appointed as ministers.

We find this contrast between the bureaucrats of low origin who are endowed with enormous power and the landed aristocracy, formally placed high but in fact trembling under the bureaucracy and in secret hating it, in all stages and periods of the development of bureaucracy: in medieval France, in eighteenth-century Germany, in the Muscovite State, in the empire of the Romanovs, exactly as in Rome and *Byzantium*. The latter is interesting as history's first and virtually most perfect specimen of a highly elaborate and broadly ramified *bureaucratic hierarchy*. Byzantium provides the first example of a Table of Ranks (*Notitia dignitatum*), similar to that subsequently issued in Russia by Peter I (see below), only much more complex. In Byzantium there had already been formed a dual hierarchy characteristic of later bureaucratic regimes: one of positions and one of *ranks*. The position carried the right to a "rank" (with a title which very exactly corresponded to our prerevolutionary ones: "Grace," "Excellency," "Highness," and so on). But the "rank" alone did not give any power, and even Byzantium had "privy counselors" from whom no one sought counsel and "assessors" who took part in no conferences. The dismissed official was being consoled with a high rank and splendid title, while "section heads," seemingly modest, actually ran everything. Byzantium was the true home of "officialdom"—the concept which in the Russian language became a synonym for bureaucracy.

The medieval states of Western Europe stood on a much lower step than that on which Byzantium stood in the fifth and sixth centuries. The government of the French kings of the eleventh and twelfth centuries differed little from the management of large serf patrimonies. So much the easier it is for us to observe in the history of French bureaucracy how its rise was connected with the economy of the patrimonial lands on the one hand, and the growth of merchant capital on the other. The first officials were inseparable from the manager and the stewards of the royal domain. The king's confessor, the chaplain who headed the king's private church, used to sign letters patent and sometimes did so immediately below the king's signature. As the only fully literate man in the royal residence, he also composed these letters and gave them final legal form by affixing a seal on them. Owing to this final act, the most important in the eyes of the world at that time (without a seal the document was invalid), he received the title of the "keeper of the seal," *chancellor*. The officials of his chancellery were, in part, sextons and sacristans, and, in part, the literate courtiers. Gradually the latter came to *write* the documents: the chancellor merely signed it. Later the *secretary* (a title which came from the Byzantine Table of Ranks) began to sign; one of the French kings of the sixteenth century, Charles IX, even granted his secretary the right to sign in his stead—because, he said, "in any case I do not read what I sign." In addition, the "state secretary" was transformed from a sexton or literate slave into a distinguished person: he began to dress like a noble and his wife began to ride in a coach; and, as in the Roman Empire, this change in the social position of the bureaucracy especially annoyed the feudal aristocracy. At the same time the conditions under which the bureaucracy was working continued for a long

time to recall its patrimonial origins; as late as the beginning
of the seventeenth century, the French ministers still had no
ministries; each was working at his own home on his own
means (more precisely on the "sinless incomes" [bribes] he received, which were so great that one state secretary requested an
annuity of 30,000 *livres* for having yielded his position to another person), hiring clerks, and so forth. In the records the
secretaries were listed like all other court servants and received
the same presents on holidays as the king's valets. If as late as
the seventeenth century, up to the reign of Louis XIV, the
chancellery bureaucracy reminded one of its origin among
"manor serfs," so the *financial* bureaucracy bore equally
definite traces of descent from elsewhere. In the "counting
houses" of the French kings as late as the sixteenth century
half of the members were clergy. But a merchant can count
better than a priest, and the last churchmen who actually managed the finances of medieval France were the *Templars,* military men, knights, clergymen, and the largest moneylenders of
the day. From their ranks came Louis VII's minister of finance,
Thierry Galerand. A century and a half later the Templars
fell, and the minister of finance of Philip the Fair who had put
them to death was a "Lombard"—that is, a professional moneylender, by this time already a layman, Bettino Cassinelli. And
in the beginning of the sixteenth century Francis I entrusted
the reorganization of his finances, which were severely ruined by
war and the king's revelries, to the Touraine merchant, Jacques
de Beaune, who became "Seigneur Semblançay," joined the
ranks of aristocracy, and commanded the royal treasury with
unlimited authority. His career ended on the scaffold, as did
the careers of many representatives of the early bureaucracy.
Neither in this, nor in other respects was he an exception, nor
was he the only one in whom the close connection between
commercial capitalism and absolutism became evident: this
connection could be observed before him in Jacques Coeur,
and also after him, down to the last minister of finance of the
old French monarchy, the banker Necker.

Toward the end of the seventeenth century, simultaneously with the triumph of commercial capitalism and absolu-

tism, the bureaucratic regime became the norm for the entire European continent. Only in England did both absolutism and a bureaucratic regime—the former in the person of the King, Charles I, and the latter in his minister Strafford—suffer a defeat which cost their representatives their lives. In France, its homeland, the continental bureaucracy preserved longer than anywhere its medieval patrimonial forms. The modern bureaucracy, characterized by Marx, arose there only as a result of revolution—primarily during the rule of Napoleon I; in earlier times the king's and state's economy, the court and chancellery, the influence of mistresses and favorites, and the power of ministers were intermixed in a completely chaotic way. Central Europe, especially *Prussia* and *Austria,* became the classical land of the new bureaucracy. Here more than anywhere else the bureaucratic regime paved the way for rising capitalism and was its tool. With the help of bureaucracy, capitalism was breaking down the last remnants of the Middle Ages—local liberties, feudal privileges, "customary law," and finally (in Prussia in the beginning of the nineteenth century, in Austria still later) even the serfdom economy. The very *theory* of the bureaucratic state rose here, finding its apotheosis in the Hegelian philosophy of law which, according to Mehring's perfectly correct observation, reflected the realities of Prussia in 1821—the age of the greatest flourishing of the Prussian bureaucratic system.

The eighteenth century was the heroic period of bureaucracy. The bourgeois historians glorified the bureaucratic regime, which was famous under the name "enlightened despotism," as an age of rational and humane government, beneficial to the masses. It was believed that the happiness of the people directly depended on the rationality and purposefulness of the structure of the government mechanism (as in Leibniz's celebrated comparison of the state with a watch). In reality the welfare of the masses was the least consideration. The government of "enlightened despots" above all else cared about increasing its revenue. The most consistent of those despots, Joseph II of Austria, introduced barbarian punishments (whipping, branding, etc.). The emancipation of the peasants was in fact their expropriation to the advantage of the landlords, and besides it was completed in Prussia only under the impact of Napoleon's defeat of the Prussian army, and in Austria still later, after the revolution of 1848. The best side of the bureaucratic regime was its struggle against the intolerance of the Catholic Church, along with other remnants of the Middle Ages; however, the Church had long since ceased to be the main enemy of the masses and had itself been transformed into an auxiliary tool of the bureaucratic state. "Enlightened despotism" was in essence an endeavor to exploit the masses "rationally," that is, to the greatest advantage of the state, and it represented a perfect analogy to the conversion of the feudal estate into an enterprise, the transformation of a "knight" into a "landed proprietor." It was a political reflection of the economic change which was proceeding at the same time. Industrial capitalism very soon felt itself cramped in the bounds of the bureaucratic state, and at the very time when the state was being elevated by Hegel into an ideal, liberalism began to get a hold among the bourgeoisie, thus preparing the revolution of 1848.

In *France* the remnants of the Middle Ages were not swept away by bureaucratic reforms, but by the movement of the masses; therefore they were swept away much more thoroughly than in Central Europe, even though a bit later. Bureaucracy was needed again, however, since after the brief period of the Jacobin dictatorship, power had slipped out of the hands of the masses. The state that was created on the ruins of the French revolution was a state of class oppression nevertheless, but for the benefit of another class—not the landlords but the bourgeoisie. However, the bureaucratic system established by Napoleon I, and designed with a purely military straightforwardness from top to bottom, was free of those vestiges of the patrimonial system in which the France of the "old order" abounded, and which the "enlightened despotism" of Prussia and Austria was ultimately powerless to take away. France entered the nineteenth century with a more complete and rationalized system of bureaucratic government than any other country had known, and in its essential features has kept this system to the present day. At the head of every department a state official, a prefect, was placed without whose authorization it was impossible to build any road, construct any school or hospital, and most importantly, whose hands controlled all *police*. The administration of the police by the bureaucracy is the most important manifestation of the French system—even in Paris the police is completely independent of the local administration (corresponding to our city soviet): it is headed by an official designated by the central power, a prefect of police. Owing to this, the class dictatorship of the bourgeoisie stands out with a nakedness which is found in no other country in the world. The words spoken by Marx in 1871 have retained all their force until this very day: "At the same pace at which the progress of modern industry developed, widened and intensified the class antagonism between capital and labor, the State power assumed more and more the character of . . . a public force organized for social enslavement, of an engine of class despotism." [6]

In *Russia* the course of the development of bureaucracy reflects the very same social-economic changes as those in the West and shows a great number of features which even externally resemble those in the history of the French bureaucracy. Our first officials, the *d'iaki* of the fifteenth and sixteenth centuries, as their very name shows, were taken from the lower clergy (*d'iak, d'iachok*—the lowest religious rank of the Orthodox Church), and were close to peasants in their social position. In the wills left by princes one finds sextons mentioned among those who were being freed. As in the West, the role of bureaucracy grew in proportion to the growth of a money economy and the appearance of commercial capital. As it had also been there, the bureaucracy was hated by the feudal aristocracy; the latter used to recount as early as Ivan the Terrible's reign how the new men of confidence appeared around the grand prince of Moscow—the clerks (*d'iaki*) who "with half [of their income] were feeding him, and taking the other half for themselves." And during the reigns of Ivan the Terrible's immediate successors, there were clerks (the Shchelkalov brothers) in Moscow who were large shareholders of an English commercial company and who, owing to the extent of their influence, appeared to foreigners to be the real "tsars." Officials of this class already became members of the Tsar's Council (*Boiarskaia Duma*), and, although formally they occupied the very last place in it—they did not even sit in it but merely witnessed its proceedings while standing—they were in fact the most influential of its members. Boris Godunov became tsar with the help of a clerk, one of the Shchelkalovs; another clerk of the Council of merchant birth, Fedor Andronov, governed the Muscovite State under Vladislav. At this time nobles of good lineage were petitioning for the position of clerks and were not ashamed that clerk was a "poor rank," unworthy of a nobly born man. The clerks of that time, along with the clergy, were the first Russian intelligentsia: a history of "The Time of Troubles" was written by the *d'iak* Ivan Timofeev. The style of this work led V. O. Kliuchevskii[7] to suppose that Timofeev had been thinking in Latin; in any case his contemporaries from the same circle not only knew Latin but also Greek. Later the clerk's assistant Kotoshikhin produced one of the most remarkable descriptions of the Muscovite State.

The flourishing commercial capitalism in Moscow in the seventeenth century inevitably pushed forward considerably the growth of the Muscovite bureaucracy. This growth was shown by the complaints made in the Assembly of the Land (*Zemskii Sobor*) in 1642 about the dominance of the *d'iaki* who built themselves "stone mansions of such a kind that it is ungainly to speak of them,"*—and the appearance among Muscovite departments of a single, perfectly bureaucratic Department of Secret Affairs where everything was controlled by the clerks and to which the boyars who were in charge of other departments "did not go and whose business they did not know"

---

*A sample of such a mansion stands to this day on the Bersenevskii embankment of the Moskva River: this house is now being occupied by the Institute of Ethnic Cultures of the Peoples of the East; earlier it housed the Moscow Archeological Society, and in the seventeenth century the house was built by the *d'iak* Merkulov; even though an addition was made in the eighteenth century, according to present-day standards it is a rather modest building.

(*Kotoshikhin*). And it is especially marked if you take into account the fact that in the other departments *d'iaki* were often the actual masters. The extent to which the social consciousness of this group had risen can be seen from a fact that goes as far back as the beginning of the seventeenth century. In a matter involving a question of *precedence*—that is, in a suit between persons who were of "noble" and "distinguished origin"—one of the judges, a *d'iak,* beat the defendant with a stick, and there is no evidence that the boyar judges had enough civic courage to intervene on behalf of their fellow nobleman.

It is possible to speak about the real Russian bureaucracy only from the age of Peter, who was the very first representative in our country of absolutism in the West European sense of the word, that is, a representative of *personal* power which was not restrained by the traditions of feudal society. Our first real bureaucratic institution was Peter's Senate (1711) which replaced the Tsar's Council (*Duma*). The latter had been an assembly of the greatest vassals of the Muscovite tsar—men whose ancestors themselves had been rulers at one time; and although towards the end of the seventeenth century many new people had joined the ranks of this aristocratic group while the descendants of the former appanage princes already constituted its minority, the Council nevertheless remained an assembly of the large landholders who maintained a social importance even independent of their "rank." The Senate was an assembly of officials, appointed by the tsar without any attention to their lineage or social position (one of its members, a prince, was promptly replaced by Sheremetev's former serf, Kurbatov; another former serf, Vasilii Ershov, was instructed to administer the province of Moscow), and these officials were subject to the strictest bureaucratic discipline. Legally, the tsar could not give orders to the Council: the verdict of the boyars, even at the end of the seventeenth century, formally ranked parallel to the sovereign's decree. ("The Lord has decreed and the boyars have judged.") Such was, however, only the *form* of what had had a real significance in the sixteenth century: the tsar commanded in fact, though not in

law. Even prior to the establishment of the Senate, Peter nevertheless managed without any boyar verdicts. The decree on the
establishment of provinces (*guberniia*) (December, 1708) began
with the words: "The great sovereign has decreed. . . . And
according to the said decree of the great sovereign, these provinces and cities belonging to them are assigned to the chancery
of the Tsar's Council (*Blizhniaia kantselariia*)."[8] And the tsar
spoke to the Senate in the following manner: "With great sur-
prise I received a letter from St. Petersburg that 8,000 soldiers
and recruits have not been delivered there, and if the governors
fail to make amends soon, let them be treated for this as befits
criminals, or else you yourselves shall suffer . . ." (Decree of
July 28, 1711).[9] Or: "Deliver troops to the Ukraine, so that
they duly arrive by July; all that is needed for war should be
provided for by the Senate, with a cruel penalty for noncom-
pliance" (Decree of January 16, 1712).[10] Possessed by the idea
that the Senators were idlers, loafers, and pilferers, Peter had
officers of the guard brought into the Senate as surveillants, and
then created a special position, "the eye of the tsar," in the
person of the *procurator-general* whose duty it was to see to it
"that the Senate acts in its calling justly and sincerely" and
that not only business is conducted on the desk, but also actions
themselves are implemented according to the decrees, "truth-
fully, zealously, and honestly, with no loss of time."[11] And for
the surveillance over the entire administration the institution
of *fiscals* was created to "watch over all matters secretly."[12]

The institution of the fiscals brings us back again to the
social meaning of bureaucracy. The new Petrine institutions
not only disregarded a man's inherited rank, but also had a
definite bourgeois character. The "ober-fiscal" Nesterov, who
had also been a serf, wrote the tsar about those under his surveillance: "They are a common company of nobles, and I, thy
slave, am mixed among them with only my son, whom I am
instructing in the job of the fiscal and have as a clerk. . . ." In
addition to his work as a fiscal he also distinguished himself
by a plan to establish a merchant company which would defend
the "fatherland's" merchant class from the dominance of foreigners. Incidentally, about half of the rank and file fiscals were

chosen "from among the merchants." In order to mollify the nobility, it was stated in the decree that they would "watch over the merchants," but we have seen how Nesterov regarded his position. Looking closely at the program of the Senate which Peter left to this institution when he was setting out for the Pruth campaign, we see that almost all of it consisted of financial-economic points ("to examine expenditures throughout the entire state . . . ," "to collect as much money as possible . . . ," "to reform letters of exchange," "to take inventory of goods . . . ," "to try to farm out the salt [trade]," "to farm out the China trade to a good company," "to increase trade with Persia").[13] In this enumeration general questions such as "sincere justice," or special military matters (the formation of officer reserves) are lost. The Petrine Senate bore the clearest stamp of commercial capitalism that one could ask for.

The bureaucracy in Russia, during the age of Peter, not only acquired a West European form, but also exuded an enthusiasm almost equal to that which was to be found then in the West. In the rules for the police (1721), we read: "[The police] maintains laws and justice, good order, and moral instruction; provides security to all from robbers, thieves, criminals of violence and fraud, and their like; drives away dishonorable and indecent ways of life and compels everyone to work and engage in honest trade; it promotes good homebuilders, and painstaking and good-willed servants; it designs cities and their streets in an ordered way; it blocks a rise in prices and brings satisfaction in all human needs; it wards off all diseases that occur, enforces sanitary measures in the streets and in homes, and forbids excess in domestic expenditures and all open transgressions; protects the low, the poor, the sick, and the others in need, defends widows, orphans, and strangers; educates the young according to the Lord's commandments in chaste purity and honest studies; in short, in all these respects the police is the soul of citizenship and of all good order and the fundamental support of human security and comfort."[14]

This "poetry" of bureaucracy conceals the filthy and cruel prose of "primary accumulation" which was being served by bureaucracy. Those who like to compare the revolutionary (it was in form) breakthrough of Peter with the destruction of the old regime by our revolution cannot be reminded too often that the revolution raised the well-being of the broad masses, and this was clearly expressed in the decline of the death rate, whereas Peter's "revolution" lowered the well-being terribly and led to a colossal increase in the death rate and reduction of the population almost by 20 percent. Peter's reform was an attempt, fully analogous to Western "enlightened absolutism," more rationally to exploit the people's labor for the benefit of the growing capitalism. Hence the very attempts to construct the state administration rationally (the projects, realized in part, of Fick, Luberas, and others). Leibniz's comparison of the state to a mechanical clock pleased Peter very much—he used to send special agents to inquire about the way some particular department was organized in one or another country, so that he might adopt and establish them for himself in case of need (in this way the fiscals were copied from a foreign model). The reach of Russian capitalism at the beginning of the eighteenth century, however, was broader than its grasp, and soon there remained almost as little of the "clock-mechanism" introduced by Peter as of the Petrine factories. Often there were left only titles and external forms, or something which actually impeded the development of bureaucracy, such as the *Colleges,* which weakened personal responsibility. In practice, the Russian system of government of the eighteenth century was more patrimonial than those of Prussia or Austria in the same period. The attempt to create a solid hierarchy of bureaucratic positions by means of the *Table of Ranks* (1722)[15] was frustrated by the patrimonial traditions without any difficulty. Even the middle nobility easily jumped above the lower steps of the Table by registering their children for service from the cradle; they were being promoted regularly, and by the time they came of age they often already were "field officers." As for the court aristocracy the decisive factor was one's personal closeness to the emperor or—in the eighteenth century—more often to the empress. The cornet who became involved in an "affair" moved up higher than any of the privy or actual privy counselors who would occasionally kiss the cornet's hand. The favorite valet of Paul I, Kutaisov, almost instantly became both actual privy counselor and a knight of the Order of St. Andrew, but when Suvorov indiscreetly asked him for which services he had achieved this, he had to answer modestly that he "shaved His Majesty."

The bureaucracy of the eighteenth century was thus more similar to its seventeenth-century predecessor than to what Peter had designed. The halt in its development precisely reflected the halt in the development of Russian capitalism in the first decades after Peter. As soon as the economy began to move forward at a faster speed, this immediately reflected itself in the upsurge of bureaucracy. The post-Petrine bureaucracy experienced two such upsurges. The first—right at the end of the eighteenth and the beginning of the nineteenth centuries, during the periods of Paul and Alexander I—was distinguished by a new sweep of Russian commercial capitalism (the formation of the world grain market and the transformation of Russia into the "granary of Europe") and the rise of a large-scale machine industry. The most prominent figure in the Russian bureaucracy during this period was Speranskii, who put forth anew a series of projects to make Russia happy by resetting the administrative mechanism and very carefully raised the question of the abolition of serfdom law. Speranskii moved in a circle of prominent members of the St. Petersburg bourgeoisie and considered the managing of the "manufactures," i.e., the ministry of industry, to be one of the basic departments of the state; in foreign policy he was a supporter of France and opponent of England, that principal competitor of the growing Russian industrial capital—this was the basic reason why Speranskii fell into disfavor before the War of 1812. During the reign of Nicholas I the Russian bureaucracy flourished almost as much as it had in Peter's regime, a fact closely related to the heyday of Russian industry whose interests had by that time begun to determine in part tsarism's foreign policy. Korf, Nicholas's most trusted secretary of state, was a pupil and admirer of Speranskii; Nicholas's "chief of staff for Peasant Affairs," Kiselev, greatly resembled the Prussian bureaucratic reformers of the preceding period. Thus, in the Nicolaevian bureaucracy there existed uninterrupted continuity from the age of Speranskii to the new upsurge of the Russian bureaucracy—the famous "reforms of the sixties," when the abolition of serfdom, and *zemstvo* "self-government," and the new courts were all instituted exclusively by bureaucratic methods, provoking extraordinary bitterness among the landlords, who were finding that "the official-bureaucrat and the member of society constitute two beings totally opposed to each other." The new vigor in bureaucratic work, again, corresponded precisely to the new upsurge of capitalism which was brought about by the expanding internal market, owing to the partial emancipation of the peasants, railroad construction, and so on. It should be added that no reform was completed, they all remained half-measures; rather than to weaken it, they all reinforced the oppression which hung over the masses.

After the age of "reforms" the bureaucracy gradually became a direct apparatus of capitalism. The ministers of Alexander II were, without doubt, more "left" than their tsar, and at the conference which took place after March 1, 1881, they declared themselves for the constitution by a large majority (Valuev, Loris-Melikov). The feudal reaction won for a time, but it had to agree to large concessions in economic and financial policies. It is characteristic that no Russian ministers of finance at the end of the nineteenth century were career bureaucrats: Bunge was a professor; Vishnegradskii, a big stock-exchange operator (this he also combined with a professorship); Witte, one of the most prominent railroad men, on the eve of his appointment to highest bureaucratic posts held the modest rank of titular counselor. As in the eighteenth century, "The Table of Ranks" yielded, only this time not to feudal customs but to the demands of capital. All kinds of police, both central and local (the governors, ministry of the interior, and, especially, *the department of the police,* which became the real center of the all-powerful bureaucracy), retained bureaucratic features to the highest degree, thus emphasizing the fact that in Russia "the State power assumed more and more the character of . . . a public force organised for social enslavement." [16]

Therefore, as one of its first tasks, the proletarian revolution had to break down the bureaucratic machine.

"The workers," Lenin wrote in August–September, 1917, "having conquered political power, will break up the old bureaucratic apparatus, they will shatter it to its very foundations, until not one stone is left upon another; and they will replace it with a new one consisting of these same workers and employees, *against* whose transformation into bureaucrats measures will at once be undertaken, as pointed out in detail by Marx and Engels: (1) not only electiveness, but also instant recall; (2) payment no higher than that of ordinary workers; (3) immediate transition to a state of things when *all* fulfill the functions of control and superintendence, so that *all* become 'bureaucrats' for a time, and *no one,* therefore, can become a 'bureaucrat.' " [17]

III

Bourgeoisie in Russia

The beginnings of the Russian bourgeoisie go extraordinarily far back into the depths of Russian history. As far back as the treaties between the princes of Kiev and Byzantium—the monuments of the tenth century—we find the names of "merchants." Inasmuch as these names accompany the names of the representatives of the princes themselves, it is absolutely clear that we do not have here before us a peddler-merchant, but the large-scale organizers of robber trade, for whom even Solov'ev[1] had correctly found an analogy in the African slave trade of the nineteenth century. In later times, in the twelfth and thirteenth centuries, in large city centers, in Kiev or in Novgorod, we find organized merchants who had—in accordance with the character of the commerce of that day—primarily a regular military organization. It was divided into "hundreds," and at the head of all the "hundreds" in Novgorod stood the milliarch ("thousand-man")—the commander in chief of the city's militia and at the same time the head of all the merchants. In Novgorod, as early as the twelfth century, we also find an *economic* organization of merchants like the well-known guild of John the Baptist, with a charter of its own, from which we even learn of the average size of commer-

First published in *Bol'shaia sovetskaia entsiklopediia* (1st ed., Moscow, 1926–48), vol. VIII, cols. 181–94.

cial shares of the time—ten thousand rubles in present-day currency. The Novgorod merchants already were a definite social force with their own special political interests. The landholding aristocracy which ruled the Novgorod Republic, and held in its hands huge reserves of valuable raw materials and silver, usuriously exploited the merchant masses; and by its foreign policy, constant wars with Moscow for Novgorod's colonies, the *Zavolochye*,[2] it obstructed the Novgorod merchants' trade with central Russia where the foreign goods imported into Novgorod were sent and from where grain came to Novgorod. The Novgorod bourgeoisie, therefore, gave lukewarm support to its boyars in the struggle with Moscow, thus contributing to a considerable degree to the victory of the latter.

The colonial wars conducted by Moscow—which in the final analysis were wars for valuable raw materials and silver—testify to the fact that its bourgeoisie was being formed at precisely this time and that commercial interests had made themselves felt. Contemporaries attributed the very rise of Moscow to her economic-geographic importance as a trade center. As far back as the fourteenth century we find there merchants who traded with the Crimea, and Genoese traders from the Crimea, the latter to all appearances a regular corporation. At exactly the same time a merchant from central Russia, Afanasii Nikitin, reached India in his Eastern travels; if he was the only one to describe it, this does not at all mean that no one else had taken such journeys. The influence of the Muscovite bourgeoisie was already felt with absolute certainty during the last struggle between Moscow and Novgorod at the end of the fifteenth century. Its interests affected the drive of the Muscovite State to the southeast, to the Caspian Sea in the following sixteenth century—a drive marked by the capture of Kazan' and Astrakhan', which very significantly had begun with the customs war between Moscow and Kazan'. And the struggle for Livonia, which took up the entire second half of Ivan the Terrible's reign, had already assumed the character of a real trade war. In internal policy the influence of the Muscovite merchants counted just as strongly; even then they

possessed features of a real *class,* which was breaking down
into several groups ("the *gosti*"—large-scale wholesale traders,
"the merchant and cloth hundreds"—large retailers who traded
in foreign manufactures, and, finally, *"the black hundreds"*—
petty shopkeepers and artisans, between whom it was hard
to distinguish because every artisan himself sold his produce).
The *Oprichnina*[3] owed its rise to a considerable extent to the
support of this class: Ivan the Terrible addressed his appeal
from Aleksandrovskaia Sloboda precisely to the Muscovite
bourgeoisie. The Terrible may be considered the forefather
of "protectionist" policies in Russia: he gave a subsidy to the
merchants who traveled to Germany, Holland, and England
to trade. With the latter country he set up stable trade relations which formed an important chapter of his foreign policy.
Also, his confessor, the archpriest Sylvester, was the forefather
of commercial education in our country: his pupils traded "in
diverse lands in all sorts of goods." At the end of the century
the Muscovite large merchants were interfering even in the
tsar's family affairs, and although some of them paid for this
with their heads, nevertheless, the fact was very indicative of
the political activity of the Muscovite bourgeoisie at the end
of the sixteenth century. In the beginning of the seventeenth
century, the influence of the bourgeoisie, especially that not
only in Moscow but also in the north, above all the *Zavolochye*
(whose significance as a source of raw materials added to its
importance as a road to Western Europe), reached its max-
imum for the Muscovite period. Without the consent of the
bourgeoisie it was impossible to retain the Muscovite throne.
The Godunovs[4] fell because the burghers of Moscow did not
support them. The Pseudo-Dmitrii, in spite of his enormous
popularity among the masses, did not manage to last for more
than a year, and he was succeeded by the nominee of the
bourgeoisie, Vasilii Shuiskii, who relied mainly on the financial
and military aid of the northern cities. At this time the first
definite bourgeois notes began to be sounded in Russian
political literature: bourgeois patriotism can be detected, and
events were given a concrete, materialistic interpretation
which resembles the literature of the Italian Renaissance.

However, the outcome of the struggle was determined by the development of the essential fact of the age—the peasant revolution—which penetrated even the cities and roused the masses of artisans and unskilled workmen against the merchants. The bourgeoisie assumed the role of organizer in the struggle against the revolution; we find its representatives in both counterrevolutionary governments—both in the defeated government of Vladislav, in the person of the rich Muscovite merchant Fedor Andronov, and in the victorious government of the Romanovs, in the person of the Nizhnii-Novgorod merchant elder, Koz'ma Minin. However, for this purpose the bourgeoisie was forced to enter into a coalition with the remaining boyars and with the heads of the insurgent peasant masses, the Cossack chiefs, and principally with the middle-rank service landholders, the gentry, who got the lion's share of the spoils. The costs of the unsuccessful peasant revolution, a thorough devastation which was brought about by "pacifiers" of all kinds and nations, struck a heavy blow to the economy of Moscow which had been developing rapidly in the sixteenth century. The process of accumulation did not come to a halt, of course, but it continued more slowly; the external defeats of "the Troubles" (the loss of Smolensk and of the access to the Baltic) slowed down the development of foreign trade. Nevertheless, twenty years after "the Troubles," Russian commercial capital had increased by half; its turnover rose from 14 to 21 million rubles in today's money. As always, the crisis hit the lowest strata most and furthered the concentration of capital in the higher strata of merchants: throughout the entire seventeenth century we simultaneously hear the wails of the provincial merchants who were brought to ruin and we also meet the first millionaires in Russian history, the Stroganovs.

The process of reconstruction after the unsuccessful peasant revolution was completed only toward the last quarter of the seventeenth century; in the so-called Petrine reform we have a new upsurge in the rise of the Russian bourgeoisie, greater than anything before. Peter's entire foreign policy was marked by commercial capital. In the name of its interests

Peter carried on a twenty-year war with Sweden—the principal commercial rival of Russia on the Baltic Sea—and not only regained the position held in the days of "the Troubles," but also took away from Sweden two-thirds of the eastern shores of the Baltic. In the name of that same interest, toward the end of his life, he began the less successful struggle for the Caspian Sea. Be that as it may, toward the end of his reign the great trade route from Europe to Asia lay entirely in Russian hands: from the Baltic Sea by way of the Volga to the Caspian Sea. In internal policies at the beginning of the Petrine age the bourgeoisie again, for the first time since "the Troubles," stepped forth in the role of organizer: the merchants' "town hall" became the financial center of the state. Men of bourgeois extraction turned up in the highest state posts. The official literature of Petrine "schemers" overflowed with bourgeois ideas, taken in part from West European books, but also in part conceived independently under the conditions of a great economic breakthrough (Pososhkov).[5]

However, even the "Petrine reform" had its price, one which had to be paid until the second half of the eighteenth century. The population of the country fell below the level at which it stood on the eve of the "reforms": this alone did not promise a rapid economic development. The period of decline in the seventeenth century also had its effect. In the meantime the "maritime" commercial countries—England, Holland, France—had made enormous progress, and the outmoded Russian commercial capital, engaging in a struggle with them, was quickly defeated. The attempt to create a Russian commercial fleet failed. The export trade fell into the hands of foreigners, primarily the English, who subsidized the Russian government, including chancellors and members of the imperial family. In internal trade, which had already developed heavily in the course of the seventeenth century and continued to develop in the eighteenth century, especially in connection with the rapid growth of the large city centers of Moscow and St. Petersburg, the landlord became the successful rival of the merchant; more and more frequently he appeared at the market either in person or through his peasants. The landlord even took over the industrial enterprises: the landlord, who had large reserves of peasant labor at his disposal, owing to the agrarian overpopulation of the central provinces, constructed manufactories and organized domestic industries, thus easily driving out the merchant who did not have free labor at hand. In general, the rent, and not the entrepreneur's profit, was the chief source of accumulation in this period. Merchants made capital on *farming out;* the tax-farmer became the typical Russian millionaire at the end of the eighteenth century and early nineteenth century. But the tax-farmer had become almost a noble: he carried a sword and received a rank; his children sometimes served in the Guards. He stood further apart from the provincial merchants than had the rich *gosti* of the seventeenth century. By the middle of Catherine's reign, the bulk of the merchants were clearly in the opposition. The commission of 1767 heard only complaints from them. Liberal publishers (like Novikov) viewed the merchants as their principal public since the upper nobility read only French and the provincial nobles did not read at all. During the Pugachev rebellion[6] the provincial merchants proved to be the stratum that was closest to the insurgent peasantry; Pugachev protected them and they supported him. Traces of this mood of opposition continued even into the nineteenth century—echoes of a merchant opposition were still heard before the Decembrist uprising. This mood of opposition on the part of the bourgeoisie was a transient phenomenon, however, and did not reoccur until the end of the nineteenth century. It was a peculiarity of the Russian bourgeoisie that its growth was closely connected with the growth of tsarism. The most prominent representatives of commercial capital in the seventeenth century, the *gosti*, were agents of the tsar; not only did they directly exercise commercial monopolies of the State treasury, but they were also in charge of the collection of taxes from the other merchants. As for the latter, they controlled the collection of all indirect taxes: the custom, "tavern," and other revenues were collected by the agents selected from among local merchants. It was so in Muscovite Rus'; under Peter, as we have seen, the bourgeoisie became the direct financial apparatus of the tsar's regime. In the eighteenth century commercial capital was accumulated chiefly by means of farming out (the former "tavern" revenues) which gave a fourth of the total budget of Catherine II. The issue of promissory bills initiated by the government of Catherine increased the amount of money in circulation, provided a new impetus to the commercial turnover, and facilitated accumulation in money. There was nothing specifically Russian in any of these phenomena. The very same connection between merchant capital and absolutism can be noted everywhere; but, while in Western Europe this phenomenon was characteristic of the end of the Middle Ages, and by the eighteenth century the bourgeoisie had already detached itself from autocracy, in our country this alliance of autocracy and capital continued far into the nineteenth century. *Industrial capitalism*, which was beginning to develop in the first years of that century, proved to be even more dependent on tsarism than its predecessor, commercial capitalism. The first textile factories, which served a consumer market (the landlord manufactories chiefly worked on government orders) appeared in our country during the period of the so-called Napoleonic Wars, when the Russian market was artificially isolated by the Continental Blockade from all foreign competition. The wars ended, but it was necessary to maintain isolation, and the period of 1823–57 was the first period of intensive tariff protectionism that we have had in Russian history. The competition of English textile goods was almost completely eliminated; but the protection of Russian large-scale industry by the state was not limited to this passive defense. While the empire of Peter and Catherine only knew wars for commercial routes, the empire of Nicholas I opened the age of wars for markets, one of which, the Persian, very quickly fell almost entirely into the hands of young Russian capitalism. By the 1830's people had been dreaming about a campaign to India, and practical preparations were being made for the capture of all the Near Eastern markets. All of this led to a protracted conflict with England and, in the end, to the *Crimean War*. Under Nicholas I, as under Peter, the direction of foreign policy was determined by the interests of

Russian capitalism, this time industrial, however, and not commercial. Later it will be seen that the latter had by no means departed from the scene, but, on the contrary, by and large prevailed. Yet industrial capitalism proved to be tied to autocracy's chariot as strongly as its predecessor, and politically this was of enormous importance.

There could be no question, to be sure, of a complete peace between industrial capitalism and the feudal system. Subordinating itself meekly to the military dictatorship of tsarism, Russian large industry could not but collide at every step with the social base of the latter, serfdom economy. The "free" workers in the merchants' factories were in reality serfs whom the landlords released for quitrent, and the wages they earned, in addition to providing their subsistence, also included the tribute which they paid to their master. Owing to this the wages in Russia in 1830–40 were higher than in Germany. At the same time the owners of serf estates, by lowering the "subsistence minimum" of their peasants almost to the level of work animals, were hindering the expansion of the internal market; the serf-peasants were returning to a natural economy against their will: they could not be buyers; on the other hand, for the landlord, the menial artisans, men and women, were to a certain degree a substitute for large-scale industry. While it had not become an antagonist of autocracy, from its very first steps industrial capital had to become an enemy of serfdom law. Even the official literature which represented the interests of industry (*The Journal of the Manufactures and Commerce*) was instrumental in the agitation for the emancipation of peasants. The factory owners freed their serfs (the "possessionary peasants")[7] on their own initiative—the first such case in Russian history. On the basis of rising industrial capitalism there appeared a whole series of progressive trends, which still were not liberal in the precise meaning of this word, because they did not aim directly at autocracy, but were in any case undermining autocracy's social base by lashing out at serfdom.

As always and everywhere, it was not the entrepreneurs themselves but representatives of the intelligentsia who stepped forth as the ideologists of the movement—these were in that time primarily university professors and liberal officials who expressed the interests of the bourgeoisie, as they also did in later periods, more clearly than the bourgeoisie itself was capable of doing. The most prominent of the first group, the professors, were: Chicherin and, especially, Kavelin; the liberal officials were represented on the one hand by the associates of "the chief of staff for peasant affairs," the minister of state domains Kiselev (such as Zablotskii-Desiatovskii), and on the other, by N. A. Miliutin and his circle. However, the "peasant reform" also involved several characteristic figures directly from the capitalist world, of whom the most prominent were the large tax-farmers Koshelev and Kokorev. It is interesting that the "emancipation" thus brought forward from the bourgeois milieu the representatives of commercial and not industrial capital. This clearly testifies to the fact that the former also was interested in the "emancipation"—and indeed the reform resulted in an enormous intensification of Russian grain exports: 376 thousand tons of wheat in 1850 and 1573 thousand tons in 1870, and such an expansion of the internal market that Russian industry could not fill it on its own. English imports to Russia grew faster, up to the middle of the 1870's, than did the output of Russian factories. This renewed competition from the English was a result of the autocracy's failure in foreign policy at Sevastopol—the failure which forced a lowering of the customs barrier (the tariff of 1857).

There was thus a crack in the alliance of autocracy and capitalism, and autocracy felt it. Having scarcely recovered from the consequences of the defeat at Sevastopol, it renewed its advance in Central Asia, and in the beginning of the 1870's again launched an active policy also in the Near East. In each case it was equally defending the interests of both commercial and industrial capitalism; however, the introduction of duties in gold currency in 1878, i.e., the raising of customs tariffs by 50 percent in one step (the paper ruble at that time was worth only 66 gold *kopecks*), marked the beginning of a new era of protection, this time especially of industry, and a new alliance between autocracy and the industrialists. The protection policy reached its high point in the tariff of 1891 which surpassed the record of even the "protectionist" tariffs of Nicholas I; and this new alliance found its political crowning in the ministry of Witte (1892–1903)—the direct successor of those officials under Alexander II who knew how to unite in their own persons a loyalty to autocracy with a devotion to the interests of capitalism. In this sense the most characteristic of Witte's reforms was the introduction of the gold standard in 1897, which cost the landlord a pretty penny and also in part the merchant—the strata interested in selling grain abroad—and was advantageous to the factory owners who bought machines from abroad.

The close alliance between autocracy and capitalism explains why in the course of the whole nineteenth century the liberal movement in our country was not represented by the bourgeoisie in a proper sense but by progressive groups of landowners who had become to some extent entrepreneurs; this, however, does not at all mean that these landowners had completely lost all their feudal traits. The Prussian *Junker*—the most distinct type of this kind of landowner—carefully preserved the basic feudal privilege, the monopoly of land and the remains of personal rule over the peasants, and this did not prevent him from organizing his economy rationally, using machines, artificial fertilizers, and so forth. The Russian variety of this type, in just the same way, never refused to take advantage of the remains of serfdom law, and in particular of his monopoly of land: and yet, even he strove to organize large agricultural enterprises with farm labor, machines, and so on. However, the extremely high prices of equipment, which were created by the "protective" customs tariff, stood in the way of this rationalization. The temporary and incidental pittance on the part of the government did not solve this problem, and during the entire nineteenth century the progressive landowners found themselves in a state of suppressed opposition to autocracy, which from time to time emerged as open hostility (*Decembrists, Zemstvo, Zemstvo movement*).[8] In the beginning of the century liberal, even radical, political organizations sometimes arose in this milieu, but for the most part they were friable, unstable, and short-lived, so that the very existence of some of them has been a subject of controversy. However, in the course of the entire nineteenth century the bourgeoisie in the proper sense did not even have such organizations; and as for the political formulation of its class aims, it even stood behind the proletariat, which had developed only in the second half of the nineteenth century. By the 1870's the proletariat had its own rudimentary political organizations; in the 1890's it had a whole network of them; and from the beginning of the twentieth century it had its own political party—the first political party altogether to arise on Russian soil. The first political party of the bourgeoisie appeared not only after the proletarian party had already been in existence for several years, but even after the proletariat had gained its first large victory in the strike of October, 1905.

This fact of the *political backwardness* of the Russian bourgeoisie constitutes one of the principal historical peculiarities of the Russian revolutionary movement, and explains to us why in Russia "the victory of the bourgeois revolution was impossible *as a victory of the bourgeoisie*" (Lenin).[9] While the bourgeoisie was leading revolution everywhere in Western Europe, in Russia it was *plodding along* behind it. It was, nonetheless, completely inevitable even for Russian capitalists to move toward a bourgeois revolution inasmuch as the "infinitely inveterate and antiquated autocracy" (Lenin) was proving itself evermore an unfit instrument for the protection of capitalist interests. The rapidly growing proletariat, which had reached 10 million toward the beginning of the twentieth century, was forcing the bourgeoisie to adopt measures for "self-protection." The bourgeoisie of the whole world was finding this "self-protection" especially in deceiving the working masses and in bribing their upper ranks. To do this certain institutions such as freedom of association, freedom of assembly, labor unions, a legal workers' party, and so on were necessary. Without them all, one could practice neither bribery nor deception. Autocracy, on the other hand, with its feudal-police methods of government, approached the matter in such a way

that even the most naïve and unconscious worker very soon
came to understand the class nature of the society in which he
lived and the class contradictions that were tearing it apart.
The tsarist government either shot down the strikers, in this
way momentarily clarifying the class consciousness of the
masses, or resorted to coarse demagogic methods, establishing
"yellow" workers' unions where no unions whatever existed
and where police organizations became in this way, by an irony
of fate, a school for class struggle. The Russian bourgeoisie
*began to sense the necessity of a transition to a political system
of the West European type,* in brief, to a constitution, for the
sake of its own class interests. In the early years of the twentieth
century, for the first time after a century-long break, the bourgeoisie again began to join the opposition, while individual
capitalists even went so far as to support revolutionary organizations materially, on the one hand, and to publish illegal literature abroad, on the other (*Osvobozhdenie,* the newspaper
and the union).[10] While pursuing this course the bourgeoisie
began to form an alliance with the liberal nobility, the "left
Zemstvo men."

The bourgeoisie's oppositional sentiments reached their
high point in the summer of 1905, when a participant at the
Moscow province congress of manufacturers suggested that a
lockout be declared "in order to draw the workers out to the
streets." The Russian bourgeoisie was hoping in this way to
follow in the footsteps of its elder West European sister, forcing the autocracy to grant concessions with the help of a
workers' revolution. We have already seen, however, that the
methods of the West European bourgeoisie were little suited
to Russian conditions owing to the extreme political backwardness of the Russian bourgeoisie. In addition, the alliance
of the latter with the left wing of the large landowners proved
fatal for the bourgeoisie; for these landowners, having become
liberal, did not cease to be feudal and found themselves in the
most severe conflict with the peasant masses on account of land.
Conditions were thus created in our country which favored
the *hegemony of the proletariat,* inasmuch as the peasants,
who had followed the bourgeoisie in West Europe, could

follow only the working class in our revolution. When the workers' and peasants' movement reached its apogee in the last months of 1905, the bourgeoisie had ceased even to plod along behind the revolution: it became openly reactionary and fought the workers by means of a lockout, not in order to "draw them out to the streets" but to suppress the workers' movements. It asked for field courts-martial and did not mind leading the struggle against the revolution. This was precisely the meaning of the attempt to create a Kadet ministry in the time of the first Duma in the summer of 1906. The Kadets,[11] a bourgeois political organization standing farthest to the left among those formed in the fall of 1905 and representing the interests of the most advanced industry and banking capital, at first tried to fraternize with the victorious proletariat (they greeted the October strike), but subsequently spoke in defense of the monarchy and entered into close contact with General Trepov, the chief bodyguard of Nicholas II. The Octobrists,[12] who stood to their right and reflected in part the interests of commercial and usury capital, in part, of heavy industry—but mainly those of the Russian Junkers (see above)—from the very start made no advances to the revolution; instead, they furiously demanded a state of siege. It was one of autocracy's main mistakes (and one of the main proofs of how hopelessly obsolete tsarism was) that, failing completely to take advantage of the "loyal allegiance" of the Russian bourgeoisie (this allegiance was suddenly revived under the blows of the democratic revolution), it did not form a bourgeois ministry. Tsarism could not do without informers, feudalists, and men of "personal confidence" participating directly in the administration; the very idea of a party-based government seemed preposterous to the autocracy. But, nevertheless, even men of "personal confidence" could not help but make bourgeois policy. Trepov has been mentioned already. Stolypin, who replaced him in the summer of 1906, even though his government was not formally Octobrist followed the policy of the right Octobrists, destroying the remnants of those institutions which most impeded the development of capitalism (*land commune*) and pushing forward the differentiation of the peasantry. Thus, on the one hand he was expanding the internal market for industry, and on the other providing cheap labor for the latter. This policy had to be crowned with a resumption of active foreign policy. Foreign policy, owing to the predominance of "Junker" interests in the Stolypin regime, had to take up the traditional struggle for Constantinople and the Straits, thus simultaneously assuring the export of Russian grain and extending the foreign market for Russian industry (owing to the agreement between Russia and England in 1907, Persia again became, as under Nicholas I, almost an exclusive possession of Russian capitalism).

It would seem that complete accord should have been reestablished between the bourgeoisie and tsarism. In fact this did not occur. The whole period of Stolypin was filled with an undercurrent of ferment in the bourgeois circles which began immediately after the revolutionary movement had been forcibly suppressed. This ferment openly expressed itself in the Kadets' parliamentary opposition and press, and in a more secretive form in the Octobrists' activities, in various Duma commissions, conferences, and so on, which had this additional significance that close relations were established at these conferences between the representatives of large capital and the members of the military high command. The main cause of the friction between the bourgeoisie and autocracy was that while the bourgeoisie was getting more and more "Europeanized" (in Russia syndicates were appearing and an attempt was even made to establish trusts, close ties were established with international banking capital which actually began to direct Russian industry, and so forth), autocracy was becoming more and more old-fashioned. It was returning to the methods of personal rule, forgotten since the time of Paul I, under which the autocrat finds himself in the position of a puppet controlled from behind the stage by the various completely medieval figures of magicians, miracle workers, and so forth. The degeneration of autocracy in this direction was crowned, as everyone knows, by the regime of Rasputin. What is more, along with all the other Asiatic features, there continued to prevail in the apparatus of autocracy bribery, embezzlement, technical incompetence, and so on. More than at any other time the bourgeoisie had grounds for not trusting the tsar and his officials. Among the latter Stolypin himself was the most acceptable to the bourgeoisie: the court camarilla saw to it that he was removed from the stage by the act of an anarchist. Following Stolypin's death (1911), the new conflict between the bourgeoisie and autocracy assumed an even clearer shape. One of its symptoms was the formation of the Progressive Party in the following year; the Progressivists were bolder in their opposition than the Kadets, who until then had stood at the extreme left. The more serious character of this new opposition was only emphasized by the fact that in their program the Progressivists, who represented in a social sense the large-scale textile industry, primarily of the Moscow region, were more moderate than the Kadets.

The bourgeoisie's distrust of autocracy and its apparatus proved to be entirely justified after the outbreak of the war, the main effect of which was to raise the Russian bourgeoisie to the height of genuine "European" imperialism. Even the leaders of the bourgeoisie did not realize until much later that Russia had been a tool of imperialism, and the bourgeois rank and file understood it only after the October Revolution. One could not but understand one thing, however—that the hopelessly antiquated autocracy was a system absolutely not suited for the conduct of imperialistic wars under conditions of a highly developed industry. Russian metallurgy, which remained in any case far behind the German (in 1913—19.2 million tons in Germany vs. 4.7 million tons in Russia, four times less), was not utilized at all in the beginning of the war; its skilled working personnel was sent to the front; the industrialists who offered their services were told that their services were not needed; they hoped to conduct the war as it had been done in the middle of the nineteenth century, using provisions stored up in peacetime that scarcely sufficed for a month. The result was the defeat, exceptional in its immensity, of the Russian army in the summer of 1915 which compelled the autocracy, after several convulsive gestures, to capitulate before the bourgeoisie in fact, handing over to it the whole organization of the home front (The *Union of the Zemstvos* and the *Union of Towns, Special Council for Defense, War Industries Committees*,[13] and so forth). However, even then autocracy did not want to renounce formally its rights and privileges, and the medieval figure of Rasputin continued to head the whole system. The bourgeoisie could not help but sense the complete frailty of its achievements; and it set a formal removal of autocracy as its next task. The bourgeois parties in the State Duma, from the extreme left to the extreme right, aligned themselves into a Progressive Block,[14] which was openly exposing the defects of the autocratic regime in the Duma sessions, and, using its connections with the high army commanders, was preparing a conspiracy for the overthrow of Nicholas II by means of a coup d'état. It hardly needs to be said that the struggle against autocracy arising from the class interests of the bourgeoisie did in no way push the bourgeoisie's other class interests to the background. The war opened up various possibilities for exploiting the proletariat under the pretext of "military necessity" and under the cover of the most thorough destruction of all proletarian organizations—opportunities about which, it seemed, one could not even think after the revolution of 1905. Toward the end of the second year of the war the real wages of the Russian worker were cut in half, in some places even by two-thirds. Strike after strike followed; the new workers' revolution was approaching with catastrophic speed. But the bourgeoisie did not notice this: it had been encouraged by the fact that it had managed to draw the highly skilled upper sections of the working class into war industries committees; it was also carried away by the pursuit of the unprecedented profits of the war; and, finally, it was busy carrying on its own war with autocracy. Under the revolution, the bourgeois politicians whose lips never stopped uttering this word naïvely imagined a successful coup d'état carried through with the support of the workers and the army. The genuine popular revolution, which broke out in February–March, 1917, was for the bourgeoisie like a thunderbolt out of a clear sky. The mistakes and cowardice of the intelligentsia organizations (*Mensheviks, Social Revolutionaries*),[15] which found themselves in the first moments at the head of the insurgent masses, and the low level of consciousness and poor organization of the masses themselves helped the bourgeoisie to survive the autocracy, which had fallen in February, for two months; as early as May, however, it was forced to camouflage itself in Kerenskii's "socialist" government; the bourgeoisie was no longer capable of ruling in its own name. Camouflaged in the "coalition," it held out for another half year.

From the very beginning of the 1917 revolution, the bourgeoisie took up a definite counterrevolutionary position. In the days of February it tried with all its strength to save the Romanov dynasty, and it stepped back only when it had become clear that the defenders of the dynasty would perish along with it. It was putting off the convocation of the Constituent Assembly in every way possible, even though in the first months of the new regime, when the masses had still not come to any understanding of their position and were gripped in the ardor of "honest defensism," this clearly would have been advantageous to the bourgeoisie: the alliance with "the Junkers" and the fear that the peasants would demand land at the Constituent Assembly were dragging the bourgeoisie to the bottom. When the ardor began to be dispelled, the bourgeoisie absolutely insisted on continuing the war which had been coming spontaneously to a standstill from the very start of the revolution. The bourgeoisie continued to regard the worker as its enemy, threatened him with the "gaunt hand of starvation," i.e., with a general lockout, and enforced a partial lockout on the sly, closing factories and sabotaging production. In short, it seems that no class in the world tried so hard to destroy itself as did the Russian bourgeoisie in 1917.

By the time of the October Revolution the bourgeoisie was completely disorganized politically, having disorganized the national economy beforehand. It was only natural that the bourgeoisie was unable to organize any kind of systematic resistance to the victorious workers' revolution; without support from abroad, without foreign intervention, the second revolution of 1917 would have gone through exactly like the first—almost without civil war. If civil war took place after all, and the counterrevolutionary fronts held out for three years, it was not because of the Russian bourgeoisie, but because of French, English, and American imperialism. The latter did not act, however, through the bourgeoisie, whose political insignificance was completely evident to them: as a tool for the overthrow of Bolshevism, they used the remnants of the Russian Junkers and the petty-bourgeois intelligentsia which had been confused by "democratic" slogans. The Junkers provided the commanders of the White armies, the petty-bourgeois intelligentsia and the kulak layer of the countryside, their cadres. The bourgeoisie dragged itself behind these armies in the same way as it had dragged on behind the revolution at the beginning of the century, organizing various sham conferences and councils whose counsel nobody sought, and governments which governed nothing, because the real government was always the staff of the White army and its organs. And on this side of the Red front, the remnants of the bourgeoisie were organizing equally effective "centers" and "councils" whose greatest achievement was to provide espionage service for the White front. One cannot in any way attribute to the bourgeoisie itself in this period a single attempt, serious to any extent, at an anti-Bolshevik coup; even the few terroristic assassination attempts of this time may be attributed wholly to the petty-bourgeois revolutionaries and anarchists. The bourgeois counterrevolution in Russia proved to be as ineffective as the attempts at a bourgeois revolution in the nineteenth century.

Thus, the bourgeoisie in Russia did not play the role that fell to the lot of its West European sisters and predecessors. It did not manage to create a bourgeois democracy after the examples of England or France; it did not even manage to become a co-ruler under a feudal monarchy, as had been the case in imperial Germany. And if the German bourgeoisie succeeded for a time in suppressing the workers' revolution, the Russian bourgeoisie did not succeed at this for one minute, for the revolution of 1905 was put down by the Junkers and the apparatus of the tsarist regime, and the revolution of 1917 hurled the bourgeoisie to the ground. This fate of the Russian bourgeoisie, so unlike that of others, needs to be explained.

Above all, the Western bourgeoisie possessed a revolutionary character during certain periods only and not for the whole length of its existence. Each country's bourgeoisie had been allied to absolutism at the start, and it ended everywhere by becoming a counterrevolutionary body; the former corresponded to the period of commercial capital, the latter, to the period of monopolistic capitalism. The bourgeois democracy was always established by the bourgeoisie during the high period of industrial capitalism, and the longer this period lasted, the more solid was the democratic superstructure erected by the bourgeoisie. In England, where this period took up a whole century, the bourgeoisie entrenched itself in power most firmly. On the continent this period was already shorter, and if the French bourgeoisie nevertheless managed to create the Third Republic, in Germany it never got beyond the role of a deferential counselor to the emperor. The period of the dominance of industrial capitalism in Russia was particularly short. For the first three-quarters of the nineteenth century industrial capitalism had existed in our country, but it did not determine the basic line of development of the national economy: Russia still remained, above all, an agrarian country. The talk that to consider Russia an agrarian country was a "superstition" was started only in the 1890's; only "the age of Witte" began the real rule of industrial capitalism in our country, and the following decade already saw the rise of imperialism on Russian territory. Thus, the Russian bourgeoisie did not have at its command even two decades in which to create the political superstructure peculiar to industrial capitalism: it withered, so to speak, without managing to blossom. Thus, we arrived at the paradoxical, but historically absolutely correct position that the backwardness of the Russian bourgeoisie can be explained by the unusually rapid growth of Russian capitalism at the end of the nineteenth century through the beginning of the twentieth century. This is the basic reason. Two others may be added to it. First, in Russia, which was after all an agrarian country, especially up to the last quarter of the nineteenth century, the landowner vastly outweighed the manufacturer. All institutions were being established by the landowners to serve their needs; the landowners' state possessed an enormous power of inertia: it had been difficult even in Prussia for the bourgeoisie to overcome this inertia; in Russia, even more so. We have already seen above, in a series of concrete examples, what effect Junker inertia had had. And the last point: Russia entered on the road of capitalism later than all other European countries; Russian capitalist industry had to grow under conditions of severe competition, both on the internal and, especially, on the foreign markets, with the powerful industry of Western Europe which had taken shape earlier. For this reason the autocracy's "military-feudal imperialism" was an indispensable condition of its development and even its very existence. The vast concentration of military forces and resources that was achieved by tsarism with the help of unbelievably brutal methods which ultimately hindered the economic development itself nevertheless helped Russian capitalism to "repulse" its competitors. The Russian bourgeoisie lacked the strength to create its own military dictatorship as the French bourgeoisie had done in the days of the First Empire. Tied by a marriage of convenience to the rotting corpse of autocracy, the bourgeoisie itself was infected by its decay and perished from senility at an age when the Western bourgeoisie had been in its prime.

IV

The Revolutionary Movements of the Past

Russia of the old regime is thought to have been the least revolutionary country in the world. It is said that the Russian revolution began only at the very last moment under the influence of ideas which had come in from the West.

This legend was strongly maintained by the tsarist government and the historians who were on its payroll. The autocracy needed this legend because nowhere was a government threatened by such dangers from revolution as in Russia. (They feared revolution so much that they tried to ban the word itself from Russian history; and this fear shows how strong revolution was.)

In reality, Russia, starting from the sixteenth century, was in all likelihood the most disturbed, the most revolutionary country in Europe. From the middle of the sixteenth century to the beginning of the nineteenth century, all Russian governments were living on a volcano. At every moment, beneath their feet, an abyss filled with boiling lava was about to open up. This abyss did open many times, and it was not merely autocratic government which fell into it.

First published in *Ezhegodnik Kominterna: Spravochnaia kniga . . . na 1923 god* (Petrograd and Moscow, 1923), pp. 229–32.

Only in the first years of the nineteenth century could rather firm ground be found under the feet of autocracy—particularly during that time when our revolutionary movement was supposedly just beginning. In fact, the revolutionary outbursts of the first three-quarters of this century did not present tsarism with any serious danger. Only the events of the first of March, 1881, when Alexander II was murdered, called to mind the possibility of a new eruption, and only in the twentieth century did a new catastrophe break out, the greatest of all, which carried off into the flaming chasm not only the last autocratic government, but even that bourgeois pseudodemocracy which was trying to spring up on its debris.

In order to assess the relative revolutionary character of old Russia, it is enough to cite one fact. Every European country, in the period of the breakdown of feudalism and the rise of the capitalist system, had its *peasant revolution:* in France—the *Jacquerie*, in England—the uprising of Wat Tyler, in Bohemia—the Hussite wars, in Germany—the great Peasant War of the sixteenth century. In every country, however, there was *one* such revolution. Russia, in the corresponding period of her economic development (falling for us between the seventeenth and eighteenth centuries), experienced *four* of them. Three were in Great Russia: the so-called Time of Troubles in the very beginning of the seventeenth century, the uprising of Stepan Razin in 1670–71, and the Pugachev mutiny in 1773–74. The first brought down a series of governments, one after another; the last was not far from achieving its aim: Catherine II had no more dangerous rival than Pugachev. To these one must add the fourth, grandiose and successful revolution in South-West Russia, in the Ukraine, in 1648–54—the uprising of Bohdan Khmel'nyts'kyi, which put an end to the Polish dominion in these parts and was, in fact, the start of the disintegration and fall of old Poland.

What can explain such an exceptionally strong revolutionary excitability among the Russian people—a trait that also explains something about recent events and explains why the socialist revolution of the twentieth century was able to begin in Russia? Certainly it is not any kind of Russian national trait. "National peculiarities"—this is not something that explains, but something that is itself subject to explanation. What can explain this "national peculiarity" of the Russian people, its revolutionary character?

Solely the peculiarities of its economic development. In the fourteenth century, when merchant capitalism was already taking shape in Western Europe, a handicraft and guild industry was flourishing, and a national state arose with a bureaucracy, moneyed taxes, and a permanent army, in Russia the prospering of purely feudal relations could be observed. This was the so-called appanage period in Russian history. Each small town, and even each large village with its surrounding countryside, was a separate "principality." Every landlord was the sovereign of his own estate: "every church tower has its own law." From his "subjects," this sovereign collected taxes in sheep, cheese, and eggs, and if it was far to go by himself after all of this—the principalities were not only very small but even mixed up with each other in the oddest way— he gave up the farthest village in the fief to one of his "serving people," or vassals.

Under the pressure of European merchant capitalism, which, personified by the Hanseatic merchants, for a long time had been opening a way for itself into this wild country, at first through Novgorod, then through Moscow in the guise of the Italians who built the Moscow Kremlin at the end of the fifteenth century, and finally in the guise of the English, who opened the sea route to Russia through Archangel in 1553 (in the seventeenth century the English were replaced by the Dutch, the teachers of Peter the Great)—under the fiery rays of this rising sun of capitalism, Russian feudalism was melting away like snow in the spring. What had resulted in the West from a slow, prolonged, and persistent struggle in individual localities, rose up suddenly and throughout all territories in a Russia which was united rapidly by the native merchant capitalism being formed. The countryside did not have time to adapt itself in any way to the new economic conditions. The landlord, who was in Russia, more than anywhere else, a tool of primary accumulation and was intoxicated by a greed for profits which had been completely unknown to his grandfather, was robbing the peasants sometimes in the most literal sense of the word. Moscow was rolling in luxury; the countryside began to starve. Having lost its bearings because of the unexpected misfortune, the peasantry wandered from one landlord to another, finding everywhere one and the same lot. The more passive majority sold itself into slavery simply for the sake of bread, looking for an escape from starvation. The more active minority went off to the borders of the state and there organized free settlements of Cossacks, equally frightening to its neighbors and to the Moscow State itself.

The conflict of the state with the Cossacks of Eastern Russia—like the conflict of the Polish State with the Western Cossacks forty years later (the "Zaporozhe Cossacks")—was the signal for the first peasant revolution. The merchant-capitalist state, which had not yet managed to take shape, was weak. The Cossacks easily obtained a victory, and the peasant uprising was spread like a stormy sea across the land, wiping out the serf law that was just emerging. The uprising went under the slogan: "Destroy the lords, take their estates for yourselves." So read the proclamations of the peasant leader Bolotnikov.[1]

Many landlords were annihilated, but in Great Russia the peasants and Cossacks did not know how to build anything on the ruins of the landlord's state. They themselves did not have any political ideal other than tsarism. In 1613 the Cossack army put forward as a candidate to the throne an old feudal family, the Romanovs, who promptly proceeded to betray those who had seated them on the throne. Under the first Romanovs, Michael and Alexis, the peasants were enserfed once and for all. It is true that economic concessions had to be made: in the middle of the seventeenth century the Muscovite peasant had more land than at the end of the sixteenth century, but in return, legally he had become a complete slave.

The Western Cossacks were closer to Europe and more aware. Having overthrown the old yoke, they did not go under a new one so obediently. For several decades the Muscovite tsar had to restrict himself to the role of the suzerain of the Ukraine. Gradually, however, he took it in hand; the Ukrainian peasants who had revolted were taken in hand by the Cossack "chiefs" who turned from leaders of the uprising into a real landowners' class that was even more greedy and oppressive than the landlords of Great Russia.

The later Cossack-peasant uprisings were already encountering a much stronger state power, armed with weapons which the poorly organized rebellious masses did not have the strength to cope with. For several months the uprising of Razin controlled the main commercial artery of the Muscovite State, the Volga River. Its ripples reached the northernmost end of the commercial route, the White Sea, where Razin's Cossacks inspired the uprising of the Solovki monastery. The movement of Razin was more conscious than the first peasant revolution. Razin had a definite purpose—to replace the bureaucratic state with a Cossack republic, with a tsar as a figurehead, who would execute the will of the Cossacks. At the service of the real, and not imaginary, tsar, however, there was by that time an army equipped and organized according to the West European model. Neither the Cossack detachments nor the bands of rebelling peasants who were accompanying them were able to survive its clashes with that army. On the sixth of June, 1671, Razin was executed in Moscow. His comrades were for the most part killed off even earlier. With the capture of Astrakhan within a few months, the main trade route of Muscovite Russia was again in the hands of the merchant-capitalist state.

The new Cossack-peasant revolution, almost exactly one hundred years after Razin's death, encountered in its course a still more solid military-bureaucratic organization. It was very characteristic that in this revolution the Cossacks were already not playing the foremost role: the participation of the future proletariat in the form of the working population of the Ural mining works—this is what frightened autocracy. These plants were the industrial base from which Pugachev got his cannons and shells. Catherine was extraordinarily afraid that the Moscow and Tula works would join the insurrection and deliberately placed large orders with the latter to secure stability among the workers. Pugachev lost time and the government won it. Against the rebels an army was assembled which formerly had been used only against a strong foreign enemy, as Catherine II herself admitted. Pugachev's troops were crushed, and on the eighth of January (Old Style), 1775, he met the fate of Razin in Moscow.

The Pugachev rebellion was the last Cossack-peasant revolution and in general the last large mass movement in Russia before 1905. After the Pugachev rebellion, the serf law in Russia was established for good. It fell in 1861 not beneath the blows of a peasant uprising, but under the pressure of a new wave of capitalism coming from the West—industrial capitalism. Under such conditions, the emancipation of the peasants was in fact an expropriation of them. The answer to this expropriation was a whole series of separate peasant uprisings (in all, including the minor outbreaks, no less than 2000 throughout the whole of Russia), but they did not merge into a general revolution as the revolutionary intelligentsia had expected.

However, even these were still more dangerous to autocracy than the Decembrist uprising (December 14, 1825), so highly valued in Russia by the bourgeois liberals, in which there had been, properly speaking, no uprising, because the conspirators, having gathered several regiments of guards on the Senate Square, deliberately refrained from attacking the government troops, firing back only when these were attacking. The Decembrist conspiracy had an exceptionally great significance for the development of the revolutionary ideology of the Russian intelligentsia—we will be concerned with this in the following essay—but it takes a very secondary place in the history of the mass popular movements in Russia.

V

Tsarism and the Roots of the 1917 Revolution

It is commonplace to regard Russian tsarism as something "primitive," as some remnant of hoary antiquity, something like patriarchal despotism, that has lived on until our days under the protection of the general economic and political backwardness of Russia.

But although this view of Russian autocracy as a vestige of patriarchal despotism has been expressed by people who are great authorities on the problems of Russian history—for example, the well-known Kavelin in his *Thoughts and Observations (Mysli i Zametki)*[1]—it is nonetheless incorrect. Russian autocracy is a fact of relatively recent times and represents an East European parallel to such phenomena as the absolutism of Louis XI or Henry VIII in Western Europe.

The backwardness of Russia manifests itself mainly in the fact that absolutism flourished in Russia in the beginning of the eighteenth century—when it had already fully acted out its role in England, and in France had been transformed into the new, higher form of autocracy of Louis XIV which resembled Russian absolutism at the time of Nicholas I. However, in its *type,* the rule of the Russian Romanovs (whose

First published in *Ezhegodnik Kominterna: Spravochnaia kniga . . . na 1923 god* (Petrograd and Moscow, 1923), pp. 232–40.

direct line had died out in 1761) was completely identical with that of the Tudors or the Valois.

This was far from being the earliest type of state authority on Russian territory. The written tradition of Russian history, reflected in the chronicles, had even found remnants of a genuine patriarchal despotism personified by the tribal princes of some or other Drevlians or Viatiches,[2] whom the chronicle even knew by name. The contemporaries of the first flourishing of Russian culture (Kievan Rus' eleventh to thirteenth centuries) were not these, however, but the newly arrived Norman princes and their guards. They were representatives of the "robber trade," of a precapitalist exchange, who from being leaders of bands of slave traders had become rulers of the areas they were exploiting, having first annihilated or subjugated their native patriarchal chieftains. This was already the second type of state power that the Russian Slavs knew.

Toward the thirteenth century even this appeared obsolete. The Russian prince, having become settled, was transformed from a vagrant robber and merchant into a large landowner and feudal seigneur, similar to those who were known in Western Europe as early as the tenth century. After the researches of Pavlov-Sil'vanskii (who died in 1908), no one in Russian historical scholarship any longer seriously questions that Russian feudalism was as much a variety of the type mentioned as was English, French, or German feudalism. The most persistent opponent of this view was N. Rozhkov, but in the latest edition of his *Russian History from a Sociological Point of View,* he regards "the feudal period" of Russian history as something that is self-evident.

However, Muscovite autocracy was connected with feudalism only in the same way as Russian feudalism was connected with the Varangian principalities of the earlier period: one of the feudal princes, the Muscovite, became at first a suzerain and then the sovereign of all Great Russia.* This happened not because he was a feudal prince, however, but because he was unlike the other feudal princes.

*The Ukraine joined the Muscovite State only in the middle of the seventeenth century, and Belorussia was annexed only at the end of the eighteenth century. [Pokrovskii's note.]

The prince of Moscow separated himself from, and rose above, the other feudal lords, owing to his close alliance with *merchant capital,* which in Russia of the fourteenth and fifteenth centuries had assumed the rudimentary forms known in Western Europe as early as the eleventh century (the so-called Crusades).

In another essay we have examined the role this invasion of merchant capital played in the development of the *revolutionary* movement in Russia. Its influence was no less, however, in the formation and development of *state* power.

Moscow was situated exactly at the crossing point of the commercial routes which in the fourteenth century were connecting Western Russia (Belorussia) with the Volga region and Northern Russia (Novgorod) with the rich grain regions of the south (Riazan'). The protection of these routes was the chief function of the Moscow prince: the chronicler of that century recorded that there had been no war in Muscovy for forty years. Commerce could not but appreciate this.

Gradually the prince of Moscow took a more active part in commercial operations. Even the first Muscovite princes had been lending money—we learn about this from their wills. The Muscovite tsar of the sixteenth century gave subsidies to the merchants trading with foreign countries, and was himself a large shareholder in a foreign (English) trade company. Concerning the second Romanov,* Alexis, one foreigner said that he was "the first merchant of his state." And another foreigner compared the court of his son, Peter "the Great," with a merchant's office in which one spoke no less about commerce than about politics.

"Primary accumulation" accompanied commerce. The autocratic regime, under which no one had any rights, was adapted to the needs of primary accumulation better than any other form of government. Under what other regime could one stroke of the pen change the peasants of a whole country into serfs, depriving them not only of property but also of freedom, as was done to the Ukrainian peasants under Catherine II (in 1783)? But in Russia this was considered so natural that Rus-

---

*This dynasty assumed the throne in 1613. [Pokrovskii's note.]

sian historians were for a long time explaining even the rise of Russia's serf law in general by such a stroke of the pen by a predecessor of Catherine. Only the studies of Kliuchevskii have shown that the Muscovite tsar enjoyed little of the power of an eighteenth-century emperor and that the enserfment of the peasants in Great Russia had proceeded in a much more complicated and prolonged manner than in the Ukraine.

In principle, autocracy bore a personal character. This character was manifested with especial sharpness in Peter (1672–1725), who claimed that the tsar could dispose of his realm like his private, acquired property: he could, for example, arbitrarily bequeath the state to whomever he wished. But this was only the clearest way of showing the unlimitedness of power and the subject's total lack of rights. Even earlier, when autocracy was still being formed, the same thought was expressed by the church, which taught that the tsar was God on earth. In fact, the tsar did not, of course, acquire divine omnipotence from this [teaching]—and a whole series of events from the same period in which the tsar was being declared an earthly god demonstrates the fact that he was nothing more than a mortal (the suicide of Boris Godunov, the murder of his son Fedor and of Pseudo-Dmitrii, the dethronement and the exile to a monastery of Vasilii Shuiskii, and so on). Similarly Peter's successors, despite their theoretical absolutism, were in fact only a tool in the hands of a group of magnates, proprietors of enormous estates, who were carrying on trade through figureheads, their clients. It was they who owned the first large industrial enterprises, with thousands of serf workers—the Ural mine works or the huge textile manufactures which were working almost exclusively on government orders for the army and navy.

During the first period after Peter, frightened by the open attempt of the domineering "Transformer" to turn theory into practice, these oligarchs also made attempts formally to limit autocracy for their own benefit (the so-called constitution of the "Supreme Lords," 1730). But they did this incompetently, and immediately began to fight for power among themselves, so that nothing came of it. Then they became convinced that it wasn't worth the trouble—with the help of regiments of guards the matter could be settled much more simply. A tsar who was objectionable to the oligarchs immediately fell from the throne and turned up in prison or in the grave—with a speed that no constitution could provide.

Only the Pugachev rebellion (1773–74) set a limit to this sporting with the heads of tsars. Having caught sight of the peasant's hatchet over their heads, the oligarchs understood that it was impossible to play any more—and surrendered without demur to the yoke of Catherine II's favorite, Potemkin. Catherine's son, Paul I (1796–1801), abused the obedience of the formerly rebellious aristocracy and fell victim to the last palace revolution in Russian history. His sons (Alexander I and Nicholas I) knew how to spare the pride and interests of the higher nobility; they became, in substance, the first real autocrats—embodiments of *the dictatorship of the nobility* over Russia. Though by this time the form was already a strictly personal one, it was nevertheless a dictatorship of a class, and not of persons. When addressing the representatives of great landowners, no tsar forgot to mention that he was the first nobleman of his state, the greatest landholder of Russia! Catherine II sometimes even called herself a landlady from Kazan' province—since there were, of course, crown estates also in Kazan' province.

In the beginning of the nineteenth century, however, the noble class itself no longer formed a single whole. The opening of the world market to Russian grain (in particular, much of Russian wheat was imported to England after the industrial revolution of the eighteenth century) transformed the Russian landlord estate into a "factory for the production of grain." On the virgin soil of the south and southeast, where the earth, known as black earth, was yielding enormous harvests without any fertilization, on this factory nothing was required but the hands of laborers: here the estate enterprise was turning into a likeness of the American plantation; the part of the Negroes was played by the Russian enserfed muzhiks. But in densely populated central Russia where the soil had already been under cultivation, *capital* was also required; as early as the first years of the nineteenth century individual landlords were beginning to establish a complex economy based on alternation of crops and to order machines from abroad (they began to discover that an estate worked by farmhands was more profitable than a slave plantation).

A battle between the landlord–"planter" and the "Manchesterist" noble began. On the side of the latter stood industrial capital, which had great successes in Russia from the beginning of the nineteenth century and especially after the Continental Blockade (for Russia 1807–12; however, the "protectionist system," with some vacillations, held out to the middle of the century) when factories and plants began to mushroom. In 1761 there was only *one* cotton weaving factory in Russia; in 1804 there were 199 of them, and in 1814—423. The number of workers in them increased over the latter ten years from 6500 to 39,000. Cloth factories numbered 155 in 1804, and in 1825—324; there were 26 cast-iron foundries and iron works in 1804, and 170 in 1825. Also on the side of industrial capital stood the "intelligentsia," which had just begun to form—a stratum of educated *contremaîtres*, capitalist organizers of the economy. It is no accident that among the leading "Decembrists" we meet the business manager of the Russian American Company Ryleev, the engineer Batenkov, the manager of a factory Steingel', and the writer-economist Nikolai Turgenev. Even the military in the group of conspirators were not alien to economic interests. General Orlov was very much involved with the banks: his friends were complaining that having completely given up politics, he didn't even want to talk about anything else.

The first clash of "Manchesterists" with "planters," the aforementioned "Decembrist conspiracy," was completely unsuccessful for the former. The St. Petersburg group of conspirators (the so-called Northern Society), which had rather substantial forces at its disposal, completely lacked the knowledge of how to launch them—and the Ukrainian group (the so-called Southern Society, headed by Colonel Pestel', which was not composed of Ukrainians but of Russian officers who belonged to the troops that were stationed in the Ukraine) favored armed insurrection but was upset by arrests and managed to raise only one regiment. Thus the Decembrists did not succeed in accomplishing anything: traces of their program and propaganda remained, however—and the *Russian liberal tradition* originated with them. The main demands of its program were: emancipation of the peasants and limitation, if not complete abolition, of autocracy.

The attempt by Nicholas I to oppose the demands of the "Manchesterists" with a firm "no" turned out to be a failure. The growth of the economy supported the "Manchesterists." Exports of Russian grain grew at an enormous rate (wheat: in 1820, 14 million poods, in 1860—42 million; rye: in 1820, 4 million poods, in 1860—20 million. Russian pood = 15 kilograms). The struggle for Constantinople (the Crimean War, 1853–56), begun by Nicholas partly to please industrial, but still more, merchant capital, immediately cut off these exports and dealt a hard blow to both the "Manchesterist" of central Russia and the "planter" of the south. The war was terribly unpopular—these years saw the first occurrence of "defeatist" attitudes in Russian society. At the same time even the peasantry became agitated. You could feel revolution in the air again.

Nicholas I did not survive this.* His successor, Alexander II, concluded the Peace of Paris, which was extremely disadvantageous for Russia, and immediately took up the struggle with the domestic movement against tsarism. Having learned from the bitter experience of his father, he did not resort to open force from the very beginning, but decided to win by ruse. The peasants were emancipated (in 1861) according to a plan which was incomparably more advantageous to the landlords than to the peasants themselves; in those places where the deception was already too flagrant, the peasants rose up, but the broad popular movement had been frustrated. For the "Manchesterist" wing of landlords, as well as for the intelligentsia,

---

*The version of his *suicide,* disputed by Professor Schiemann, was corroborated by the testimony of the Grand Duchess Elena Pavlovna which was preserved in the notes of Senator Semenov.[3] [Pokrovskii's note.]

certain institutions of the West European type were introduced (trial by jury; local self-government, partly copied from the Prussian system; a new censorship statute, borrowed from the France of Napoleon III; a new university statute, etc.: all these bourgeois reforms were carried out in 1862–64). For the "Manchesterists," this, along with the peasant reform, was enough to extinguish their opposition completely: from that time on even the most liberal of the nobles expressed their political attitudes only by means of the most loyal addresses and petitions. Moreover, Alexander II's government very cleverly used the Polish uprising (1863–64), which was completely harmless for Russia, to dispel the last remnants of defeatist attitudes in a chauvinistic fervor. The more radical journals (*The Contemporary* [*Sovremennik*], *Russian Word* [*Russkoe Slovo*]) were simply suppressed; the more radical publicists (Chernyshevskii, Mikhailov) were exiled to Siberia.

It seemed that the revolution had been uprooted. Even Russian "publicism" from abroad, which immediately after the Crimean War had acquired a colossal popularity among the widest circles of Russian society and had become a formidable force (Herzen, Ogarev, Bakunin—*The Bell* [*Kolokol*] and *The Polar Star* [*Poliarnaia Zvezda*]) lost its revolutionary pungency. Now, after the bourgeois reforms, it did not know what to say. Russia seemed to be completely transformed. On top of everything, at the time of the uprising Herzen had taken the side of the Poles, and as a result he brought down upon himself an avalanche of political dirt, which had cleverly been prepared by the government's policy. Belated actions of the small revolutionary circles—the most important of these was Karakozov's attempt on Alexander II's life (April 4, 1866)—completed the triumph of this policy. The last radicals were exiled; the last liberals hid themselves in their holes. On the scene there remained a triumphant autocracy which, it seemed, had completely accommodated itself to the demands of industrial capitalism.

Yet, it was precisely the development of the latter that was fostering tsarism's most formidable enemies. Above all, the peasant reform again split the nobility along new lines. While on the whole very advantageous for the nobility as a *class*, it was chiefly designed for the needs of *large* landed property: the small landlords, who had primarily been exploiting the enserfed peasant as a *person*, having lost their rights to free labor, were no longer able, for the most part, to manage their estates. This part of the nobility which had been brought to ruin was the first to reinforce the ranks of malcontents. Moreover, local self-government, which fell into the hands of the economically progressive landlords who began to build schools and hospitals and to introduce improved methods of farming and management, was bringing many educated men—doctors, teachers, agronomists, statisticians—to those remote places where formerly it would have been rare simply to meet a literate man. All of this intelligentsia, which was recruited from the ranks of the small nobility, minor officials, village clergy, and sometimes even from the higher strata of the peasantry, and which was, in addition, poorly paid, was rapidly becoming the champion of the petty-bourgeois democratic movement opposed to tsarism. The appalling excesses of *gründer*-capitalism which transformed the construction of the Russian railroad network in the period between 1860 and 1870 into a real bacchanalia of plunder were making even socialist theories popular among the petty-bourgeois democrats: utopian socialism already had its spokesmen in Russian literature, beginning with Herzen and Chernyshevskii (even earlier—Petrashevskii and his circle in the 1840's).

The new revolutionary army grew rapidly, and the development of industrial capitalism was automatically forming its cadres. At the end of the 1860's in Russia the industrial workers already numbered more than half a million, and after the emancipation of the peasants they almost became a real proletariat in the European sense of the word. In particular, the workers in the St. Petersburg factories and plants, having come from far away and being in part quite isolated from the land, represented a class completely unknown in serfdom Russia. And since the excesses of industrial capitalism were not smaller than those of railroad capitalism, very early we begin to see this new class acquire a new, European form of protest against exploitation—*the strike*. The strikes in St. Petersburg in 1870 made the government apprehensive; the minister of the interior distributed a circular to the governors calling his subordinates' attention to the horrible conditions in which the Russian workers lived: the long workday, low wages which moreover were being paid out very irregularly, various abuses on the part of the proprietors, such as fines, compulsory sale of provisions in factory stores, and so on. Yet even the officials from the liberal "Manchesterist" nobility did not consider it possible to infringe upon the "rights" of the factory owners. The first factory laws appeared in Russia only fifteen years later.

Yet if these strikes passed without changing the condition of the workers, they made a deep impression on the Russian revolutionary movement. It is no accident that from the beginning of the seventies the revolutionary movement was spreading and growing stronger among the Russian intelligentsia—especially in St. Petersburg (where a wave of strikes lasted throughout the seventies). Several propagandist circles were formed and began to spread socialist ideas, primarily among the workers (the very earliest of these was Chaikovskii's circle, whose most prominent member was Kropotkin; but this same circle was in general the breeding ground for the revolutionaries of the seventies). True enough, the socialism of these circles was petty bourgeois; on the whole they were strangers to Marxism (although individual theoreticians among them knew and appreciated Marx), and they saw the seeds of the future socialist system in a remnant of feudalism—the commune; also, they considered the main arena for their propaganda to be the countryside, where young revolutionaries were going by the hundreds (the so-called going to the people, 1873–74). However, the propaganda had almost no success among the peasants, whereas among the workers two revolutionary organizations arose: one in the south, in Odessa, the other in St. Petersburg. The latter, "The Northern Union of Russian Workers," led by the workers Khalturin and Obnorskii, was the first genuine political organization of the proletariat in Russia.

These organizations, needless to say, were routed by the government, but it was not they who drew the most attention.

The essential enemy for autocracy in these years (the end of the 1870's) was *the petty-bourgeois intelligentsia* among whom the revolutionary mood intensified even more than it had in the beginning of the 1860's. The cruel persecutions which had befallen the revolutionary propagandists (the trials of "193," "50," and others—in all, up to 1000 men were arrested and exiled) showed the latter that they could expect no mercy from the government. And the mood of the bourgeoisie, who after Alexander II's unsuccessful attempt to capture Constantinople in 1877 had again started to grumble as it had done after Sevastopol, inspired the hope that all of the "educated society" would support the revolution. The revolutionary society "Land and Freedom," formed in 1878, was replaced in the following year by a much stronger revolutionary organization "People's Will," which chose *terror* as the principal weapon leading, in its opinion, most rapidly and correctly to the goal—the overthrow of autocracy.

The "Executive Committee of the People's Will" (Zheliabov, Mikhailov, Perovskaia) declared a real war on Alexander II. On March 1, 1881, the tsar was killed by a bomb on a street of his capital. Even before this the government had completely lost its head. Alexander, before his death, was prepared to sign a constitution. His son, Alexander III, simply did not know what to do, listening at the same time both to constitutionalists like Loris-Melikov, and reactionaries like Pobedonostsev.

The inertia displayed by the bourgeoisie, whom terror had frightened almost more than it did the autocracy, and the dull indifference of the broad masses, who, left alone, were still too little conscious politically (while the members of the People's Will, carried away with terror as they were, shunned agitation and propaganda), encouraged the government of Alexander III. The tsar resolved to follow the course that had been tried with such success by his father in 1861—the course of *bribing* the people. The poor peasants were won over by the abolition of the poll tax and the regulation of redemption payments owed by the peasants following the 1861 reform. For the prosperous segment of the village a "Peasant Bank" was established, which made it easier for the well-to-do peasants to purchase land from these landlords. Finally, the benefactor-tsar provided the workers with factory laws which, pitiful though they were in comparison with Western Europe, all the same to some extent restrained the previously unlimited exploitation by the employers.

In contrast, however, to the 1860's, the intelligentsia was not shown any indulgence. In April, 1881, the new tsar issued a manifesto which categorically declared the inviolability of autocracy. The bourgeois reforms of the sixties were sharply curtailed—in the Zemstvo, where until this time everything rested on the *property* qualification, the *estate* principle was introduced. In the village the Justice of the Peace was abolished and Land Captains from the nobility were introduced, and so on. The empire of Alexander III was closer to the serfdom state of Nicholas I than to the half-bourgeois state of Alexander II.

This became possible because the "Manchesterist" noble had suffered a decisive defeat in these years. The crisis caused by [the decline of] grain prices that had begun in the 1870's made capitalist agriculture almost impossible. The landlord was dreaming, as though about paradise, about the unpaid, compulsory labor of the peasants which he had forfeited in 1861, but in fact he was making ends meet with tips from the public purse (available through the "Nobles' Bank" established in 1885). The pro-serfdom outlook definitely prevailed here; not only revolution but progressive tendencies of any kind were met by nothing but ridicule. Anti-Semitism which began to develop among the Russian nobility and even a part of the bourgeoisie precisely during those years (the first "pogroms" took place in 1881) represented an especially clear manifestation of this new mood.

The government of Alexander III hoped to get the better of the petty-bourgeois intelligentsia, isolated in this way, exclusively by police measures. It seemed to the intelligentsia itself that the government was successful in this course. The despondent mood of the intelligentsia corresponded to the embittered reactionary mood of the propertied classes. "The man of the eighties" in Russian literature became synonymous with a despondent, melancholic man who had thrown up his hands in helplessness. The works of Chekhov are filled with this type—one can learn best of all from them what the Russian intelligentsia of the age of Alexander III had experienced.

As a matter of fact, the solid foundation of the Russian revolution was laid precisely in these years. The failures of the intellectual-terrorists had very little effect on the working class which, as personified by its leaders, for example, Khalturin, had hardly attached more significance to terror than to the utopian socialism of the "populists." The revolutionary propaganda among the proletariat did not stop for a minute: in the course of the eighties in all large St. Petersburg factories there were propaganda circles which in extreme cases operated by their own strength, altogether without the intelligentsia. When the propaganda of the Emancipation of Labor Group[4] reached Russia and the first Marxist propagandists appeared in the St. Petersburg factories, they found that the ground had been fully prepared for them.

At the very same time, the agrarian crisis accomplished what the populist propagandists could not obtain in the early eighties: it stirred up the peasant masses. The sharp fall in grain prices forced the peasant to throw on the market not only the surplus product but also the necessary product of his farm. The proletarianization of the peasantry proceeded by giant steps. From 1888 through 1893 the peasantry of nine central agricultural provinces lost 25 percent of its horses. The famine of 1891–92 merely revealed what had been coming for a long time: the complete ruin of the widest segments of the country-side.

Toward the beginning of the twentieth century the ground was fully prepared for the action of the revolutionary parties and for the ascendancy of the proletarian ideology over all others.

VI

"The Prison of Nations"

Thus that basic force was being prepared which several years
later was to assume the leadership of the masses who had revolted against the landowners' autocracy. Oppression by the
latter was unbearable for the peasants, and even more so for
the workers, yet they were not the only victims of oppression.
The store of enslaved and dissatisfied which Russian autocracy
had accumulated by the end of its days was not restricted to
Russian peasants and workers. The condition of the non-
Russian peasants and workers was even worse, precisely because in addition to everything else they were not Russians.
This condition was so striking that it can be described in the
words of the *official* sources, in the words of the Russian officials
and generals and their authorized agents. Not to notice it
would be impossible.

Here is how the tsarist minister Witte described the *general* situation. Naturally, he expressed himself in a way that
was to be expected from a prominent tsarist official, but we
should not be disturbed by his expressions. The important
point is that even that official understood things which later,
in 1917, proved to be inaccessible to the understanding of the

This chapter is section III of *1905 god* first published in Moscow,
1930. Reprinted in M. N. Pokrovskii, *Izbrannye proizvedeniia* (Moscow, 1965–67), IV, 129–35.

Russian bourgeoisie. Here is what Witte wrote around 1911: "Our failure to realize that since the time of Peter the Great and Catherine the Great Russia no longer exists and there is a Russian Empire has been the reason why our policies of the past decades, up to the present, have been entirely mistaken. When approximately 35 percent of the population are non-Russians and the Russians themselves are divided into Great Russians, Little Russians, and Belorussians, then it is impossible to carry on a policy in the nineteenth and twentieth centuries that ignores this historical fact of capital importance, the national identity of the other nationalities which have become part of the Russian Empire—their religion, their language, and so on."[1]

It does not matter that Witte through his own ignorance included Ukrainians among the Russians and even called them "Little Russians." What could one expect if subsequently, while leading the struggle against the revolution, he did not even know the name "Bolshevik" and talked about some kind of "anarchist revolutionary party of Russia" which had never existed. What does matter is that even Witte ought to have properly written the name "Russia" in quotation marks, as I am writing it now; for the "Russian Empire" was not at all a national Russian state. It was a collection of several dozen peoples, among whom the Russians constituted a clear minority (about 47 percent), peoples who were united only by the general exploitation on the part of the ruling clique of landowners, and united moreover through the help of the most brutal oppression.

Even the Muscovite State of the seventeenth century, in spite of the opinion of bourgeois historians, was no longer a national state of the Great Russian tribe. Besides the remnants of the Finnish tribes, who were enslaved as early as the pre-Muscovite period (the Karelians in Tver, and before the eighteenth century also in the Kaluga province), the Tatars, Mordvians, the Mari, Chuvash, and Bashkirs were conquered; at the same time the "conquest of Siberia" was begun, i.e., the forcible annexation of many small northern peoples to Moscow. The enslaved peoples had been revolting at the first opportunity: the Mari annihilated entire Muscovite armies with their commanders. However, the superior military organization of the Russians always prevailed in the end, and the uprising was put down. Here are two examples from the history of the "pacification" of the Bashkirs. After the uprising of 1735–41, "the Bashkirs were beaten, executed, they died in captivity, were sent to work, their wives and children . . . given away for resettlement in Russia, all in all 28,452 persons." And do you know how this author—a landowner, a relative of that Bibikov who had participated in the suppression of the Pugachev uprising and whose much-praised biography he wrote—how he estimated the total number of "Bashkirs"? Just about one hundred thousand men! And this was only one uprising! In 1754 the Bashkirs "revolted again," and again this time "in order to pacify them they were beaten and deported . . . in numbers up to thirty thousand."[2]

You will say: but this was long ago, in the eighteenth century, when customs were cruel, torture existed, people were flogged with whips on the public square, and so on. Later customs grew milder. Well, let's take a look at how mild they grew. Let us take the dispatch of the Russian commander in chief in the Caucasus at the beginning of the nineteenth century—a tsarist general who had no reason at all to slander his own subordinates. He writes about the relations of the Russians to the Kabardians (now the Kabardino-Balkar Autonomous Republic): "the extension of the Caucasus line [the area of Russian colonization] at the expense of their best land has made the Kabardians distrustful of us. . . . Because of the vain desire of some of the local commanders to distinguish themselves militarily against the Kabardians rather than by winning them over with gentle and just rule, it has become common to undertake military action every year against them or some other peoples, frequently without any cause. Such measures have embittered the Kabardians to the point that although they do not have even a shadow of their former might after their last utter defeat, they are still nourishing to this day their invincible spirit of revenge against Russia." This "spirit of revenge" was kept alive as if deliberately also among those

nationalities of the Caucasus who had the misfortune to subject themselves to the Russians. Here, for example, is the order
issued by another supreme commander in the Caucasus at that
time, Ermolov, with regard to the "peaceful" Chechens (the
Russians themselves called them "peaceful" because these
Chechens had already ceased resisting): "In the event of theft
every settlement is obligated to deliver up the thief, and if he
goes into hiding, then his family. But if the inhabitants provide
a means of escape to the entire family of the thief, then the
whole settlement is to be set on fire." If the "plunderers" (i.e.,
the mountaineers who continued to resist) took a Russian in
captivity and the inhabitants of the "peaceful" settlement did
not recapture and rescue him, "from such a village for every
Russian taken in captivity, it is ordered that two men from the
natives be conscripted." In the event of a regular raid by the
"plunderers" that the "peaceful" natives fail to resist, "[their]
village is destroyed, and the wives and children slaughtered."[3]

After this, one can believe the words of a Chechen historian (an officer in the Russian service, i.e., more than merely
"peaceful") that "having been constantly ruined by the Russians, the Chechens grew accustomed to being resettled from
one place to another to such an extent that this forms their distinguishing national characteristic."[4] But you will say again:
after all this was still in the time of serfdom law, when even in
"Russia" itself people were being exchanged for dogs and
horses; later "customs grew milder." Very well, let us take the
"annexation of Turkestan," the conquest of Central Asia
(the present-day Kazakhstan, Uzbekistan, Turkmenistan).
This came in the 1860's and 1880's, after the "liberation." One
thoroughly "Black-Hundred" Russian traveler at the end of
the nineteenth century found that the population of present-
day Uzbekistan was given to "trembling" before the "Russian
name." We will see presently that "trembling" might also be
given a different name, but first let us recount, in the words of
this traveler, how this "trembling" was achieved. It "was
achieved with difficulty and its cost was heavy. Before the
present state of complete security could be established in the
country, it had been necessary to deal mercilessly with the

natives after the slightest attempt on their part to attack the Russians. Entire villages were burned to ashes if a single body of a murdered Russian was found in their vicinity." In addition, the population was brutally exploited: the taxes introduced by the Russians (who had come to "emancipate" the local population from the "yoke" of the native rulers) were increased two, three, four, in one case even fifteenfold! Under this, the population was simply dying out. Where before the arrival of the Russians there had been 45 settlements and 956 households, twenty years later there already were only 36 settlements and 817 households, and of these as many as 225 were empty. Small wonder if according to the "Black-Hundred" traveler mentioned above "all around one could sense an exasperated and discontented feeling. Hundreds of angry eyes full of a disapproving severity kept watch on our ceremonial processions; it felt as if one could reach out and grab the evil rays which were piercing us from all directions." In the end our "Black-Hundred" man began to ponder the fact that "if some sort of great political or military confusion were to occur in Russia, in Turkestan a popular movement against the Russians would start immediately."[5] Witte was not the only one who resembled the cat that knew whose meat it had swallowed.

In the East, in the Caucasus, in Central Asia, later in Manchuria (Russian acts of plunder in Manchuria were in no way different from those in the Caucasus or Central Asia, and this is why I do not speak about them separately) direct coercion was applied more often, of course, than in the more civilized Western or South-Western provinces of the "Empire." But even there in some places, for example, in Poland, after its "insurrections," its attempts to overthrow Russian rule, direct coercion was used very often and a great many Poles ended their lives in Siberia. Everywhere the "alien," i.e., non-Russian, was an inferior creature and an "outcast" to a greater degree than even the Russian peasant. At least no one stopped the latter from speaking in his own language, and in the court or at a *Zemstvo* board he heard the language which he understood. But in the non-Russian provinces—Poland, Latvia, Estonia, the Ukraine, Transcaucasia—all "public business" was conducted in Russian: the literate Latvian peasants, like some savages in Central Africa, had to make themselves understood before Russian judges through an interpreter! In the Ukraine for a long time even the Gospel was not permitted in Ukrainian, although this would have been clearly advantageous to the priests in stupefying the Ukrainian peasants. In Poland the Polish language was taught in schools, but it was compulsory to do so in Russian: the teacher was forbidden to discuss a Polish writer, for example Mickiewicz, in the children's native language because in a Polish school only Russian could be spoken. The children were deprived of a meal if they were "caught" speaking Polish among themselves. Needless to say Ukrainian, Belorussian, Georgian, etc. schools did not exist. If a Ukrainian or Georgian wanted to be literate, he had to study Russian. Moreover, this was done to nations which not only have their own written language (sometimes older than Russian), but also have their own literature and classical works which frequently have been translated into other languages. One unwittingly asks himself: What can explain these savage attempts to turn back the history of culture, to make already literate peoples illiterate? An answer to this can be found in the history of the Jews—a people who were the outcasts par excellence of all "outcasts" in the tsarist patrimony.

In the Western and South-Western parts of the "Empire" they sometimes constituted a majority of the urban population. They could not be driven out but they were locked up there. The Jews were forbidden to take up residence in villages or to leave the "Pale of Settlement." The others were not allowed to study in their native language; for Jewish children, admittance even to Russian schools was almost completely denied. There was a fixed "percent" [quota] of Jewish students for each district: in those places where Jews were in a majority it reached up to 10 percent; in other places it fell to 3 percent. Jews were denied entry to the state service so that they could in no way get into the ruling class (the landowners and bourgeoisie from among the other "aliens" could enter). In military service, no matter what feat a Jew may have performed, he was never promoted to the rank of officer. And to top it all, from time to time the illiterate urban bigots, small shopkeepers and artisans of the towns where the Jews lived, were incited against

the Jews and a Jewish pogrom followed. Such a pogrom occurred in Kishinev, the capital of Bessarabia, in the spring of
1903, and it shook all of Europe; up to a thousand Jews were
killed or maimed by the enraged bigots. We shall see that later,
in the period of revolution, the pogroms were a favorite weapon
of the tsarist government.

The pogrom offers us the very key to the nationality policy
of that government. Why was the Russian or Ukrainian petty
bourgeoisie and peasantry being incited against the Jews? In
order to turn the eyes of these unfortunate people from those
who were really responsible for their misfortune. The real
culprits were those who were milking the people dry for the
sake of the ruling stratum, who imposed on the peasants taxes
ten times as high as those paid by the landowners, and so on.
Instead of this, they showed peasants a prosperous Jew and
said: "Look how rich he is getting! He is getting rich off you,
and that is why you are so poor!" And the illiterate, ignorant
fellow believed that all the evil was in the Jew, and he did not
see the real source of evil. Neither did he see that for every
rich Jew there were a thousand poor ones.* Admittedly, this
worked less well as time went on, and already by 1902 the
peasant, when they tried to incite him against the Jew, began
to raid the landowners. For the time being, however, the discord between nationalities which the tsarist government zealously supported was obstructing the unification of all the
workers and the exploited into one mass. The Russian was
incited against the Pole ("he is always rebelling!"), against the
Tatar or Uzbek ("infidels, non-Christians!"), against the
mountaineer of the Caucasus or the Turkmen ("he only thinks
about how to slaughter the Russians!").† In Transcaucasia the

---

*Here is what the organizer of the pogroms himself, Plehve, said
about this at a conference: "Whole families consisting of many members live for weeks on stale bread alone, and a herring, divided into
small cuts, is a luxury which one can allow oneself only on holidays."
[Pokrovskii's note.]

†Not only the illiterate were incited—in Russian "classical"
literature we find the very same motives. In Lermontov, for example,
in "A Cossack Lullaby": "the evil Chechen crawls to the bank and
whets his dagger." Now we know why the "Chechen" became "evil."
[Pokrovskii's note.]

Armenian was incited against the Turk, and the Turk against the Armenian. In Finland, the Finn against the Swede, in Latvia, the Latvian against the German, and so on, and so forth. The low cultural level of the masses who were being incited was the primary condition for the success of such instigation. A literate, self-conscious population cannot be stirred up against anyone you choose; and the Latvian peasants in the end did not oppose Germans in general but the German landowners, the most greedy and merciless of their kind in the whole "Russian Empire." And since it was easy to exploit an illiterate population, in this way tsarist policy also assisted the plunder of the "aliens" by Russian capitalism. It was not accidental that the Bashkirs were even sent to France so that they could be exploited in particularly hazardous work there.

However, we will be very much mistaken if we think that this oppression of "borderlands" (some of these "borderlands" began at 500 kilometers from the center—and this was in a country through which one could travel 10,000 kilometers without crossing a border) was only a subsidiary means for autocracy, that it only somewhat facilitated its struggle with the popular masses by splintering them, inciting one part against another, keeping them in ignorance by artificial means. No, the colonial policy of the ruling class of landowners (Lenin called it "military-feudal imperialism") was one of the basic reasons why the landowners' dictatorship itself existed in our country for such a long time. The availability of colonies, i.e., "the borderlands" (the land inhabited by the "aliens"), for exploitation helped to preserve backward forms of the economy in the center. "The development of capitalism in depth in the old, long-inhabited territories is retarded because of the colonization of the outer regions. The solution of the contradictions inherent in, and produced by, capitalism is temporarily postponed because of the fact that capitalism can easily develop in breadth. Thus, the simultaneous existence of the most advanced forms of industry and of semimedieval forms of agriculture is undoubtedly a contradiction. If Russian capitalism had possessed no range for expansion beyond the bounds of the territory already occupied at the beginning of the post-Reform period, this contradiction between capitalist large-scale industry and the archaic institutions in rural life (the tying of the peasants to the land, etc.) would have had to lead quickly to the complete abolition of these institutions, to the complete clearing of the path for agricultural capitalism in Russia. But the possibility (for the millowner) of seeking and finding a market in the outer regions in process of colonization, and the possibility (for the peasant) of moving to new territory, mitigates the acuteness of this contradiction and delays its solution."[6]

Thus wrote Lenin at the end of the nineteenth century. The dictatorship of the serf-holding landowners was not only a reflection of our country's economic backwardness, it was also one of the causes of this backwardness. As it rested on outmoded forms of economy, it did not let the economy move forward at the same time. As long as it was not overthrown, "Russia" had to remain a backward agrarian country.

VII

Russian Imperialism in
the Past and Present

When these lines appear in print, the name of General Liman von Sanders[1] will, perhaps, already have been forgotten, or perhaps it will have become historic. As the reader remembers, that is the name of the Prussian general who became the de facto commander in chief of the Turkish army. This appointment, foreign newspapers report, has generated great excitement in Russian "public opinion" (read: *The New Times* [*Novoe vremia*]).[2] The fact that a Prussian general was made a Turkish pasha would alone hardly be worth the interest of real public opinion in Russia. The historian, however, instinctively remembers another incident which took place in this very same Constantinople sixty years ago [i.e., 1854]. That incident deserves comparison with "the penny candle"[3] even more than the present one: the keys to the church at Bethlehem (who remembers this now and who knew very much about it then?) were taken from the pockets of the Orthodox monks and put into the pockets of the Catholic monks.[4] Moreover, within a few years because of these keys a cannonade roared at Sevastopol. Nicholas I went to his grave in a tragic way, and the age

First published in *Prosveshchenie*, 1914, no. 1, pp. 18–27. Reprinted *Vneshniaia politika* (Moscow, 1918) pp. 153–61.

of "the Great Reforms of the Sixties" began in Russia. Moscow had been burnt down by a penny candle. Will General Sanders be such a penny candle? This does not depend on him, of course (nor on *Novoe vremia*), but on the "economic basis" upon which he stands, not so much in the capacity of its "political superstructure" as in the role of a political weathervane pointing out the direction of the wind. In any case it is worth the effort to compare the "economic basis" of the Bethlehem keys with that of the Prussian general, and we have no fear of boring the readers of *Enlightenment (Prosveshchenie)* with our historical inquiry.

In our country the view is widely held that Nicolaevian, "pre-reform" Russia was a noblemen's feudal country where everything, and every one, was determined by the interests of the landowners who at that time were also the masters of the peasant "souls." Such a presentation is absurd enough in itself, and especially so for a Marxist: after all, the age of "the Reforms" followed immediately after the Nicolaevian period— and no matter whether we regard these reforms as "great" or not, it is impossible to deny their strongly pronounced bourgeois character. The replacement of class ranks by property qualifications of various forms and kinds (in the Zemstvo, in the courts of justice, and so on) alone was enough to dispel any kind of doubt regarding this point at least. How did these bourgeois reforms suddenly appear against this purely feudal background? Then, too, if it is remembered that the projects for reform preceded their implementation (the plans of Speranskii, the Decembrists, the peasant and legal reforms under Nicholas I), no other course is left to the materialist historian than to acknowledge the existence of some sort of bourgeois environment which nourished these plans and projects. We shall not refer in full to the political role of this pre-reform Russian bourgeoisie. Extremely characteristic facts are available on this. Many know, for example, that on the eve of December 14, [1825] at the dinner tables of the most prominent St. Petersburg merchants "speeches were being made in the most liberal spirit" (the Steingel' memoirs).[5] But if we occupy ourselves with them, they will lead us too far from our proper task. It will suffice to show what an enormous influence young Russian capitalism had on the *foreign policy* of Nicholas I. All students of history know of the "victories and conquests" with which the reign of this sovereign began: everyone has heard about his Persian and Turkish wars, about Dibich-Zabalkanskii, about Paskevich-Erivanskii, about the Treaty of Adrianople. Yet in no historical work—not merely textbooks—will you find any attempt to provide not only an economic but simply a sensible explanation of all these campaigns and conquests. In the meantime, however, contemporaries long had noted the economic basis for this—and in the Russian Council of State in the Nicolaevian period this matter was being discussed with complete clarity. The well-known English publicist of those days, Urquhart (a name the students of Marx's life have of course come across) wrote that after Russia's victory over Persia, the Persian market proved to be practically in the monopolistic possession of Russian capital: English goods were forced to wage a desperate and, at first, by no means always successful struggle against Russian products; Russian currency and Russian commercial usages held complete dominion in northern Persia. Moreover, a well-known Russian statistician of that period, Arseniev, testified that a number of Shuia textile factories lived off the Persian market. One of Shuia's largest firms, the Posylin's, became so acclimatized in Transcaucasia that it was considered in Tiflis to be a native, local firm—its Shuia factories having apparently been quite forgotten. The merchant decorated with the Persian Order of the Lion and the Sun has become an anecdotical figure in our literature. Only rarely does one now surmise that this anecdote, like Don Quixote's armor, recalls the distant heroic age of Russian industrial capitalism; Posylin was the first among Russian merchants to be awarded this Persian decoration. For the Nicolaevian factory owners, however, Persia was not enough. From the secret correspondence (published at a later date) of the South Russian administrators (the governor-general of Odessa, Vorontsov, or the commander in chief in the Caucasus, Rozen, and others) with Kankrin, the minister of finance, we have learned about the extensive plans of the Nicolaevian government to capture not only the Persian but also the Turkish market and to expel the British from Trebizond, the main port of entry for English goods on the southern coast of the Black Sea. To achieve these goals, Nicholas's diplomacy put an ever increasing pressure on Turkey, and as a result of the so-called Treaty of Unkiar-Skelessi (1833), the Russian emperor became almost as much the master of the Bosphorus shores as he was of the banks of the Neva. This was too much for the English, and war appeared imminent. Within a few years Nicholas Pavlovich had to give up the Unkiar-Skelessi treaty, and the danger of a war with England was averted, though by no means eliminated forever. In the last months of his life, the summer of 1854, Nicholas I had a chance to see, from the window of his palace at Peterhof, what he had been preparing for in 1835: the English navy cruising before Kronstadt.

The conflict was prolonged and stubborn, and it could not be settled amicably because it was not at all a local, Eastern conflict: the struggle for the Turco-Persian market was only the most striking symptom of discord—the area of this discord was incomparably broader. At the beginning of the nineteenth century Russia could not be counted as an industrial power. For Western Europe, above all for England itself, Russia was a great supplier of raw materials: timber, fat, hemp; Russian wheat also was becoming increasingly important on the European market. In exchange for these raw materials "punctilious London" was furnishing the nobility and officialdom of Russia with finished products—from cloth to writing paper and toilet requisites. The peasants wore only what they had made themselves at home. There were factories and plants, of course, but for the most part they employed compulsory serf labor and lived not so much off the market as off government orders. Industrial capitalism in the proper sense, just as the industrial proletariat, did not yet exist. The brief period of an imposed Russo-French alliance and unwilling break with England (1807–12) changed the picture beyond recognition: under the influence of the "Continental Blockade" (which prohibited imports of English goods to the Continent) which Napoleon had forced Russia to join, the Russian *textile industry* was rapidly born in some five or six years. As late as 1809 Russia was importing in total only a half million pounds of American cotton; by 1811 nine and a half million pounds were imported. In 1808 the first mechanical spinning machine appeared in Russia (a private one—before that there had been only government-owned ones); and before the French invasion in 1812, there were eleven in Moscow alone. The War of 1812 put an end to the Continental Blockade for Russia, but England was no longer able to regain the place she had lost on the Russian market. The "national" Russian industry stood on firm ground: in 1812 there were 2332 factories in Russia, by 1828 already 5244; in 1812 workers numbered 120,000 and fifteen years later there were already 225,000, half of them free. This was real capitalism, and very soon, after hesitating for several years, it determinedly went over to the offensive. In 1822 the Russian border was practically closed to English goods: the tariff introduced in that year directly prohibited the importation of some, while high, "prohibitive" duties were imposed on the majority. Within six years, from 1820 to 1826, imports of foreign cloth into Russia were reduced: cotton by half and woolens fivefold. There was a corresponding increase in the output of Russian factories. And since the internal Russian market was growing with difficulty, owing to serfdom and the natural-economic relations supported by the latter, large-scale industry, which had just begun to spring up, started to search for foreign markets. Persia and Asiatic Turkey were not in the least the only objects of its greed: the Moscow and Vladimir industrialists managed to have the entire Caucasus and Transcaucasia, where trade had been previously free, included in the Russian customs boundary; Russian reconnoiters even appeared in Afghanistan. Perovskii's campaign against Khiva (in 1839) was the start of the conquest of Central Asia; finally, a Russian "spiritual mission," which quite obviously was covering up the same commercial reconnaissance, was dispatched even to China; and one could find schemers who were already dreaming of ousting the English from China as well. English

free trade was confronting Russian protectionism almost everywhere across the face of the earth. Not only sensation-seeking
journalists, like Urquhart, but even English statesmen began
to look with alarm upon this Russian flood. The struggle
against "Russian expansion" became the main task of the English bourgeoisie, and its political leader Palmerston personified
the anti-Russian policy. Since the road to Russian capitalism
was paved everywhere by Russian bayonets, the matter also
had to be settled by bayonets. At Sevastopol, the "brave bayonet" gave out: a year after the Peace of Paris, which ended the
War of Sevastopol, Russian protectionism surrendered too; in
1857 Russia received a new "free-trade" tariff which again
permitted the importation of foreign goods into Russia with
a more or less moderate customs duty.

As we see, in the first half of the nineteenth century,
Russia knew *imperialism* in its most authentic form: high customs duties which gave the "home" industries a monopoly inside the country; the urge, behind the cover of these duties, to
expand its economic territory on an immense scale; a series of
aggressive wars and "expeditions" resulting from this urge—
everything which we are accustomed to include under the term
"imperialism" was there, even the political reflection of this
economic fact. Imperialism in contemporary Europe means a
taste for a strong central power, mighty and "magnificent,"
before which "foreign peoples" humbly bend their knees, and
one which in return is forgiven much at home. The might and
magnificence of power was the main aim of Nicholas Pavlovich:
he impressed upon his subjects the idea that the Russian sovereign was the master of all Europe, that there was no power
that would dare to get in Russia's way—and, apparently, toward
the end he himself came to believe this. The tragedy which
ended his reign was to a significant degree the result of this
self-deception. Yet if the mastery of Russia over Europe was an
illusion, the "might and magnificence of power" inside the
country was a completely real fact. Foreign nations did not,
perhaps, fear the Russian emperor as much as he would have
liked; but his subjects were unquestioningly obedient, above

all the merchants. The reputation for unshakable loyalty, which this class has had, stems precisely from those times: the liberal enthusiasm of an earlier age (when all hope for the internal market had not yet been lost) had vanished without a trace. It is exceptionally characteristic that in subsequent Russian history the awakening of imperialistic passions always coincided in time with political reaction. The conquest of Central Asia was proceeding during the same time as, after the Polish uprising in 1863, the government and the bourgeoisie turned sharply to the right. The reaction of the 1880's was contemporary with the attempt at economic conquest of Bulgaria, the most curious episode in "Russia's expansion," which right now we have no time to consider in greater detail. Finally, the greatest wave of imperialism in prerevolutionary [i.e., pre-1905] times, the Manchurian-Korean *épopée,* coincided exactly with the regime of Sipiagin and Plehve inside Russia. The flourishing of the latest Russian imperialism, therefore, is completely natural and in order against the background of the Stolypin reaction. The literary representatives of the Russian textile industry (Mr. Struve, and *Russkaia mysl'* in general) showed the greatest lack of judgment in demanding that the Russian government at one and the same time "establish the great power of the state" and be "liberal." That meant to demand from one and the same plant that it bloom with roses and bear tasty pears. . . . You can only have one; and, naturally, the practical bosses of Mr. Struve have always preferred pears to roses. First you must have enough to eat—and the various pleasant things in life can wait.

Russian imperialism, as in the days of Nicholas I, is chiefly cotton imperialism. While iron metallurgy in Russia made almost no progress during the first decade of the twentieth century (the quantity of smelted cast iron in Russia in 1900 was 176 million poods; in 1910, 185 million poods), the textile industry displayed an unprecedented sweep (the quantity of cotton processed by Russian factories in 1900 was 16 million poods; in 1910, 22 million poods). It faced no crisis, with the exception of the short hitch caused by direct engagement in war and by the revolution: the views on the industrial crises in prerevolutionary [pre-1905] Russia were based upon the study of "heavy industry," which, strictly speaking, is not Russia's representative industry at all. However, the similarity to the period of Nicholas I is not confined to "the stuff of imperialism," if we may put it that way: it goes much further. Then, as now, Russia made an unsuccessful attempt to change her political structure; in other words, she attempted to free her productive forces which were gripped in the clutches of an obsolete state mechanism (in Nicholas's time this would have resulted in the destruction of serfdom, which had been a part of the Decembrist program). The delay in the development of productive forces was, however, both then and now, equivalent to a delay in the expansion of the internal market: the textile industry is particularly sensitive to this because its consumers are the popular masses. *When production grows faster than the internal market, it means that a foreign market is necessary.* The nationalism of Stolypin followed logically from his victory over the revolution. And a victory of the revolution would have slowed down the development of imperialism for a long time: the reaction is not only conditioned by the successes of imperialism, but itself conditions the latter.

Until recently, the Far Eastern theater of Russian imperialism has attracted the greatest public attention. There was so much noise over Mongolia that one can hardly not have heard about it. But we always try to help matters with noise precisely at those times when they are not moving by themselves. In Manchuria and in Mongolia the prospects are very great, but in reality, there appears to be nothing as yet: the Russian trade balance with China remains by and large passive since as before we buy more from China than we sell to it. Matters are completely different in the *Near East,* that old arena of Russian imperialism. Here there is less noise, but the results obtained, at least in one respect, must be described as enormous. If Urquhart were to rise from the grave, he would be horrified to see what has happened in Persia, where already during his lifetime the Russians would not leave the English alone. *Today the Persian market is entirely in Russian hands:*

in terms of its turnover with Persia, Russia occupies the first place by far among the European states. The following account shows this turnover in 1906–7:

Countries	*Thousands of* *Pounds Sterling*
Russia	8.292
England	3.128
France	0.700
Austria	0.277
Germany	0.182

And yet Russian merchants grumble that the Germans are "outdoing" them in Persia. The English source from which we took these data openly recognizes not only Russia's absolute superiority in the business of exploiting the Persian market but also her unceasing advance. While the Anglo-Persian trade of 1906–7 was remaining in almost the same position as in 1897, it says, "trade with Russia was rising from 3½ million pounds to 8¼, or by 137 percent."

Since 1906–7, if things have changed, it has not been to Russia's disadvantage, as is shown by the following small table of imports to Persia:

Countries	*Thousands of* *Pounds Sterling*	
	1910–11	*1911–12*
Russia	4.391	5.355
England	3.793	4.414
Germany	0.279	0.332

Germany and England together export less than does Russia alone. In short, Russian capitalism in Persia occupied *relatively* the same place as it did in the 1830's: relatively, because the absolute turnover then and now is not comparable. Under Nicholas I the entire Russo-Persian trade has been estimated at 4 million rubles—today it comes close to 100 million.

There was good reason why the cotton processed by Russian factories was then counted in millions of pounds, and now is in millions of poods [one pood = 36 lbs.].

Eighty years ago Russian imperialism, setting out from Persia, advanced on Turkey, there to meet a defeat. Now, after the occupation of Northern Persia, the occupation of Armenia is next in line, as it economically and strategically commands the eastern half of Asia Minor; the road from the Black Sea to Persia and to the upper Tigris and Euphrates passes through Trebizond and Erzurum, cities in the Armenian uplands. In foreign newspapers the planned advance of the Russians on Armenia is mentioned quite openly, quoting the words of Russian ministers, since they have talked more willingly, as is well known, with French journalists than with any others. They have given to understand that St. Petersburg is ready to see Armenia as a compensation for the incident with Liman von Sanders. It is exactly the same as in 1853, when Nicholas I found a compensation for the keys of Bethlehem in the "Danube principalities," the present-day Rumania. The Sevastopol war, as it is well known, began with the Russian occupation of Rumania. But let us not run ahead. Let us consider what Turkey represents for Russia right now—from the economic point of view. Here is another small table of imports to Turkey from the same three states: England, Germany, and Russia:

Countries	Thousands of Pounds Sterling 1905–6	Percent of Total Imports	Thousands of Pounds Sterling 1908–9	Percent of Total Imports
England	9.642	(35.05)	8.257	(30.0)
Germany	1.163	(4.22)	1.698	(6.16)
Russia	1.597	(5.8)	2.188	(7.94)

As we see, England is still first and foremost, as she was throughout the entire nineteenth century. However, not only her share of imports to Turkey, but even the *absolute volume* of English exports to Turkey has been rapidly falling: in its stead, Russian and German exports are growing both absolutely and relatively, Russia's being larger absolutely and growing more rapidly. In subsequent years the rapid growth of Russian exports has shown itself even more sharply: in 1909 Russia exported to Turkey goods worth 26 million rubles (as against 21.5 million the previous year—the Russian and Turkish fiscal years do not overlap); in 1910, 26.5 million rubles; in 1911, 32 million. Since 1905 the Russian exports have doubled. It is true that in comparing Russian and German exports one must make serious adjustments: the figures cited refer only to exports directly from Germany itself. Undoubtedly, however, a significant part of German goods—it is difficult to determine how much—comes by way of Austria: the latter exported, for example, 6.772 thousand Turkish pounds worth to Turkey in 1910–11 (Turkish pound = $\frac{9}{10}$ English pound sterling). In total, of course, Austro-German exports exceed the Russian by far. However, we did not intend to inspire patriotic feelings in the reader with a picture of how the Russians are overpowering the Germans. For us what matters is that Russia is one of Germany's rivals in Turkey and claims a share in the English succession—and, for the time being, a rival that is not doing badly. From here, it is but one step to the question of dividing the inheritance.

But, the reader will object, first of all, what does the benefactor think of this matter? At first glance it appears clear that the conflict should again, as in 1830–40, arise between England, on one side, and Russia and Germany jointly, on the other. After all, are not the English being squeezed out of the market? Yes, but today they are inclined to regard the fact much more calmly than eighty years ago. What matters is that commodity exports have lost the importance for England that they used to have. Since 1875 their volume has increased merely by half, whereas Germany has increased her exports during the same interval by two and a half times, and the United States threefold. English exports to the European continent have fallen from year to year,* but the English have no grounds for losing

*For example, the English machines exported to Germany in 1907 were worth 2,365,000 pounds sterling, and in 1911, only 1,934,000 pounds sterling. [Pokrovskii's note.]

their composure by such an event: first of all, their own colonies are growing and growing gigantically—it is these that chiefly account for the increase in English exports; and, second, and much more importantly, *from a country which exports goods, England is becoming more and more a country which exports capital.* In 1910 English capital in investments abroad amounted to 3192 million pounds sterling. England's trade balance has been passive for a long time, i.e., it imports more than it exports, but owing to the interest on capital invested abroad, England still gets increasingly more from abroad than it pays there.* English businessmen, of course, suffer from foreign competition, especially German. It is not they who direct English policy, however, but the banking aristocracy; and so Persia was given over, one might say, to Russian capital for plunder, while as for Turkey, the late Salisbury said as early as the 1890's that it really made no difference to England if Russia should establish herself on the Bosphorus. On the other hand, Germany cannot regard this fact with indifference: in contrast to England, its balance of trade depends basically on the export of goods. Germany also has its capital abroad (according to different data, from 26 to 33 billion marks, i.e., roughly half as much as England), but the returns from this capital almost fail to equal the balance. While exporting 5.8 billion marks annually, Germany imports 7.4 billion, and if it were not for the "earnings" of the German marine (300–400 million marks annually), not only would it fail to make a "net profit," but its balance would close with a loss in the hundreds of millions. Thus, for Germany the sale of commodities has a tremendous significance; one should see with what distress a German consul reports that from the export trade of German cloth to Persia, which had once been very extensive, there has remained, owing to Russian competition, only the name, only the empty sound. The Lodz tricot is being sold at the Tabriz bazaar under the name of "Meseritz cloth," and only this

*Imports to England exceed exports by £178 million. In interest it receives from abroad £155 million, plus £20 million commissions and bank fees, plus £91 million in freight and insurance charges. [Pokrovskii's note.]

name recalls the fact that at one time good German cloth from Meseritz (in Silesia) was sold there. For a long time now the commodity has been Russian while the name is German. German capitalism does not relish the prospect of having only German names left in Constantinople as well. One must, at least, not allow the Russians into Turkey if by now there is nothing that can be done about them in Persia. Thus, the conflict lies right here—not a conflict between England, on the one hand, and Germany and Russia, on the other, but precisely between Germany and Russia.

But, the reader will protest, is the sale of German goods in Turkey, which is, as we have just seen, rather negligible in absolute figures, really so important that it can itself determine the policy of the German Empire? Of course not—but, after all, even before Sevastopol the fate of English capitalism did not in the least depend on whether the Russians would be forced from Asia Minor. England was fighting against Russian expansion in general, and not with this or that separate detail: Russian imperialism was in the way of England's path, and its embodiment was Russian protectionism, the tariff wall which shut Russia off from the capitalist world. It seemed that it would be most convenient to make a break in this wall from the East. The wall stands even now, but England cares little about it—Germany, on the other hand, cares a great deal. No one loses more than Germany from Russian protectionism. The altogether passive trade balance of Germany is particularly marked with regard to Russia. While buying almost one and one-half billion marks annually from the Russians, the Germans are selling them a total of one billion, according to the most optimistic figures, but pessimists even talk about one-half billion. The "honest Michel" overpays Russia a good three-quarters of a billion marks out of his own pocket—and these billions in gold, which the Russian finance ministers so like to boast about, these billions which have been set aside precisely in case of a war with Germany, have been accumulated at the expense of Germany. Is this not an insult? And, by the way, the customs barrier is constantly being extended—and exactly in the most unfavorable direction for German capitalism. The only part of the Russian Empire with which Germany has traded profitably until the present day—i.e., where her balance was not passive, but active—has been Finland (in 1910 German goods imported there were worth 74 million marks, and exports to Germany, only 26 million marks). And now, the Russian government is openly preparing to include Finland in the Russian customs area.* Then it will be Armenia's turn, and then, perhaps, still another country's. And in 1917 the term of the Russo-German trade agreement will expire—the barrier may rise even more, or, on the contrary, be lowered. Will that year be a repetition of 1857 or 1822? Will Russia again be forced to enter the free-trade path (and then, willy-nilly, open the way for the development of productive forces inside the country: the tariff of 1857 was followed by the nineteenth of February), or will Russian protectionism and imperialism prevail? As the reader can see, the similarity between the situation at the beginning of the twentieth century and that in the middle of the nineteenth is striking: substitute "Germany" for "England," and Urquhart's articles become vitally topical. At that time England had to keep waiting until she found an ally in France, and until the latter would need the keys of Bethlehem. Judging by the incident with Liman von Sanders, Germany has an opportunity to act more directly and does not want to wait. The eruption of the conflict is not far off.

*In principle this question was already decided by the Russian government in 1894. [Pokrovskii's note.]

VIII

Historic Mission

Today it is hardly necessary to point out to the reader that the war between Russia on the one side, and Germany and Austria on the other, is being waged over the Turkish succession. At first, until Turkey had appeared on the scene, this simple truth was wrapped up, in part deliberately, in part through incomprehension, in every sort of superpatriotic (and sometimes even super-Marxist) argument. Now the truth is shedding one cover after another, returning to the natural state of all truth—sheer nakedness. This nakedness sometimes even assumes too philistine a character, resembling not so much an ancient statue as the Russian bathhouse: some good professor is already imagining the splendid dachas that can be built between Batum and Trebizond. . . . Yes, of course, it is too early for building, besides this is not the season—who thinks about a dacha in December? However, it is the right time to examine the "historic mission of Russia on the Black Sea." The general public, without distinguishing any shades, accepts this "mission" in its entirety: how can one do without the keys to his own house! Russia needs the Straits—the development of Russian capitalism is impossible without them. But how can one keep the

First published in *Golos* (Paris), no. 95, January 1, 1915, and no. 96, January 3, 1915. Reprinted in *Imperialistskaia voina* (1st ed., Moscow, 1928; 2d ed., Moscow, 1931).

Straits if one does not rule Constantinople? And around Constantinople one needs *ein Hinterland,* to put it in the language of the enemies of freedom and civilization. The matter is clear: the Dardanelles, Bosphorus, Tsargrad [Constantinople], Asia Minor—all or part must be Russian.

In such a summary representation, like in those heaps of "broken earthenware" that have served prehistorical archeology so well, pieces belonging to quite diverse periods have been put together. For this reason, as with broken earthenware, we are able to find in the lowest tier an object which had accidentally fallen down from the very top. At first glance it might seem that the most archaic of all possible motives for the conquest of Tsargrad is a religious one: the erection of the cross on Hagia Sophia. This, it would seem, is the most ancient of those "missions" bequeathed to present-day Russia by Muscovite Rus': but in fact, if we consider Russo-Turkish relations of the Muscovite era as they actually were, we find scarcely any mention of this "mission." In spite of constant urgings from the West in this direction (by the Pope of Rome and the German Emperor, at that time still head of the "Holy Roman Empire"), the project for the conquest of Tsargrad was raised only once during the whole epoch in any sort of serious way: when Dmitrii,* that "heretic and defrocked monk," the pupil of the Arians and Jesuits, sat on the Muscovite throne. The truly Orthodox sovereigns of Muscovy were deaf to such entreaties. One does not have to search long for the reason, that is, from our present point of view. Constantinople fell on May 30, 1453: in the eyes of devout Muscovites it had fallen fourteen years earlier, when the Church of Constantinople recognized the supremacy of the pope over it (the so-called Union of Florence, 1439). The material destruction of the Byzantine

---

*In textbooks called "Pseudo-Dmitrii I." In any event, it is easier to show the authenticity of his descent from Ivan IV than it is to show that of Nicholas II's descent from the Romanov boyars. The latter is absolutely indemonstrable, whereas the former is only relatively so—depending on what value we attribute to one or another piece of historical evidence.[1] [Pokrovskii's note.]

Empire was only the logical consequence of its moral fall. After 1439 Moscow became the center of world Orthodoxy—the "Third Rome." To return from the "Third Rome" to the "Second" would have been nearly the same as to look for last year's snow. True, the Orthodox patriarch continued to live in Constantinople, and the spiritual center of Orthodoxy, Mt. Athos and its monasteries, remained under the jurisdiction of the Turkish Empire; but the Greek hierarchy got along excellently with the Turkish "yoke" (the Mt. Athos monasteries recognized the supremacy of the sultan even before the fall of Constantinople). As they came to Moscow for alms, the patriarch and the Mt. Athos hermits were able to see the Muscovite regime as it was, and this hardly inspired them with a particular desire to become direct subjects of their northern protector. In talk they did not mind longing for an Orthodox sovereign; but in fact they remained loyal subjects of the *padishah* right up to the nineteenth century. The recent fate of the Mt. Athos monks testifies to the unquestionable sagacity of their predecessors.[2]

The farther the Russian sovereigns drifted away from Orthodoxy, the greater became the role that Tsargrad played in their policy. The son of the patriarch Filaret, the most pious Michael Fedorovich, could in no way be induced by the Don Cossacks into a war with the Turks, no matter how much they tried. His grandson, Peter I, who made a "masquerade show" out of the Orthodox liturgy and dressed his chief jester as an Orthodox patriarch, had conducted a series of wars with Turkey, not always successful, but occasionally highly resolute (the Pruth campaign of 1711). And during the reign of Catherine II, who corresponded with Voltaire and subsidized the Encyclopedists, the question of erecting a cross on the Hagia Sophia became quite urgent: an extensive plan was devised for the reestablishment of a Byzantine Empire with a sovereign from the house of Romanov (or Saltykov—in any case from the offspring of Catherine II) as its head. There is no need to search for the key to this strange sequence—the decline of Orthodoxy and the rise in the interest in Hagia Sophia: it was detected long ago by the historical literature even of the pre-Marxist period.* Beginning with the reign of Peter, Russian foreign policy was dominated by commercial capitalism. The struggle for trade routes became its chief concern. Peter himself had to fight mainly for the northern route—the Baltic Sea—but even during his reign the restoration of the old Genoese route across the Black Sea (a route well known to the Muscovite traders with the Crimea of the time of Dmitrii Donskoi) was being contemplated quite openly. For the time being, however, this was the more distant and roundabout route, and one could wait awhile with it. The colonization of the South Russian steppes made the matter urgent. Even at the very start of this process, in 1760, the landowners of Southern Russia were heard complaining that they could not do anything with their wheat since Russia had no port on the Black Sea. As a matter of fact, the wheat could have been exported even then, though under very unfavorable conditions. Today the Turks seem to us to be a people exceptionally sluggish and passive economically. This was not the case one hundred and fifty years ago. At that time Turkey was stubbornly holding its monopoly of navigation in the Black Sea; only the Ottoman flag—and no other—could be flown on it. The Turkish shipowners did not, of course, refuse to carry Russian goods—they lived mainly by shipping them—but Russian commercial capital had to share its profits with the Turkish: the middleman's services cost so much that in the end trade became "disadvantageous." A series of wars had to be fought to force the Turks into relinquishing their monopoly. The very first war, which was ended by the peace of Kuchuk-Kainardji (1774), made a notable breach in the Turkish monopoly: the Russian flag was given equal rights with the Turkish flag on the Black Sea. There remained, however, the question of freedom of navigation in the Straits, of the access of foreign vessels to Russia's new harbors on the northern coast

*See especially the work of Ulianitskii, *Dardanelli, Bosfor i Chernoe more v XVIIIv*. If the work had been published around 1900, the "objective" *Kadet* historians would have raised quite a clamor over "the manipulation of facts," "flagrantly stretched interpretations," etc. But it came out in 1883. [Pokrovskii's note.]

of the Black Sea, and so forth. The Turks held out against every step, interpreting every vague phrase of the treaties to their own advantage. Only the peace of Adrianople (1829) definitely resolved this whole confusion to Russia's advantage. Article seven of the Treaty of Adrianople made navigation from the Mediterranean to the Black Sea and back absolutely free for merchant vessels of all powers at peace with Turkey. Once and for all the Porte undertook never to close the Straits for commerce, accepting responsibility for losses if this obligation was violated.

Thus, the "historic mission" which is now being advertised to a public not much concerned with history, with discourses on the necessity of a "free outlet" for Russian commerce, etc., had essentially been settled quite satisfactorily as early as 1829. Reading the Treaty of Adrianople, one wonders what more could be wanted. The only objectionable matter would be violations of this treaty by the Turks. But, first, such violations (except for the incidents in the Russo-Turkish wars, which in the nineteenth century had always been initiated by Russia and never by Turkey) occurred very rarely. Second, even this was not at all an irreparable evil. As early as the end of the past century, a famous expert in international law, Professor Komarovskii of Moscow (an Octobrist) and his disciple Zhikharev suggested a plan for the neutralization of the Straits —to make their status in international law similar to that of the Suez Canal. It would not be legal to blockade the Straits; military actions would be forbidden in and around them within a certain distance, etc. It would have been all the more easy to achieve this because Russia is not the only country interested in free navigation through the Bosphorus and Dardanelles, nor is it the country that is most interested. In tonnage of vessels that entered the Constantinople harbor in 1909–10, 41.7 percent carried the British flag, 17.7 percent—Greek, 9.2 percent—Austrian, and only 7 percent—Russian (the Italians were a little less interested: their share was 5.8 percent of the tonnage). However, Russian diplomacy has openly shunned this line of least resistance. From the very start, even before the Turks had time to think of violating the Treaty of Adrianople (the ink had scarcely dried), Russian diplomacy raised a completely different, new question: free passage of Russian ships of war through the Bosphorus and the Dardanelles.

At the beginning of the 1830's the sultan's vassal, the pasha of Egypt (the famous Muhammad Ali, Egypt's "Peter the Great"), rose against him. Ali's troops defeated the sultan's army in Syria and were moving through Asia Minor towards Constantinople. All at once, with the rapidity of a purely theatrical trick, Russia's Black Sea fleet appeared at the Bosphorus. The "knight-tsar," Nicholas Pavlovich, had come to rescue his "friend," Sultan Mahmud. Nicholas himself, it is true, was not with the fleet, only his generals and admirals were; but they were accompanied by a corps of Russian troops which landed immediately on the Asia Minor shore of the strait and occupied the most important strategic points. Russian officers were moving about the Bosphorus and Dardanelles, making surveys, selecting points for fortifications, stores, and so on. The Turks, who had still not collected themselves following their defeat at Adrianople, did not dare object. They made their bows, said "thank you," and only timidly made bold to hint that they were not worth all these favors and troubles, that the sultan himself would somehow deal with the Egyptian rebel. Nicholas was determined to bestow his favors to the full upon these people who did not understand what was good for them. The Russian army began to converge on the Danube; to protect Constantinople it had to go by the land route, taking corresponding protective measures with regard to Shumla, Varna, and other Turkish strongholds. With utmost panic the sultan hurried to yield to the Egyptian pasha things that he had not even demanded, simply to remove any pretext for Russian intervention. Only a determined action by England and France (the latter acted with especial zeal) put an end to the intervention. Realizing that he would have to go to war with the English and French over the Straits and feeling that he was not yet ready for this, Nicholas gave in. The Russian troops left the Bosphorus, but before they did Nicholas's plenipotentiary (Count Orlov) made the sultan sign the so-called Treaty of Unkiar-Skelessi (1833). In the public part of the

document, the contracting parties guaranteed each other terri-
torial inviolability (at times even Nicholas could be a joker).
The treaty's real significance was contained in a secret article
in which the sultan pledged himself to close the Dardanelles,
upon Russia's demand, to foreign (read French and English)
war vessels. In order to leave no doubt that this would not at
all apply to Russian warships, it was agreed that the Russian
squadron then at sea in the Archipelago would pass trium-
phantly through the Dardanelles and Bosphorus and enter the
Black Sea. The perfidy of our rivals spoiled the ceremony: the
Russian ships had to perform this journey very modestly, going
one at a time, as though incognito.

Yet even without a dramatic finale, the political sense of
the Unkiar-Skelessi venture is quite obvious. This was Russia's
first (and for a long time the only) attempt to step forth in the
role of a great Mediterranean power. When she confronted
the real sea powers along her way, Russia became bashful and
retreated. On land neither England nor even France made
Nicholas panic, but he did not yet have a navy capable of defeating that of England or France. On the other hand, it was
precisely the naval character of the Russian venture that roused
the Anglo-French counteraction: a Russian navy in the Archipelago, based in Sevastopol and Nikolaev (which were inaccessible to the rivals since the Dardanelles and Bosphorus had
come into Russian hands), would have been the master of the
eastern half of the Mediterranean. This idea had been strongly
impressed in the minds of the English and French statesmen,
and they did not rest until the possible base of the Mediterranean Russian navy was destroyed—until Sevastopol itself was
taken (1855). Even the formal abrogation of the Treaty of
Unkiar-Skelessi (in 1837) did not quiet England. The economic
sense of the venture is no less obvious; quite recently it was
characterized in Russian literature, at somewhat greater length,
so that now we may limit ourselves to the briefest reminder:
the reign of Nicholas I was the first spring of Russian manufac-
turing capitalism. Restricted in the internal market which was
growing slowly because of serfdom, it looked for foreign markets and found them, it seemed, in the backward areas of

Western Asia. "There is no doubt that with a real improvement of factories and manufactories, our merchandise can begin to compete with the foreign merchandise prepared especially for the Asiatic trade," argued the State Council of Nicholas I as early as 1836. A European will not buy Russian goods, of course, but perhaps the Asiatic could be tempted, especially if cannons were placed along the Bosphorus in suitable places. In Russia, the enserfed peasant constituted the economic base of the pyramid; why, as a counterpart to him, shouldn't one have a servile customer abroad for those "improved" Russian cottons and calicos? In such a case the serfdom economy would have gotten along excellently with the successes of Russian industrial capital.

The striking similarity (including even petty details) of the situation in the 1830's, following the defeat of the Decembrists, and that of the 1910's, following the defeat of the Russian Revolution, was analyzed in detail in "Russian Imperialism in the Past and Present" [chapter VII]. At that time the dilemma had been either the abolition of serfdom, or the conquest of new markets; now it's either full completion of the bourgeois revolution, the triumph of bourgeois relations in the Russian countryside, or a "great Russia" defeated at home but defeating abroad. Then, after Sevastopol, the first alternative was triumphant; now, we are told, it will be just the reverse. There is a saying, however, that one should not count one's chickens before they are hatched; also that he who laughs on Friday, cries on Sunday. However, what matters is not who will be laughing or crying; understanding, not crying or laughing, is important. We have acquired even now some facts for understanding the new "historic mission" (which dates from 1833). Political conquests last only when they consolidate an economic supremacy that had been established, or was being established, earlier, in peacetime. In this, conquest and revolution are similar to each other: both give a legal form to the material conditions that already exist. What does Russian capital have as it advances on Turkey? Until now Russia has been exporting sugar there (Count Bobrinskii)[3] and kerosene in large quantities. But neither Russian sugar (which owing to the monopoly inside the

country is selling abroad for next to nothing) nor Russian kerosene (which in Turkey will always be cheaper than American
and better than Rumanian) has faced any competition: it is not
for either of them that the market needs to be conquered. How
do matters stand, then, with those goods which, in the opinion
of the Russian Council of State, had been sufficiently "improved" by 1836?

There exists a special American study concerning the sale
of cotton goods in Turkey.[4] In the statistical tables to be found
in it regarding imports of cotton goods to Turkey, we find
diverse countries, from England, which exports $21 million
yearly, to Holland, whose exports do not exceed $321,000.
(Italy takes second place after England—$3,146,000; Austria
comes third—$2,645,000). You will not find Russia there: it is
hidden in the category of "all other" countries which all together export less than one million dollars' worth of goods.
Only in a special table for exports of yarn can one find Russia,
with the modest figure of $3,000. This was how matters stood
less than ten years ago (the figures refer to 1906). From this time
on Russian exports have risen, but it will take a rather long
time to wait until, on a natural course, they catch up with
England or even surpass Italy. However, if the stupid Asiatic
does not see the advantages of Russian cotton over English or
Italian, one can always force him to buy Russian cotton by
driving him with a bayonet behind the Russian customs border.
The question remains: how will the English and the Italians
regard this? That is the first part. And the second: why talk
about keys to one's own house when it is clearly a case of breaking into someone else's trunk?

IX

The Beginning of the Proletarian Revolution in Russia

In considering the revolution of 1905 which we are recalling now, I will take as a point of departure the positions which we Russians held when this revolution began to draw near. You all know, comrades, that of course I would not say "We Russians," except that the Russian intelligentsia was always distinguished by excessive modesty with respect to Western Europe. To a certain degree this modesty might be compared with that awesome trepidation with which the West Europeans themselves regarded the ancient world. The colossal monuments of ancient culture made an overwhelming impression on people who were incapable of creating such monuments in the present age and drove them to imitate what were called the ancients, to imitate them so that they might at least attain the level of these ancients, if not surpass them. You yourselves know this, of course, because many among you are graduates of the classical *gimnaziia* where this reverence before antiquity was instilled into young brains. And likewise the Russian intelligentsia, traveling abroad and seeing not the ruins but the living monuments of West European culture like Paris or

First published in *Krasnyi arkhiv,* vol. XI–XII (1925). Reprinted in *Izbrannye proizvedeniia,* IV, 59–72.

London, fell into a certain awesome trepidation and thought: it's beyond us, how can we do that, it's beyond us country bumpkins from the sticks. And, thus, when roughly from 1901 on it became quite clear that we would be speaking French, and not German, i.e., that there would come a real revolution, with fighting in the streets, armed insurrection, and so on, we chose the most timid of all examples which could be found in Western Europe as we were drawing the plans for our own revolution. Even some of our leaders at that time, Plekhanov, for example, did not mention the English Revolution of the seventeenth century or the great French Revolution. For him, the model from which he was prepared to draw the Russian Revolution was the Central European Revolution of 1848. Strangely enough, on the opposite side of the barricade, the late historian P. G. Vinogradov, who became known to the wide public mainly because of the two figures which he invoked with extraordinary gusto, agreed with Plekhanov. Our Russian Revolution, he said, should go no farther than '48, and in no case must it get as far as '89.[1] It ought to be an unassuming, Central European, German, orderly, small revolution; in no way must it be a great revolution like the French. So, I repeat, reasoned the Russian intelligentsia. As for the Russian workers and peasants, they were completely unaffected by this timidity of the intelligentsia and did not draw any parallels. Neither then nor now have they been interested in any sort of parallels, but were and are interested in the heart of the matter, and have produced the three revolutions that went farther not only than '89, as the late P. G. Vinogradov had feared, but even farther than 1793–94. In the fateful moment, Robespierre did not dare, as you know, to disperse the Convention, although it is obvious from the most recent research of Mathiez that objectively he certainly could have done this,[2] for the Convention had already disintegrated and it was necessary only to prevent it from reassembling. Yet Lenin dispersed the Constituent Assembly very simply, acting as if it was something quite obvious to do, meeting with almost no resistance. It turned out that our revolution overcame that magnificent fetish of a Constituent Assembly, created by

Western Europe, with exceptional ease and speed, without any resistance or fighting; for there was no fighting in defense of the Constituent Assembly. One cannot really regard as a fight the limited shooting on the streets of St. Petersburg; properly speaking, no fight took place.

Thus, already by this one achievement, the Russian revolution had crossed a certain boundary, and without regard to how much we argue whether we have socialism or state capitalism, you may define this problem as you please, but in any case we have found ourselves beyond bourgeois democracy as it exists in Western Europe. Insofar as we have nationalized large-scale industry and transport, and practically nationalized large-scale commerce, and so on and so forth, to that extent our Soviet government never will have to face the question which the French or English government faces: now, what will be the position of this or that railroad company with regard to a change in railroad tariffs? We do not have this, and like everything else tariffs are changed according to the needs of the state as a whole and all the workers. Thus, we have already crossed over a certain boundary, I repeat, having justified both the hopes and fears of the other side to the greatest extent.

As you see, I treat our revolution as one whole, as three great episodes named after the months: December, 1905, February, 1917, and October, 1917; and this seemingly contradicts what I have already said, what I have written fairly recently, and what, in general, we all know, namely, that the Revolution of 1905 was a purely bourgeois revolution whereas the October Revolution was certainly and unquestionably a socialist revolution. But here it becomes necessary to introduce a certain correction to that correction which we had to make while fighting against the theory of permanent revolution. The latter was ready to present all three actions on the same economic plane, and claimed that as early as December, 1905, a socialist revolution was possible; and a socialist revolution presupposes imperialism, i.e., the rule of monopolistic capitalism. When one was struggling with this theory, it was necessary to stretch the point somewhat and emphasize the bourgeois character of the first revolution, which, of course, was not moving toward socialism and did not pursue socialist goals. But, nevertheless, if one were to look for a sharp line, an impenetrable wall between 1905 and 1917, one would not find it. Between 1905 and 1917 our revolution to a certain degree was developing in an "evolutionary" way, without breaks and without leaps, refuting, if you like, the "dialectic" in its extremely vulgar version, of course. The basic condition for a socialist revolution is the rule of monopolistic capitalism; this basic condition does not at all presuppose a formal break from the earlier period, the period of industrial capitalism, since industrial capitalism itself had developed from commercial capitalism without such a necessary revolution. Similarly there was also no break between our three revolutions. The same class was in the front, it was leading, it was in the vanguard of the whole movement; and even the very same party, and the very same Bolsheviks who were there in 1905, were also there in 1917. Therefore, these three actions must be regarded as a whole, and today I will dwell on the first action in order to show exactly what was original in it; for, as you will see, something original which was anticipating the second and even the third action had already occurred in this first moment.

It is necessary to emphasize here that the basic defect of all the old parallels with '48 and '89 or even with England, with Cromwell, was the failure to understand the fact that in the beginning of the twentieth century in the Russian revolution a completely new social class had entered the scene. In no previous revolution was that class the principal agent. This basic feature of our revolution should have restrained us from making any light-minded parallels. An attempt was made, in a very superficial analogy, to draw a parallel between the economic level of Russia in 1905 and the economic level of Central Europe and of Germany in particular, in 1848. Naturally, no parallel could be drawn. If we measure the development of industry by the level of metallurgy, and metallurgy by the output of cast iron, then even in 1897 Russia was on the same level as Prussia in [18]79, and not [18]48. If we take the development of the railway network which had reached 1000 km in Germany in 1848 and exceeded 40,000 km at the end of the nineteenth century here in Russia, we will get the very same picture of the economic incommensurability of Russia at the end of the nineteenth century and Germany in the middle of that century: the former stood not at the same level as Germany in [18]48, but at the same level as Germany at the time of the emergency antisocialist laws—in the [18]80's. No revolution has ever taken place on such a level, and Lenin was absolutely right when in 1917 he referred to the Paris Commune of 1871 as the single forerunner of our revolution, the forerunner from which there was something to learn, from whose experience we could draw something for ourselves. This was indeed the single case where a revolution in Europe arose on roughly the same level of economic development as that at which Russia stood in the beginning of the twentieth century; however, even this was very approximate, because above all Paris, where the entire revolution of 1871 took place, as all those know who have been there or have read about it in books, hardly was one of the large machine-industry centers of Western Europe even by the beginning of the twentieth century. In 1909 the proletariat from large industry in Paris was smaller in number than in Moscow. In Moscow there were 130,000; in Paris 108,000 or 110,000 workers employed in large-scale enterprises, while the population of Moscow then was 1.3 million, whereas in Paris it was 2.8 million. Thus, in Paris, in comparison with Moscow, the large-scale industrial proletariat was very insignificant. Paris was above all a production center for all kinds of luxury goods, women's dresses, all sorts of finery, bijouterie, etc., and all of these were concentrated in small shops that one can hardly call large-scale industrial enterprises. The overwhelming majority of Parisian proletarians were *handicraft workers;* Paris was the most important commercial center of France, one of the greatest on the whole continent of Western Europe, with the biggest banks and so on; and even though bank clerks are of course proletarians in a way, nevertheless they are not like our metalworkers or textile workers; it was a proletariat which stood very close to the petty bourgeoisie. That is why Paris was a much more backward center than Moscow and St. Petersburg in 1905. Nevertheless, this example is valid to a certain degree. It is possible to get something from it, whereas in 1905 it was already impossible to take anything from the German example of 1848. That is why the revolution—I am speaking about the revolution of 1905—destroyed in the most brutal way all hopes as well as fears; it destroyed all forecasts, among them that of Plekhanov who failed to understand our revolution and who precisely in these years began to move away from the revolution. To him it was something alien, absolutely unlike that scheme which he had drawn for himself; and since he was too vain to sacrifice his scheme to the revolution, he sacrificed the revolution to a scheme.

Let us try to ascertain what exactly was original in this revolution, how it was affected by the fact that it broke out at a certain point of development on a very high level after industrial capitalism had already developed and, this was connected with it, the large-scale industrial proletariat prevailed in industry; immediately we begin to perceive a whole series of interesting traits which show, as it were, both the impossibility of an analogy with 1848 and the incompleteness of an analogy with 1871. You know that to a considerable extent the revolution in Central Europe in 1848 was lost because nationalist contradictions among the insurgent masses were to some extent arising spontaneously and to some extent were engineered in an extremely cunning way. The Austrian revolution perished directly from these nationalist contradictions; it was split by them and it collapsed. The German revolution also suffered from them. The particularism of the individual German states greatly interfered with the course of the German revolution. When the tasks of our Commission for the study of 1905 were being formulated, I addressed, incidentally, the chairman of the literary sub-commission in one of the Union republics with the request for articles on the national movement in his area in 1905. It was very easy to get a history of such a national movement in Poland and Finland, and the comrades secured it without difficulty; now, however, both Finland and Poland for our purposes are all on their own. When I addressed this proposal to Transcaucasia, I got the anser that they had no national revolutionary movement. There had been a counterrevolutionary movement, for example, the mutual slaughter in Baku of the Tatars and Armenians, but there had been no revolutionary movement. A thorough study of documents shows that this assertion in such a categorical form is, of course, not completely true: the population did make demands for the establishment of instruction in the Georgian language and for a boycott of schools in which instruction was forcibly carried on in Russian; thus there were some such features, but to the utmost degree there is no basis for comparisons with Germany and especially Austria, where the nationalities engaged in armed combat with each other; thus there is no ground for speaking about a national movement in 1905 as a serious political factor, with the exception of Poland and Finland. This was creating illusions about the future course of the revolution. When we were arguing in Paris, in 1916, on how the revolution would proceed in Russia, I suggested that one of the consequences of the downfall of autocracy would be the separation of major nationalities from the old "Russian Empire," beginning with the Ukraine, which had been forcibly attached to it.[3] I was countered with the objection that capitalism had welded all the separate parts of the "Empire" too strongly to make any serious national movement in our country possible. This proved to be false, and you know that there was a time when the Ukraine separated itself for a whole year, Transcaucasia was separated for much longer than a year, for two to three or four years; however, in the end these countries nevertheless combined in a single Union. Only Poland and Finland found themselves outside of it, and anyway both did so mainly in virtue of the international situation; as for Latvia and Estonia, these came to stand on their own because of the international situation following the intervention of the English, partly of the Germans, etc., etc. Thus, in a sense, I was right that the national movement was possible, and so were my adversaries of 1916 when they said that capitalism had welded the Russian Empire of that time too strongly to make a serious national movement possible.

Here, comrades, is the first consequence of that economic level which the revolution found in 1905, a consequence that had colossal importance. Autocracy would have been all too glad to perform the Austrian tragicomedy of 1848–49; it displayed the greatest inclination but objectively it lacked all capacity to stage it. In Chita, and in Krasnoiarsk, Rostov-on-the-Don, Ekaterinoslav, Kiev, Odessa, and even to a certain degree and with some reservations in Warsaw and in Riga, the revolution pursued the same goal as it did in Moscow and St. Petersburg. Thus, an enormous united front came about, and autocracy rampaged in absolute panic before it. It was owing to the high economic level at which the revolution found Russia that this front was a reality. The proletariat saved Russia from a repetition of the Austrian revolution of 1848–49, even though the composition of the "Empire" as regards its nationalities was no less variegated than the national composition of Austria in 1848.

I shall not repeat myself as to the goals of the revolution, because I have already spoken and written about this subject more than once, and when one has published something an illusion rises that everybody knows about it; in fact this is absolutely not the case, it is the purest illusion; and yet one still finds it awkward to repeat what everybody supposedly knows, what has already been published. I shall not repeat what has already been printed and what—to me at least—is known about how the proletariat influenced the peasants, how it pulled the countryside behind it, how it gave its forms of struggle to the village, and so on. You can read all this; therefore it is not necessary to repeat it, it's not worth wasting time on it. Allow me to note that also in this case we were ahead of the French in '71; for one of the basic causes of the fall of the Paris Commune was the revolution's failure to extend beyond the limits of Paris's *"banlieue"*; it was enclosed within them. The other working-class centers of France—the Northeast of France, the French Donbass, or the basin of the Upper Loire, Saint-Etienne—did not manage to accomplish a revolution of their own: there was no revolution there. In our country the revolution was everywhere, and that is why it was so difficult to get the better of us, in spite of the fact that the Paris Commune had a large armed force—150,000 armed national guardsmen with 1500 to 2000 cannons, whereas we had captured only one cannon at the Presnia and then we did not know how to fire it. Yet, in spite of the fact that we were weaker than the Paris Commune of 1871 in military respects, we were much stronger owing to the spread of the revolution, because it had seized the whole country, because capitalism had united this land with an iron ring, and because at the time of the revolution this iron ring of capitalism was confronting tsarist power while it was itself being enveloped by the iron ring of the proletariat. Let me illustrate this with a small but characteristic example: the railroad workshops, which represented precisely that part of metallurgy which is attached to the railroad network and whose personnel moves across the network, became the hotbed of the movement of the metalworkers in our country. There is no more mobile, movable element than the worker from a railroad workshop: today he works in St. Petersburg, tomorrow in Moscow, the next day in Rostov-on-the-Don, and after that somewhere even farther away—in Kiev or Odessa, etc., etc. It was precisely here among this mass of railroad metalworkers, who were the living and visible embodiment of the unity of all proletariat throughout the whole land, that the demands first appeared for an eight-hour working day, the idea of a general political strike, and so on.

This was the essential feature of our first revolution in 1905, a feature which was then passed on to, and through, the two following revolutions. In precisely the same way the revolution of 1917 failed at first to create any kind of local movement; it was a "national" revolution which seized the whole land. Only then did [local] nationalist movements begin. And still later, as industry was being restored, individual parts that had separated from each other were merged again into a single Soviet Union. However, the originality of the revolution of 1905 is not, of course, exhausted by this fact; it had other original features, more profound and more interesting ones: first of all, the aspect which, apparently, struck observers, and especially struck French observers, was the absence among our revolutionary masses, among the workers and the peasants who followed them, the absence of that formal approach to revolution, so characteristic of Western revolutions, especially the French Revolution. The French bourgeois newspaper *Le Temps* expressed it in this way: the Russian people properly speaking lack political concepts.[4] According to *Le Temps* (which was receiving very good subsidies from the Russian Embassy), the basic guarantee of autocracy's stability lay in this phenomenon, and thus also the stability of those Russian securities which the Parisian petty bourgeoisie was buying on the recommendation of *Le Temps*. And, indeed, if one approaches the matter from a purely formal point of view, we were weak with regard to political concepts. To make myself clear I will again illustrate this with a couple of anecdotes.

When in the spring of 1907 I happened to participate in the election campaign in Moscow for the London Congress, I was present at a large number of workers' meetings. These were meetings of workers who were very adept in political matters—party comrades, old revolutionary fighters. They deliberated on revolution exceptionally well, about its class significance, etc., but when we had to explain to them the importance of the slogan of the Constituent Assembly, I ran up against some kind of wall; because this formal point from which all bourgeois science proceeds, that this was the embodiment of the supreme will of the people, was not clear to the workers. To them these were words, and since the slogan of the Constituent Assembly stood in our party platform, they were trying to interpret these words in their own way. The Constituent Assembly, one of them said, is a general armament of the people. The Constituent Assembly would arm the whole people and in this way consolidate the revolution. He did not suspect that he was repeating the words of Engels in a somewhat different form. In essence the worker was absolutely right, but I am afraid that in an examination in constitutional law he would get an "F" for the answer that the Constituent Assembly is a general armament of the people. Another worker said: the Constituent Assembly means an eight-hour workday. The Constituent Assembly should proclaim an eight-hour workday. At this point one was forced to argue with comrade worker and point out to him that in the Constituent Assembly there

would be not only workers but also peasants, who at that time
regarded the eight-hour workday rather coldly, and we had
feared that an eight-hour workday would not pass. This was
reflected in certain peasant instructions. All of this terribly
discredited the Constituent Assembly in the eyes of our audience, and only party discipline kept them from protesting.
Who needed the Constituent Assembly if it would not even
grant an eight-hour workday? At first glance this seems funny,
but in fact a profound and serious matter is involved here.
What matters is that the formal point of view—the urge for
the establishment of a Constituent Assembly of this kind, to
express the will of the people and so on—was so strong in the
older revolutions because they were all petty-bourgeois revolutions, with the exception of the Paris Commune to a certain
extent, though only to a certain extent. By virtue of objective
economic conditions the small independent producer is not
linked to other small independent producers, and it is extraordinarily difficult for him to unite with them politically. This
condition very vividly affected the peasant movement in 1905:
in not a single case did the peasants unite beyond the limits of
a county, and in only one case within a county—the Balashov
county of Saratov province; as far as the other areas were
concerned, *volosti*[5] did unite, though in a majority of cases even
volosti did not, and the neighboring villagers were fighting
among themselves for the landowners' property which had
fallen to their lot. In older times, when the small producers
did not constitute a detachment which followed the proletariat
but themselves represented the sole revolutionary force, some
sort of formal bond was indispensable in order to change this
whole mass of small producers into one whole. Thus originated
the petty-bourgeois urge to create at all costs an artificial form,
a bond that is not produced naturally, by the economic conditions. That is why they absolutely had to make a fetish either
out of the Convention, or emperor, or royal power, or anything
one pleased; they played this game throughout the entire
seventeenth and eighteenth centuries; and it was reflected in
the talk of our peasants about the good tsar. Some form or other
was absolutely indispensable to them, because otherwise they

would have been shattered and scattered. I said in another place and shall not repeat it that autocracy relied a great deal on the dispersion of the petty bourgeoisie. That is why the proletariat, united by production, was autocracy's archenemy. The proletariat did not need to look for an artificial expression of popular will in this or that form, more or less artificial, because for the proletariat popular will is the will of a given production unit, a shop, all the shops in a factory, then all factories in a city, the City Soviet of Workers' Deputies, and, finally, all Russia's Soviet of Deputies. To the proletariat this is what embodies popular will. In the factory the worker becomes aware of this bond with other workers, and not only with the workers in his branch of production, but also with workers in other branches; since workers produce for transport, for the railroad, the proletariat clearly sees and recognizes this bond. For him, doubtless, the formal aspect had to be put in the background, and in fact it was put in the background.

The formal aspect played a very minor role in our revolution; this fact was expressed in a feature which has attracted little attention. Virtually all of the old bourgeois and petty-bourgeois revolutionaries passionately indulged in constitution-making. After the Decembrists, as you know, almost all that remained were plans for a constitution. However, we have produced—out of necessity—only one such constitution, and we did so when it was necessary to formalize power. When it became necessary to have a written constitution, a working commission was formed and with its help the Constitution was drawn up.[6] This was a purely practical operation: when revolution is accomplished, some kind of order has to be introduced inside the country. In our country, however, nobody was engaged in composing a constitution "for storage." In our minimum program we had listed the demands of the working class, but we were not interested in such questions as how these demands would be fulfilled or what form they would assume, and we occupied ourselves exceptionally little with them. This speaks of the class which we were representing, the spirit of this class; for since this class was welded by work itself, it has had no need whatever to create any artificial soldering, any artificial formal union to express its will, and in this lies the tragedy of our Constituent Assembly of 1917–18. It all seemed unnecessary to the working masses. I remember very well the election to the Constituent Assembly in a working-class district. I was living at Zamoskvorechie at that time. It was simply embarrassing to go out and vote, just as it had been embarrassing during my student days to go to church on official holidays: for what reason, why, what is this for? It was clear that those workers among whom I lived at Zamoskvorechie were completely uninterested in the election; and while at the same time even men like Aleksinskii, the former deputy to the State Duma, were taken seriously in Western Europe, it certainly occurred to none of us to take pride in being a member of the Constituent Assembly.[7] Some were elected in a number of provinces, and it was simply embarrassing to make much of this; it was embarrassing to claim distinction, and it was particularly embarrassing to do it in front of the workers. Even the Social Revolutionaries, who played up the Constituent Assembly as their trump card, admitted that this slogan did not captivate anybody; it was impossible to drive a single soldier onto the street, and that is why their demonstration, which at first had defensive goals (to defend the Constituent Assembly from dissolution), and then in the event of a great success, also offensive, i.e., to disperse our Soviet, fell through. This demonstration did not succeed, since it proved impossible to drag a single soldier out into the street with this slogan; nor was it possible to drag out a single St. Petersburg worker. And when it became necessary to defend the Soviet from those very same insurgent S.R.'s, then the whole St. Petersburg proletariat came out to the streets, including even the worker S.R.'s, who declared: "Well, now, we are fighting for the Soviets"—and for this reason they joined the ranks of the Red Guard.

Such was the realism of the working class which formed an exceptionally characteristic trait of our revolution of 1905 and explains the originality of the political form which this revolution has created, the Soviet of Workers' Deputies, i.e., an assembly of representatives from the units of production. This was an exceptionally characteristic form which was not only peculiar to the proletariat. It was immediately passed on to the soldiers, who formed Soviets throughout their profession, and it was passed on even to the peasants, who formed peasant Soviets. Incidentally, peasant Soviets had been formed even in 1905. In Tver province there were several peasant Soviets. These Soviets had the characteristic peculiarity of having been formed with the direct participation of workers, that is, those of the Tver peasants who had been working in the Tver factories. These workers, who had moved back to the country and agitated the peasants there, surrounded Tver with a complete ring of Soviets of Peasants' Deputies, which were in fact worker-peasant Soviets, since in every such Soviet there were without fail several workers who acted as leaders.

Organization along production lines which forms the basis of our Soviet system is a feature which constitutes a world-wide achievement. When the German revolution began, it was not accidental that it manifested itself in the formation of the Soviets of Workers' and Soldiers' Deputies, and the downfall of these Soviets was at the same time the downfall of the German revolution. To be sure, if the revolution in Germany in 1919 had been successful, and not defeated, then, according to all probability, there would have been Soviets in Germany; whether or not called by that name, I do not know, but in any case there would have been representation based on production. In 1917 a conclusion that had not been made in 1905 was drawn from the principle of organizing representation along production lines, and this conclusion was logical: does he who is not attached to any productive work and in general does not produce anything, who is not a member of any production unit, does he have the right to vote? Obviously not. For where shall he vote? The Tuscan nobility who were deprived of the right to vote after the revolution of the townsmen in the thirteenth century resorted to masquerade. They registered in guilds, hung a ball of wool on the doors of their homes, or a skein of silk, and announced: I am a weaver, a silk spinner, I am a wool spinner, and so on. Such a comedy was possible in the thirteenth century, but in the twentieth century it becomes very difficult to perform. Representation based on production, by expressing the objective cohesion of the working class, an economic cohesion of the working class which does not need to be created artificially, by itself excludes the bourgeoisie, excludes from the political system that class which appropriates but does not produce. Article 65[8] of the Constitution did not appear until 1918, yet as early as 1905 it was in the air.

This, comrades, is what, in my opinion, constitutes the original features of the 1905 Revolution, and this is why, I think, we have the full right to call it *popular,* as Lenin called it, following Marx. Both he and Marx had been working to distinguish a revolution of this kind from a different type of revolution, from the earlier bourgeois revolutions; for it was clear that there was something here which did not resemble the earlier revolutions, something new. And this popular revolution of ours deserves the name Great, because it begins a new period in history. Before this period we experienced two great boundary lines: the English Revolution, which did away with feudalism in England, though on the world plane it introduced only that which had in the seventeenth century already begun to lose its practical importance—freedom of conscience; the French Revolution at the end of the eighteenth century went even farther: it advanced the idea of popular sovereignty, which in England was presented only by the extreme left wing of the movement; it advanced the idea of equality, not a socialist equality yet, but an equality which to a certain extent laid the groundwork for socialist equality, that is civic equality. And now we have the third historical boundary, our revolution of 1905–17, which has introduced a completely new idea of organization of the masses, an idea which goes beyond the formal democracy of the French Revolution as much as large-scale industrial production has superseded petty handicraft. Our revolution has for the first time linked modern economy and politics, ruthlessly shattering all those fetishes that have remained in the modern world as a legacy of the old petty-bourgeois democracy. Those fetishes were absolutely useless for our new Soviet democracy in Russia, and there will be no need for them in other countries when the socialist revolution advances there. This great movement was only beginning in 1905, and since that time we have not found any Walls of China across our path. Our demands of 1905 survived the entire interrevolutionary period under the unassuming legalized name of "uncut slogans,"[9] and in 1917 they began to be developed anew, as if from that same point at which they had been halted in December, 1905.

This process has now seized a group of countries. A person with the slightest interest in history cannot help being reminded of our 1905 by what is happening now in India or what is happening now in China. The working class is taking the lead there, too, striking the first blows and taking the first blows upon itself, and the multimillion masses of peasants, even more numerous than in our country, are following the proletariat. It is no wonder that the West European bourgeoisie which had been lending money to Nicholas II to suppress the Russian revolution is rendering all possible services to those who are trying to suppress the revolution in China. This operation is becoming increasingly difficult, however, because the hotbeds of the revolution are constantly rising in number, and because the revolution has firmly established itself in one of the largest countries in the world, a country which on some recent American maps spreads into a vast red stain that is three times as big as the territory of the United States. Neither the West European nor even the whole world's bourgeoisie is able any longer to wipe off this stain, not only with two billion or twenty billion gold francs, but even with as many billion gold dollars. The revolution which began on the streets of St. Petersburg in January, 1905, now occupies in the world's view approximately that position which the French Revolution occupied in the view of Europe alone in the first years of the nineteenth century. That was considered a world event at the time, and all progressive Europe hurried to pay homage to Paris. Today Moscow has become such a Mecca for nations. Such a development was unimaginable after the defeat of the Moscow barricades, when we were counting those wretched Brownings and Mausers that remained in our hands. Now we are counting the airplanes and battleships we have. Could we have thought then in our little rooms where we were summing up the painful results of our first action that twenty years later the revolution would be flying by plane?

X

The Prologue to the October Revolution

February 27 (March 12), 1917–21

For four years Russia has been a republic. . . . Today no one's heart skips a beat at this word: what could the RSFSR be, if not a republic? It stands to reason. It would be ridiculously naïve to go into ecstasies over this matter, like that ecstasy over the railroad which amuses us when we leaf through journals from the 1830's. In some places in the world there are "monarchs" of some sort: aren't there many odd old customs! Yet when negotiations with England are being discussed, Lloyd George is mentioned, and hardly one newspaper reader out of a thousand remembers in this connection that after all the double of Nicholas Romanov, George V, is still sitting in Buckingham Palace.

The obsoleteness of the question of monarchy and republic is exceptionally characteristic of our days—the days of the last and decisive battle between the old world and the new. Neither one nor the other world cares about the "form of government." The bourgeoisie of all lands will most readily

First published in *Vestnik agitatsii i propagandy,* 1921, nos. 7–8. Reprinted in *Oktiabr'skaia revoliutsiia* (Moscow, 1929), pp. 73–85.

give up all dynasties in return for a firm guarantee against "Bolshevism." It was not without reason that for several months before our February Revolution the foremost of all bourgeoisies, the American, was prophetically proposing to renounce monarchy (the monarchy was almost openly condemned, as far as diplomatic decorum allowed, in the famous declaration by Wilson at the end of 1916).[1] It is true that it was already too late for such a repudiation; it was already impossible to save or forestall anything in this way, but the Americans displayed a certain intuition all the same.

From the very beginning of the war in 1914, the idea of a republic in Russia was so much in the air that it was being definitely predicted two years before the revolution. In a paper that was read among the Russian exiles in May, 1915, in the Paris "Club of Internationalists," it was not only pointed out definitely that the coming revolution in Russia would lead to a republic, but even emphasized with great certainty that before the workers would win a real republic they would have to pass through a "phantom republic" of the Kadets—something like the "phantom constitution" that Nicholas II granted Russia in October, 1905. The speaker firmly cautioned the comrades against any enthusiasm for this republic, which we would have to tear down with our own hands in order to clear the way for a proletarian republic. Could he have thought at that time that he would be able to share in this work of destruction?

Plekhanov said that a revolution in Russia could win only as a workers' revolution.[2] He left unsaid that the workers' revolution could be only antimonarchical, could be only republican.

Having seized power, the workers would, without doubt, free themselves from the factory owners—this was absolutely clear. It was no less clear, however, that the worker would not spare the tsar; for tsars, kings, and emperors are the last refuge of factory owners.

The great weakness of the French proletariat, combined with the presence of a strong, numerous, robust *kulak* peasantry in France, allowed the French bourgeoisie to toy with a republic; it was no accident that the Paris garrison was always staffed with recruits from the most backward peasant districts and that during the war "order" in the capital of the French Republic was quite openly maintained by the Annamese.* However, the more developed capitalist countries, England and Germany, kept the "beloved monarch" as long as it was possible (the former still keeps him). That unquestioning blind discipline which the bourgeoisie needs in the army, police, and bureaucracy could not be based on universal suffrage. Something "divine" was needed here, higher than any parliament, something with which, in case of extreme necessity, one could even disperse the parliament, for example, if the socialists should acquire a majority in it.

The bourgeoisie has *always* needed monarchy, though more in some periods of capitalist development than in others. The absolutism of modern times, of Louis XIV as much as of our Peter, was created by commercial capital, which needed an "iron hand" to extort the surplus produce from the (legally) independent small producer, as well as for the conquest of trade routes, markets, and colonies. As industrial capitalism developed, the need for the iron hand declined: "economic" coercion inside the country superseded the "extra-economic" oppression—the capitalists began to subjugate the worker not with the hammer, as the peasant had been, but with hunger.

The first industrial-capitalist countries met almost no competition on foreign markets. In the very beginning of the nineteenth century France took it into her head to compete with England on this course, but the defeat of Napoleon quickly put an end to that, and later both countries successfully delimited their respective areas. In fact, England had a monopoly in almost all industries, with the exception of luxury goods, and this lasted until German industry entered the field in the last quarter of the nineteenth century.

English *liberalism* was nurtured by the English monopoly and spread to all countries along with English goods. Capital is a thrifty master: whoever is redundant is promptly dismissed

*The natives of the French colony of Annam, belonging to the yellow race which the French capitalists considered reliable owing to its "savagery." They were probably very mistaken. [Pokrovskii's note.]

or, at best, consigned to hunger rations. The latter occurred to monarchy. It was inconvenient to remove the crown completely from the facade of the bourgeois structure—we have already seen why. But there was no point, either, in freeing the hands of the crowned automaton. In England matters were more simplified by the fact that for a long time the automaton was a woman. Victoria reigned there for more than sixty years. During this time England was ruled by the henchmen of capital—Palmerston, Beaconsfield, and Gladstone—and Europe was accustomed to thinking that the English monarch existed only "for show."

But then Victoria died (in 1901), the throne was occupied by her by then elderly son, and the picture abruptly changed. Edward VII began to "make policies." He personally carried on all negotiations with foreign states, and the English-Russian alliance of 1907 was his doing, exactly as was the English-French alliance. How could this be explained? Just because a man sat on the throne? Of course not. However, the English monopoly on the world market had been shaken; German capital had started to flood even England with its goods. More and more often English industrial capital was forced to think about "extra-economic coercion" in foreign policy: from the beginning of the twentieth century England was preparing herself for a war with Germany and was looking for allies. Moreover, on the other hand, under the influence of the rising cost of living in England, which was due to the failures in world competition, the workers' movement there was beginning to spread ever more widely.* The iron hand was also needed inside the country. There began the age of wars for world monopoly and for the preservation by openly violent means of capitalism which had outlived its time. In a word, the age of imperialism again required a strong central power.

The peculiarities of Russian development consisted of the fact that the phases of capitalist development which have

*Between 1901–7 in England there were yearly an average of 469 strikes and lockouts, which seized in their midst 157,000 workers; in 1910 the former numbered 506, and the workers involved about half a million; in 1912 the number of strikers went over a million. [Pokrovskii's note.]

been traced here followed each other within an exceptionally short time. Until 1861, commercial capital ruled in our country —its tools were the autocracy of Nicholas I and serfdom. The emancipation of the peasants was the first concession to industrial capital which required an internal market and a "reserve army of labor." Liberalism, however—that inevitable political companion of industrial capitalism—had not yet managed to flourish in our country when, beginning in the 1890's, the workers' movement was started here, and Russia became engaged in a struggle for monopoly, though admittedly not for world monopoly which the conflict between Germany and England was, but local (initially in the Far East against Japan, in 1903–5); in a word, the age of imperialism had arrived for Russia too. The Russian liberal thus wavered between two positions. On the one hand, he cried about the arbitrariness of Plehve and demanded the rule of law; on the other, as early as 1904 he was declaring that it would be necessary to bring back Nicholas should he escape to Denmark; and when the workers' movement took on the form of a workers' revolution in October, 1905, our bourgeois liberalism wholly supported the ministry of Witte who was "pacifying" the workers' revolution—though in the end it did not decide formally to join Witte.

Autocracy suppressed the workers' movement with the help of *foreign capital*—and thus it became immediately clear, as early as 1906, that the future Russian revolution would have an international character. Not having taken part formally in this suppression, the Russian liberal bourgeoisie did not get even a scrap of power. It had to be satisfied with being tolerated, while the real power fell increasingly into the hands of foreign, *financial,* banking capital, on whose favors autocracy survived. The participation of Russia in the war of 1914 was dictated to a much greater extent by the interests of this alien, English-French imperialism than by the still very weak Russian "national" imperialism which had just begun to develop. Here, too, the fate of Russia was decided on the *international* plane.

Moreover, on the international plane a decisive clash between the proletariat and bourgeoisie was approaching. From the edge of the forest, one can see only single trees: all that occurred in our country between 1907 and 1914 has not yet merged into one general picture; we see too many details to form an integrated view. Yet historians in the near future will have no difficulty in combining into one whole both the great French railroad strike of 1910, the great German strikes in Westphalia and in Berlin itself during the immediately preceding years, the English strike movement which reached its high point in 1912—and the Lena massacre of that year with its aftermath—up to the huge St. Petersburg movement in the summer of 1914. *World Bolshevism was already being born five years before the start of the Russian Revolution.*

The process could have dragged on for as long as ten years—by speeding up the delivery, the war became history's midwife. It is a fact too well known to require emphasizing that the war was not only an armed scuffle between two groups of finance capital, the English-French-American and the German-Austrian, *but also an armed self-defense of the capitalists* in each of these two groups against their own proletariat. It was noted long ago that before any country entered the war a *state of siege* was declared within this country. Simpleminded newspaper readers were being assured that this "always happens," that "it is necessary." That was sheer nonsense: in France during the Franco-Prussian War of 1870–71, even when the Prussians were occupying almost half of the country, a state of siege existed only in the departments that were near the front; there was no thought of suspending the constitution in the rest of the country. But in this case there was a desire to *take advantage* of the war in order to suppress the too widely expanding workers' movement, to smother workers' organizations which had become too strong. They got even more than they had hoped for: the "well-tried fighters for socialism," the leaders of the parties of the Second International and trade unions, frightened by the state of siege and lured by hope for a slice of power, went running straight to the bourgeois camp and became, among the proletarian masses, agents of imperialism at war.

In any case, by 1914 two international forces were confronting each other—the bourgeoisie on the one hand, the proletariat on the other. The explosion could have occurred in any place, and no matter where it occurred, it would immediately have assumed the form of a *socialist* revolution. We already have factual evidence of this as regards Russia and Germany, and partly Italy. Why, then, did it start in Russia?

The answer to this may be seen in what we said earlier about the character and tempo (the rate of speed) of Russia's economic development. In our country the phases of capitalism's development occurred one on top of the other; industrial capital was present when commercial capital had still not faded away; and imperialism took over industrial capitalism while that was still in a period of growth. This had a definite influence on the composition of the Russian bourgeoisie. In the truly imperialist countries like England or Germany banking capital already possessed a definite hegemony in bourgeois circles: all nonimperialist interests had to take second place. In our country the bourgeoisie succeeded in achieving such a unity only during the very first months of the war; this happened because it was still thought that the war would be limited to a few months. Only when it became clear that the war was dragging on, that not only the "grain campaign" of 1914 had been lost, but that even the year 1915 would have to be sacrificed, did commercial capital, which had really begun the war (it was commercial capital above all which needed the Dardanelles; it profited from the grain export and wanted to have "the keys to its own house" in its pocket), begin to lose interest. On the other hand, with the increase in war orders, industrial capitalism, which at first was getting involved unwillingly in a venture it did not need very much anyway, began to acquire a larger and larger appetite for war. Just as all vacillation had ceased among the factory owners and industrialists, the wavering began among those at the top, where the interests of commercial capital were better seen and understood—after all, Russian autocracy had grown precisely on commercial capital—and where commercial capital had strong advocates among the large landowners who were interested in the grain export.

In his history of the Russian Revolution, Miliukov very clearly alludes to some goings-on between Nicholas II and his ministers and the Germans from the fall of 1916. We also have indirect indications of this from the opposite side, in Germany. In April, 1917, a Swiss informer reported to the government of this same Miliukov that, according to "a well-known Berlin banker," "the Russian revolution had at first made a depressing impression on the German ruling circles, because *they had been already absolutely convinced of a near* separate peace with Russia. Events in Russia destroyed this hope, and the disappointment was enormous." Among the papers of Nicholas Romanov that have become our property no documentary proof of his correspondence with the Germans has been found. But in his diary two entries have been preserved which explain precisely why it would have been useless to look for these documents among his papers. On March 9 he arrived—already the ex-emperor—in Tsarskoe Selo, and on March 10 he wrote: "looked through, arranged, and *burned* papers"; on March 11, "continued *burning* letters and papers."[3]

It was characteristic of the Miliukov government, which, it would seem, in the very first moments could and *should* have sealed Nicholas's papers, that it did nothing of the sort. The monarchy, as we shall soon see, was needed too much even by the industrial bourgeoisie which was personified by the Kadets. Miliukov had no interest in "compromising" Nicholas by disclosing his intrigues with the Germans. Nicholas, however, apparently remembering the trial of Louis XVI and knowing full well that in St. Petersburg besides the Miliukov government there was some kind of, as he put it, "workers' committee" (in one place Nicholas straightway called it "social-democratic"), did not think that precautionary measures were superfluous.

Why is it necessary to dwell on these trifles? It is necessary in order to understand why the bourgeoisie in Russia did not face the workers' revolution with a unified front, as was the case one and a half years later in Germany. Industrial capital found it convenient to unseat commercial capital in the person of Nicholas and have the war go on. Miliukov does not even think of hiding this. Speaking about the mood of "the parliamentary circles" [read: "the Progressive Bloc"], he explained it in this way: their (i.e., of "the parliamentary circles") chief motive was the desire to carry on the war to a successful end in agreement with the Allies; and the cause of their opposition was the ever growing conviction that this goal was unattainable under this government and under this regime. "The parliamentary majority struggled to the very end against the idea of attaining its goal by means of revolution. Seeing, however, that forcible means would be taken in any case, even without the State Duma, it began to make preparations for giving a peaceful direction to the coup which it preferred to get from above and not from below."[4]

One should by no means understand the words "from above" in the sense that the Kadets entertained the naïve hope that Nicholas would "go of his own will." Nothing of the sort. "From above"—meant through a *palace revolution* and not by means of a popular revolution. The same Miliukov, on a page preceding, was openly talking about a *conspiracy* aiming precisely at a palace revolution. Krymov, who shot himself after the failure of Kornilov's venture, headed this conspiracy, and the Kadet party was represented in it by Nekrasov and Tereshchenko, a fact which explains the latter's inclusion as minister in "the provisional revolutionary government"—to universal astonishment, for until then no one had heard anything about Tereshchenko.

As the Romanov throne was about to crack under the blows of the popular revolution, the Kadets had one concern: not to miss the chance to cook their own stew on this great fire. The equipment was ready. Prince L'vov (the prime minister who had been put in storage for the event of a palace revolution, and whom, of course, none of the revolutionaries on the streets of St. Petersburg even mentioned) was promptly pulled out of a pocket. What had formerly been called "the government of national confidence" was served dressed up with the sauce of "the provisional revolutionary government." Fortunately the people were personally on the scene now: the first thing they did was loudly and distinctly to express their *lack of confidence* in the Kadet clique. When Miliukov (the real prime minister) made an appearance before a gathering in the Tauride Palace, he was asked: "Who elected you?" And when he began to speak about "the public" they corrected him with: "the privileged public."[5] Miliukov took it into his head to assure them that there was no other public—and this was an obvious lie: the representatives of the revolutionary or simply democratic parties were available; and it was completely obvious that it was they whom the insurgent people obeyed. When Rodzianko (the president of the State Duma) wanted to go to Nicholas, the railroad workers would not give him a train, and he had to send his aide to request a train from the newly formed executive committee of the St. Petersburg Soviet of Workers' Deputies.

It would seem that it was clear to the point of obviousness *where real power was.* No matter how rudimentary or improvised was the first workers' organization to have risen on the smouldering debris of the Romanov monarchy, it was precisely that which the masses obeyed. As regards the attitude of the masses to the monarchy, Miliukov's mention of the latter had already caused a real scandal,[6] and for a long time afterwards the agitated crowds moved across the Tauride Palace demanding assurances from the representatives of the real, genuine power that the monarchy would not come back. The mood of the crowd was so evident and formidable that Michael, "the Emperor of National Confidence," who was pulled out of the same pocket as Prince L'vov, lost no time in abdicating.

The journey of Guchkov and Shul'gin to Nicholas, and the latter's abdication, was, as can be seen, a most immaterial detail, but it was this that made the revolution known to its contemporaries far away from St. Petersburg, including us emigrés. For Nicholas abdication was simply a railroad ticket— you can't go without it; he was up a dead end. After he signed his abdication, he was permitted to leave for Mogilev.[7]

However, and his diary leaves no doubt about this at all, even the previous day he had not used his power to the slightest extent. His entry of Wednesday, March 1, ends with the words: "Shame and disgrace. We did not manage to reach Tsarskoe." And the subsequent entry of Thursday, the second (the day of abdication), is worth quoting in its entirety. Nicholas spent the night in Pskov. "In the morning Ruzskii came and read a lengthy transcript of his conversation by direct wire with Rodzianko. According to him, the situation in Petrograd is such that the ministry from the Duma is allegedly now powerless to do anything because the social-democratic party, in the form of the workers' committee, is fighting against it. My abdication is necessary. Ruzskii reported this conversation to the Supreme Headquarters, and Alekseev did to all commanders in chief [of the fronts]. By two-thirty we had a reply from everyone. The gist is that it is necessary to take this step for the sake of Russia's salvation and the retention of the army on the front. I agreed. *A draft of the manifesto was sent from Headquarters.* In the evening Guchkov and Shul'gin arrived from Petrograd, and I had a talk with them and gave them a signed and modified Manifesto."[8]

There are four items of interest in this passage, the importance of which no one needs to be told—everything was written in the evening of the same day when impressions were still fresh: in a word, a snapshot. First of all, Guchkov and Shul'gin had not only missed the end of the show but also found the public had already left: the abdication had been definitely decided upon while they were boarding the train at the Warsaw Railroad Station. Second, the draft of the abdication act had been ready and waiting in a pocket, just as Prince L'vov and Michael had been: the plot which had been prepared in the event of a palace revolution was acted out fully. The very smallest detail was not lost. But the motivation was quite unlike what they had anticipated: Nicholas admitted to himself and his circle (it hardly entered his head that his diary would fall so soon into strangers' hands) that he had to abdicate for the sake of "the retention of the army on the front." In other words, the revolution was no longer confined to St. Petersburg, and the smallest sign of the "old despot's" (this was how Miliukov referred to Nicholas) struggle for power would have led to a situation in which the soldiers would have left the front and rushed forth en masse to defend the revolution. This was so obvious on the front that all the commanders answered Alekseev's telegram almost identically. Finally, we have a very clear picture of what Nicholas regarded as the force that had deposed him and now commanded both Petrograd and the front. It was the Petrograd Soviet of Workers' Deputies. No one on the tsar's train even thought of Miliukov, the Kadets, or the Progressive Bloc: they saw only the "workers' committee" which personified revolutionary socialism. The December barricades of 1905 [in Moscow] were resurrected again before Nicholas—and forced him to flee.

How, under such circumstances, was it *possible* for the government of L'vov-Miliukov to appear on the stage? One of the founders of this government with extreme clarity depicted its head on the day *before* it took power. "Quite alone in the Catherine Hall P. N. Miliukov was walking around, the central figure of bourgeois Russia, the leader of the only official organ of power in St. Petersburg at the moment. . . . He too found himself inactive. His whole appearance said plainly that he had nothing to do, that he did not in the least know what to do. Various people went up to him, began to talk to him, asked him questions, gave him information. He replied with evident reluctance and vagueness. They left him, and he started walking around alone again."[9]

Who would have thought that before him stood the "de facto head of the first revolutionary Government" (words which we omitted from the passage just cited)? And yet, imagine, the group of intellectuals who were in charge of the first executive committee of the Petrograd Soviet thought just that. They did not stop for a moment to think of organizing their own power, a power that the insurgent masses *recognized*. No, they set themselves a much more difficult task: how to *force* the *recognition* of the power that was helplessly pacing about St. Catherine Hall. For it was clear to the intelligentsia that the "Government that was to take the place of Tsarism must be exclusively bourgeois. Trepov and Rasputin could and should be replaced only by the bosses of the Progressive Bloc. This was the solution to be aimed at. Otherwise the overturn would fail and the revolution perish."[10]

We will not dwell on the particular and incidental reasons for this insanity into which the real holders of power in March, 1917, fell. It is, of course, quite possible that the absence from

the scene of the old and authoritative leaders of the revolutionary parties was a factor here; those people who were present were either inexperienced precisely in the revolutionary
business, or, even if they were old revolutionaries, were not
known to the masses and therefore did not enjoy authority
among them. What mattered here, however, was not so much
personal authority as a certain deficiency as a group: there was
no *revolutionary* intelligentsia on hand, and the revolution
was led by the *legal* intelligentsia.

Even in its most backward strata (the Menshevik-inter-
nationalists, the "Center" S.R.'s), the revolutionary intelligentsia was nonetheless an organizing force of the masses of the
people, first of all the proletariat. The legal intelligentsia even
in its most radical groups (the writers from *Letopis'*, the Duma
Mensheviks) was the organizing force of capitalist industry.
What mattered here, of course, was not the personal position
of one or another intellectual in industry; it was rather the
invisible, indissoluble psychological bonds which tied, in one
case, the intellectual to the revolutionary worker and insurgent
soldier, and, in the other, to the capitalist against whom this
worker and this soldier were rebelling. This proved extremely
clear in the fundamental question of the February Revolution
—the *question of war and peace*.

The correspondents of the Entente press disseminated all
over the world the lie that the February Revolution was allegedly *defensist*. And here, too, use was made of the provisions
that had been stored up in the event of a "patriotic" palace
revolution of the Kadets. This cliché was even more to the
point here than at any other time. I remember what a night-
marish impression the first telegrams about the revolution had
made on us abroad; I remember how one of us threw down the
paper in despair, shouting: "a lousy revolution!" Only in approximately one week, by lifting little by little the grains of
truth from the sea of lies, did we begin to understand what
had in fact taken place in Nicholas II's "Petrograd." In fact,
as the Menshevik Sukhanov testifies (one can believe in his
truthfulness, for no man would have been capable of writing
anything worse about himself in a political sense than he has

done in his "Notes on the Revolution"), *the revolution proceeded wholly under the peace slogan.* Characterizing the political mood that manifested itself to some degree in the spontaneous movement of the masses, Sukhanov said:

> Of course our traditional, one might say ancient, national slogan, "Down with the Autocracy", was on the lips of all the many street orators from the Socialist parties. But this was not yet a political programme; it was a negative idea that was taken for granted. The problem of *government* had not yet been put before the masses. And in particular the slogan of a "Constituent Assembly", not being on the order of the day, but merely part of the general programme of all the Socialist parties, was left completely in the shadow during those days.
>
> On the other hand, the street agitators developed at great length another slogan, with extremely grave and far-reaching implications. This was "Down with the War", which dominated all the meetings of the February days.[11]

We do not need *memoirs,* however, to establish this fact; we have documents. I do not know if and where Kerenskii's letter to Lloyd George has been printed—it was written two weeks before the October Revolution and concerned the reorganization of the Russian army (according to Verkhovskii's plan). Looking back at his attempts to revive a patriotic mood on the front, Kerenskii literally said:

> No matter how difficult Russia's situation appears from the viewpoint of our common cause [read: the prospects of the Entente victory], we may claim that it is better now than it was last spring [i.e., immediately after the February Revolution]. At that time a de facto armistice was established on the front—the result of the "fraternization" propaganda and the decline in military discipline. This situation inspired all the more fear because the Germans were respecting it, refraining from all military action on our front in the hope of employing the military forces freed in this way against our allies. Recognizing all the danger of the situation, the Provisional Government de-

cided to put an end to it in whatever way possible. Our offensive, in spite of its initial success, ended in failure. Nevertheless, one has to consider its chief aim—putting an end to the state of armistice and resuming the war—to have been achieved at the cost of great sacrifices. . . .[12]

The world conflagration began to die out in the East in March, 1917, and it was necessary to relight it in whatever way possible "at the cost of great sacrifices." Why was the Russian worker not only the first to rise up against capital, but also the first to raise en masse the slogan "Down with the War"? The witness of the March days whom we have cited before explains this by the "Zimmerwald education" of the Russian proletariat. This explanation is, surely, a bit too "pedagogical." The Zimmerwald propaganda was equally intensive in Germany, yet the German worker rose as a mass only after it became clear that the war was lost. For Russia itself it became clear that the war was lost as early as the fall of 1915: from that time on there was only the victory of the "dear Allies" to count on. Why didn't the Russian proletariat rise up at that time (as many had expected and were bitterly disappointed about)?

Because the Russian worker was completely uninterested in the victory of native imperialism. The fate of the Russian worker did not in the least depend on whether "we" would take the Dardanelles or not. But the German or English nonsocialist worker (and nonsocialists formed a majority of the working masses there) tied his own fate to the victory of "his" side, and he was perfectly right from the narrow "stomach" point of view.

By enjoying a world monopoly, the capitalist was able to *fatten up* his worker,* paying him from his own superprofit. To hope for a monopoly by his own country was to hope for an improvement in material conditions; and the loss of this monopoly would raise the question of socialism, which one-

---

*A comparison of the rise in prices and that of wages in England gives a splendid example: taking the wages in 1850 as 100, in 1900 we have (at the very beginning of German competition) 178, and for prices for foodstuffs the corresponding figures are 100 and 97. [Pokrovskii's note.]

hundredth, if not one-thousandth, of the working masses as a whole understood and accepted. The Russian worker, on the other hand, already *was* in that situation into which the English or the German worker could be brought only by the defeat of his country. The rise of wages like that of industry in our country still depended on the internal market (from 1905 through 1910 wages increased in Russia by 22 percent), and the Russian worker was much more interested that the peasants have land than the Russian tsar conquer new lands for himself.

Thus, the "Zimmerwald" character of the first Russian revolution was completely clear from its very first day. But what did these Russian Zimmerwaldians do, who as members of the first St. Petersburg executive committee actually held power? We have seen that the whole question for them was whether Miliukov, who was in fact completely powerless, would "take" or "not take" power. Only after Miliukov with his "triumphant look and suppressed smile" (how he was inwardly laughing at the simpletons who stood before him) announced the Kadet decision: "We are taking power," did the "Zimmerwaldians" breathe with relief.[13]

At last Russia and the revolution were saved. And then kindness was repaid with kindness. In response to the polite consent of Miliukov to sit in the minister's chair which had been brought to him obligingly from the Soviet of Workers' Deputies, the Soviet [read: the "Zimmerwaldians" who ran it] on its part not only failed to make the war its primary issue, but *took from the agenda, folded up and annulled all war or, more precisely, antiwar slogans* which had been unfolded at the very beginning of the movement and which would have led, had they been pursued intensively, to an inevitable breakdown of the "government combination."

Was this a betrayal? Let us repeat once more: no; for the nonrevolutionary intelligentsia it was objectively the inevitable outcome of the situation.

The government of Nicholas and the bourgeoisie which collaborated with it on the sly knew perfectly well what they had been doing when they sent all the active leaders of the 1905–7 revolution to Siberia or drove them abroad. They did

not save themselves in this way, but they ruined the organization of their enemies. The intelligentsia of the revolutionary
parties, who were gradually returning from exile or banish-
ment, had to undo the knots that had been tied. It took them
eight months to conquer what had been ready at hand as early
as March, 1917.

In that March which proved so fatal to the bourgeoisie,
the worldwide proletarian revolution was already beginning.
This is clear to everyone now. At that time it was clear to no
one in Russia and to very few outside. That explains why the
question of the "form of government" faded away so rapidly in
our country and in the rest of the world. In remembering the
days of February and March, we remember the prologue to
the October Revolution.

XI

Lenin's Role in the
Russian Revolution

In Lenin, comrades, we have buried first of all the greatest leader of the proletarian movement—the greatest the world has seen—the greatest in the history of the Russian proletariat, because he was the first man, the first sculptor, to mold the political physiognomy of that proletariat. We need only remember that less than thirty years ago it was being officially declared that the working class as a political force did not exist in Russia and there could be no workers' problem. This could be read and heard by people who at the time were not ten-year-old schoolboys, but who had already finished the university—like the speaker who is addressing you now! In the nineties I was already a lecturer at a higher educational institution when the minister of finance proclaimed to all Russia that a workers' problem could not arise in Russia. Thus, it was during less than one generation's lifetime that the workers' question not only arose, but was, for the first time in the world, resolved—resolved by the victory of the proletariat. Needless to say, there was a whole sequence of objective conditions which led to this, but after all, even a sculptor does not create

First published in *Vestnik Kommunisticheskoi Akademii,* 1924, no. 7, pp. 7–21. Reprinted with omissions in *Oktiabr'skaia revoliutsiia* (Moscow, 1929), pp. 31–41.

out of nothing; he works with marble, with plaster, with bronze—in the present case it was steel: without regard to what the sculptor makes his work of art from, his mark is reflected in this work of art, and there is no question that the ideology of the Russian proletarian movement was indeed Leninist. Simultaneously, Lenin was the greatest leader of the world proletarian movement insofar as Leninist tactics, Leninist models of organization, are necessary for every workers' movement in the world that wants to reach the first stage of the socialist revolution—the seizure of power. The theory and practice of the seizure of power by the working class were also created by Lenin.

I began with this introduction which, as you will presently see, does not bear on the contents of my lecture in order to approach a theme which may seem risky to some. All right, you say, in the framework of the proletarian movement Lenin was a great leader. But does this mean that the entire revolutionary movement in Russia that preceded him, even though it was not proletarian, even though it was petty bourgeois in relation to Lenin and to Leninism, is simply archaeology and nothing more? Does it mean that it is only an object of certain academic investigations and that we shall not get a better understanding of Leninism if we approach it from this end?

What kind of person was Lenin, not as the leader of the proletarian revolution but as the man who concluded the Russian revolutionary movement in general? I repeat, comrades, that I feel a certain, if you wish, scabrousness, slipperiness in my situation, and therefore in justification of my stand I ought to cite a few quotations from the writings of the same Vladimir Il'ich about whom we have gathered to speak. Above all, in matters of culture Lenin was absolutely alien to all guild exclusivism. He openly declared that with regard to culture communism was not something invented by the working class, or discovered by it for the first time, but rather the completion of a long chain of developments in which men had taken part long before the rise of the proletariat. Lenin put it this way:

We can build communism only on the basis of the totality
of knowledge, organisations and institutions, only by using
the stock of human forces and means that have been left
to us by the old society.

. . . [A] proletarian culture . . . is not clutched out of
thin air; it is not an invention of those who call themselves experts in proletarian culture. That is all nonsense. Proletarian culture must be the logical development
of the store of knowledge mankind has accumulated under
the yoke of capitalist, landowner and bureaucratic society.[1]

Thus Lenin understood as well as anyone in our party
understood the continuity of culture with its entire preceding
history; he understood it just as well as Marx understood.
However, we can find quotations even closer to our theme.
At one time it seemed to me personally that Vladimir Il'ich
was treating our immediate predecessors in the revolutionary
movement without very much feeling. When I suggested to
him, I remember it was 1906, that we observe the twenty-fifth
anniversary of March 1 and honor the memory of Zheliabov
and Perovskaia[2] by publishing an article in our central organ,
he received it unfavorably and said: "Well, so what? They
died. Honor and glory to them, but there is no reason to start
talking about it." It seemed to me then that this indicated a
certain coldness, a moral break with that earlier stage of the
revolutionary movement. Now I understand that it simply
reflected a tactic, an unwillingness, in a moment of intense
struggle with the Social Revolutionaries, to extol their method
of struggle, to pay even any posthumous compliments to terror.
From his point of view to do so was inopportune, and therefore he turned down my proposal at that time. Yet from the
speech of Nadezhda Konstantinovna [Krupskaia] to the Congress of Soviets, and still more from the excellent biography
of Il'ich which Comrade Zinoviev wrote as early as 1918 on
the occasion of the attempt on his life, it is evident that Lenin's
real attitude to his predecessors was different. Nadezhda Konstantinovna has emphasized that Lenin was descended from
that heroic period in our revolutionary movement which was

unquestionably represented by "The People's Will" (*Narodnaia Volia*) and its predecessors.[3] Zinoviev has devoted a whole page which I am not going to read to you—it's too long and would take a lot of time—a whole page to an account of Vladimir Il'ich's attitude to the members of "The People's Will," and has shown this attitude to have been exceptionally warm, almost enthusiastic.[4] In Lenin's opinion, Zinoviev recounted, Zheliabov was the most important figure in the revolutionary movement before Marxism. You can read this page yourselves because the brochure of Comrade Zinoviev has been widely circulated. Moreover, in matters of tactics Lenin did not draw a line between himself and this earlier period as it might seem. I will cite an excerpt from the brochure *What Is to Be Done,* which came out in 1902: "But the magnificent organisation that the revolutionaries had in the seventies, and that should serve us as a model, was not established by the *Narodnaya Volya* ["The People's Will"] but by the *Zemlya i Volya* ["Land and Freedom"] which split up into the *Chorny Peredel* ["Black Repartition"] and the *Narodnaya Volya*."[5] Above all we find here an exceptionally interesting historical discovery. That magnificent organization which the revolutionaries of the seventies had, which ought to have served as a model for all of us, was not in the least created by the members of "The People's Will" but by those of "Land and Freedom." It is a discovery, because until now all histories of the Russian revolutionary movement have traced the beginning of the conspiratorial organization precisely to "The People's Will," following in this in part the example of Plekhanov, a bad example in this regard, which was not worthy of imitation. In fact, as we know from the memoirs of Vera Figner and from the autobiography of Tikhomirov (I apologize for putting these names together but the historian needs each and every source), "Land and Freedom" had already been that conspiratorial and terroristic organization which "The People's Will" was commonly thought to have been. As a matter of fact, the split was between two parts: the terroristic organization in which, as it became evident later, a terroristic and conspiratorial leading core was unquestionably in command, and a propagandistic part, which more and more passed into the background. This, I repeat, has become clear to us only now, on the basis of new documents; yet it was perfectly clear to Il'ich as early as 1902 that the real founders of the conspiratorial and militant tactics of the 1880's were the members of "Land and Freedom" and not the members of "The People's Will." I will read further: "Only a gross failure to understand Marxism (or an understanding of it in the spirit of 'Struve-ism') could prompt the opinion that the rise of a mass, spontaneous working-class movement *relieves* us of the duty of creating as good an organisation of revolutionaries as the *Zemlya i Volya* had, or, indeed, an incomparably better one. . . ."[6]

Thus, in this instance, Lenin did not in the least repudiate the revolutionary legacy of the former generation, and twelve years later in his remarkable article "On the National Pride of the Great Russians," he wrote: "We take pride in the resistance to these outrages put up from our midst, the Great Russians; in *that* midst having produced Radishchev, the Decembrists and the revolutionary commoners of the seventies. . . ."[7] Thus, starting from the Decembrists, he united all the revolutionary movements with one thread. It was not a coincidence that the slogan, epigraph, motto, which we were reading on the masthead of *The Spark (Iskra)*, were the words of one of the Decembrists: "the spark will kindle a flame." Thus in this matter Lenin was not a man who fell out of the sky into a spontaneous workers' movement and became active in it. Lenin was a man who knew how to tie the workers' movement with the enormous revolutionary torrent which had been flowing not even from the mid-nineteenth but from the eighteenth century; for Radishchev had been a contemporary of Catherine II.

And in this connection it is very interesting to view Lenin in a role other than the familiar one of the proletarian leader whom we still will need to study for many years and many decades and, especially, whom all the world will need to study, as Lenin is important to it precisely in this respect. Allow me in my lecture to dwell on Il'ich's role in the Russian revolutionary movement. Using his words I proved clearly enough that he was close to its mainstream. There can be no doubt on this account. But this is really too general. Lenin was not only related to the whole clan of Russian revolutionaries, but he had first, second, and third cousins among them, some relatives who were closer and some who were more distant. Not long ago Comrade S. I. Mitskevich established the fact that in his days as a student Vladimir Il'ich was connected with the so-called Russian Jacobins. On this ground he even came to the conclusion—in my opinion, somewhat rash—that Lenin had been under the influence of the Jacobins and had taken over something from them.[8] This was refuted by one of the oldest members of our party and an old Jacobin, Comrade Golubeva, who spoke at an evening of reminiscences held in the Society of Old Bolsheviks. She declared categorically that the doctrines of the Jacobins, that is petty-bourgeois doctrines, had not entered into Lenin's ideology and could not have entered. She was right, of course. It was not for Lenin, of course, to learn from the Russian Jacobins how to make a revolution. It is necessary to say, however, that one problem, and a problem exceptionally characteristic for Lenin, was first considered and developed by the Russian Jacobins. This was the problem of the seizure of power.

Here is a very rough and general picture of the way people usually imagined the revolutionary movement of the sixties and seventies. There had been two currents: one, the propagandistic current, which was difficult, of course, to define exactly; it was rather variegated, but if the method of Freud were employed and an attempt made to discover its unconscious nature, then without fail one would uncover the formula: propaganda and agitation evoke the mass movement that will force the autocracy to give way. That is one formula. The other formula was for the most part held by the Bakuninists. It amounted to the following: autocracy, like all political power, must simply be demolished without any further talk. Bakunin, as you know, considered even the formation of a provisional revolutionary government as a great sin, and naturally Bakunin did not even want to think about a long dictatorship, such as the dictatorship of the proletariat that has been established in Russia.

From his point of view this would have been a perversion of the entire revolution. There were, then, two movements: one was anarchist; the other, constitutional. And yet, cutting its way through these two massifs, there was a current resembling a thin thread which set as the task of the revolution the seizure of power and a prolonged dictatorship of the party seizing power; employing terror, employing the most determined measures, the party was to force the reconstruction of the old bourgeois society in accordance with a new design. This current had its source in a well-known, but for the most part poorly understood proclamation, which, moreover, was only recently printed in its entirety, entitled "Young Russia," and issued in May, 1862. The author of the proclamation, Zaichnevskii, in his old age, if I am not mistaken, lived in Orel (later even in Moscow) and had been the head of that Jacobinist movement whose echoes had reached Vladimir Il'ich in the beginning of the nineties.

"Young Russia" in many ways was an exceptionally prophetic proclamation. I had the audacity in my lectures to call it the first Bolshevik document in our history, and it seems to me that it deserves this name. You will find in it such things as public factories, nationalized industry, public shops, nationalized trade, full and unconditional equality of women—a whole series of such exceptionally interesting openings to the future. However, in the present case, something else interests us—here is how "Young Russia" anticipates what will occur on the day after the revolution: "We are . . . firmly convinced that the revolutionary party, which (if only the movement is successful) will be at the head of the government, will have to retain for a time the present system of centralization. This will certainly be necessary as regards politics, if not the administration, in order to be able to introduce as quickly as possible the new foundations of society and the economy. It will have to take the dictatorship in its own hands and stop at nothing. The elections for the National Assembly will have to be carried out under the influence of the Government, which must at once make sure that the supporters of the present régime do not take part—that is, if any of them are still alive. . . ."[9]

Further, an example from the 1848 revolution is quoted on how the revolutionaries of that time forgot to do this and as a result got Louis Napoleon Bonaparte.

You see that this scheme very much resembles the one that we followed: the revolutionary party seizes state power and holds it in its hands until the time when the new order will have taken deep root in the ground. This is not a small, temporary revolutionary government for a few weeks, but a firm, lasting dictatorship. Zaichnevskii did not say—"dictatorship of the proletariat"; he was not a Marxist, and in his day, in the year 1862, it would have been too daring to speak about the proletariat: but he gave the scheme itself. You know that the very same line was continued in the 1870's by Tkachev, on whom I will not dwell because Tkachev's ideas, his *Alarm (Nabat)*, are too well known to everyone.[10] In the eyes of most people, Tkachev was the real founder of Jacobinism; but nevertheless its founder was Zaichnevskii, and Tkachev added yet another feature. Some of you know, and the members of the Socialist Academy all know, the splendid article in *Alarm* in which Tkachev gave an analysis of the "Trial of the Fifty" in order to prove that the Bakuninist tactic of open revolutionary communes was the greatest stupidity for a party that wanted to carry out a revolution and that the tactic of a revolutionary party, not only under the conditions of Russian autocracy (although under its conditions it must be tenfold more so), must only be the conspiratorial tactic. For this reason Tkachev was advocating in his article the most strict secrecy in the whole organization from top to bottom. Now let us turn to the brochure *What Is to Be Done,* and we will find there: "Secrecy is such a necessary condition for this kind of organisation that all the other conditions (number and selection of members, functions, etc.) must be made to conform to it. It would be extremely naïve indeed, therefore, to fear the charge that we Social-Democrats desire to create a conspiratorial organisation. Such a charge should be as flattering to every opponent of Economism as the charge of following a Narodnaya Volya line."[11] So you see also in this point Lenin drew closer to the Jacobinist tradition—this time in the person of Tkachev.

Again, comrades, I categorically disassociate myself from the idea that Lenin did not arrive at this by himself under the influence of the objective conditions of the revolutionary movement or that he was a disciple of Tkachev or Zaichnevskii (about whom he perhaps had not even heard). That would be a completely stupid way of stating the problem, but it is not necessary to deny that certain elements in the Russian revolutionary movement of the sixties and seventies flowed into the Leninist tactic and were embraced by it, regardless of whether certain objective conditions were suggesting this approach. The difference between sociological and historical analysis lies precisely in that sociological analysis gives a general scheme which tells us: without a conspiratorial proletarian organization in Russia the proletariat could not win, and for this very reason Lenin created a conspiratorial organization. Historical analysis will say, however: he created it, among other things, precisely because in the Russian soil there had already existed certain models which Lenin was not ashamed of, which he referred to as examples worthy of imitation, and which facilitated the seizure of power to a significant extent—and one of these was the idea of the indispensability of the conspiratorial organization. And if we approach Leninism from this end, having emphasized the continuing tie between Lenin and the earlier generation of revolutionaries, then we will see that Leninism was a real synthesis of the whole revolutionary movement and that as always happens with great historical figures and events, a particular event and a particular figure not only begin a new period but complete the previous one. If Marx with his "Capital" completed classical political economy, crowned and superseded it, then Lenin, with his doctrine and the revolutionary movement inspired by him, concluded and superseded all earlier forms of the revolutionary movement.

Now it seems extraordinarily natural to us, like air that we breathe or water that we drink, that any revolutionary party which engages in propaganda and agitation must be well organized and conspiratorial in the revolutionary period and that its tactic must be the militant tactic of an armed uprising—the tactic of the use of force. But only owing to Lenin does this seem self-evident to us. If you look at the Russian revolutionary movement of the sixties and seventies you will note that it resembled at that time the creation of the world as pictured by the Roman poet Lucretius, one of the forefathers of contemporary materialism. In Lucretius's description of the creation of the world, in the beginning a monster without a head but with arms and legs was born; next a monster with a head but without arms and without legs. And then, gradually, through the adaptation of these monsters to life, through their battles among themselves, that harmonious world of organisms arose that we have before us today. If we take the Russian revolutionary movement of the sixties and seventies, then we get, precisely, a picture that very much resembles the picture drawn by Lucretius. It is now exceptionally difficult to imagine that the propagandists and agitators of that time formed two factions which brutally struggled against each other, brutal to such a degree that—it is a sad fact, comrades, but it must not be covered up—their quarrels were closed at the desk of the gendarme who interrogated them. These things happened to such luminaries of the movement as Nechaev and Natanson.[12] Natanson himself was saying afterwards that Nechaev had in fact betrayed him to the police, "but in return I gave him later a good thrashing." That shows how sharp was the factional enmity of the propagandists and agitators, who in our time are managed by a single department in our Central Committee; but at that time inside the *Agitprop* a desperate battle was being waged. And so, what has been said here about conspiracy seems completely elementary to us, but at that time Tkachev was an outcast, they shied away from him, and looked upon him as something illegitimate. In the depth of their souls they most likely agreed that in essence he was right, because very soon after *Alarm* the members of "Land and Freedom" assimilated precisely the tactic of strictest secrecy: yet Tkachev, nevertheless, died an outcast and was not recognized as a leader.

If we examine this first secret organization, "Land and Freedom," we will again see an extremely unusual picture. It had two parts: the terroristic, conspiratorial, organizational—

this apparatus was located in St. Petersburg, and the second part, the "villagers" who formed the propagandistic army. The staff which sat in St. Petersburg ought to have commanded the army and directed its movements. In fact, these unfortunate "villagers" were a shackle which heavily burdened the terrorists in their St. Petersburg center. The "villagers" whined and fretted that they were not being sent literature, not being sent money. They were not sent money, because the money was going for the terrorist activities. And so from time to time the "villagers" were gathered in "Peter"; they were cajoled, were given a little money, supplied with literature, and sent back to the country; but the organizers returned to their own business, that is, the preparation of terroristic acts. And it did not enter these people's heads that it was possible to use the propagandistic army for common goals. No, it was something useless, a relic of the old tradition which they did not know how to get rid of right away. The dawdling with the "villagers" dragged on in this way until the Voronezh Congress when an effective break occurred—not the beginning of a process but the completion of something that had been dragging on for more than a year. And, finally, when the members of "The People's Will" took up an armed struggle against the autocracy in a way which seems irrational to us Marxists but which under the conditions of that time was the only conceivable one, because a group of approximately five hundred revolutionaries could only talk idly or conduct guerilla warfare—when they took up this warfare, they abandoned propaganda and agitation, except for Zheliabov, a very important figure, who grasped even this issue and led the agitation among the workers, created a program for the worker members of "The People's Will," etc. He was the single exception, however, unless you count Khalturin,[13] who doubled as a terrorist and a leader of workers but did not combine the two. Insofar as Khalturin was a labor leader, he was not a terrorist; insofar as he became a terrorist, he ceased to be a labor leader. With the exception of these two figures, the mass of terrorists, busy in their laboratories and diggings, did not engage in propaganda or agitation and, what is more, even considered certain kinds of agitation harmful. Even Zheliabov recommended a little less talk about the agrarian question because it might frighten the bourgeoisie from whom "The People's Will" was getting its material means.

And so, having considered all this, you begin to perceive clearly to what extent Lenin was the man of synthesis who knew how to coordinate into one harmonious whole, to draw together all those revolutionaries of the old days who had forgotten one another and fought against each other. Lenin was an agitator of genius, as he seemed to us at first glance, and in this respect he had a quality indispensible to agitators—an unusual sensitivity in relation to his audience. Lenin sensed from abroad, from Paris, that the proletarian grass was sprouting in Russia; for while in exile he without doubt guessed the mood of the working masses better than did many workers here on the spot. He was an agitator incomparable in his sensitivity, who knew how to tell his audience exactly what it wanted to hear and what it needed to hear. From his letter to the Swiss workers in 1917, you know that he went to Russia with the conviction that the socialist revolution in Russia was not possible because, he wrote to the Swiss workers, Russia was the most petty-bourgeois country in Europe; yet when he arrived, he came out with his "Theses."[14] He needed to look at Petrograd only for a while to see how heated the atmosphere had become, and to understand that only the slogan of socialist revolution could satisfy the masses.* Such a course was necessary if one wanted to make any revolution at all and didn't wish to remain behind, as happened to the Mensheviks and Social Revolutionaries. Right away, in the course of several days, Lenin reconstructed his plan—he did not have to change his convictions, of course, but he changed that tactic which ap-

---

*At a session of the Socialist Academy it was pointed out to me that the April "Theses" of Il'ich had already been written in Stockholm. This does all the more honor to Lenin's sensitivity; it was not even necessary for him to see the revolutionary St. Petersburg; it was sufficient to talk to people who had been breathing its atmosphere for a short time in order to grasp the situation. [Pokrovskii's note.]

parently he had in mind when he wrote the letter to the Swiss workers. Here was a man of unusual sensitivity, and therefore he was a great agitator, exceptional in his power. In addition to this, however, we have twenty-one volumes of his works, which offer a propagandistic encyclopedia such as has not existed in the world. One cannot compare them with the works of Marx and Engels, for an enormous part of these had been taken up by purely theoretical problems which had to be solved. In Il'ich you will not find one purely theoretical work without a propagandistic approach. His celebrated "Empirio-monism,"[15] a philosophical work which was a model of vast erudition and subtlety of analysis, was a purely political pamphlet directed against Bogdanov and his doctrines—no one among us can doubt this. All of his articles on the agrarian question were precisely just such propagandistic works, many purely theoretical revelations in them notwithstanding: he threw these out in passing. He is important as a pure theorist both for historians and economists, but Il'ich's aim was always propaganda or agitation.

Finally, Lenin was an incomparable conspirator (we have forgotten about this during the last years, of course, because it is not necessary to practice conspiracy), one of the best that the Russian revolution saw. In a play by Lunacharskii, which came out in 1905, there is a character who shows very well how Lenin's conspiratorial skill was reflected in the consciousness of a philistine. He says that Lenin could not be captured: first, he is young, then old, then small, then a huge lanky fellow, then a man, then a woman. This is odd, of course, but it is remarkable that Il'ich, who had frequently and seriously risked his life, and had always stayed close to the crucible of revolution, never again fell into the hands of the tsarist police after the nineties, the years when he had lacked experience. With a remarkable intuition he guessed the moment when he must leave. I was present at his departure from Finland in November, 1907. He stayed in Kuokkala, not far from St. Petersburg, for almost a year, all of 1907. And as we were living there and didn't notice anything, and it seemed to us that the situation was not changing, we could not understand why in the second

half of November, 1907, Vladimir Il'ich suddenly began to
speak about the "etheronef." Whoever has read *The Red Star*
(*Krasnaia Zvezda*) by Bogdanov, which had just been published
that year, will understand why such a term appeared.[16] He
spoke in jest, cunningly screwing up his eyes, but was nonetheless clearly "on the move." For this reason he boarded the
"etheronef"—that was an express train to Helsingfors—and left.
In a few days, approximately, the police raided our village and
paraded with throngs of prisoners. It was completely obvious
to everyone that they would have taken Lenin. For the first few
minutes the Mensheviks had laughed at him and jeered.
Martov wrote to Axelrod: "Lenin naturally left first." But—
alas!—in Martov's next letter we read: "and Dan had to
escape."[17] Therein lies the difference: Dan "escaped" but Lenin
didn't "escape"; he simply *left,* and was able to do it thanks to
his great conspiratorial skill.

I would like to make another comparison which might
perhaps not occur to us. When we see our Red Army with its
tanks, heavy guns, airplanes, and so forth, we do not think of
our armed workers, detachments of 1905, with their "Bulldogs
[revolvers]," Brownings, and so on. But the Red Army ought to
salute precisely the image of this detachment of that year, at
which all reasonable philistines were laughing so much—salute
not the detachment itself, for that has been gone for a long
time, but its image, because that was the *social* ancestor of our
Red Army. From what did it descend? From that advocacy of
an armed uprising which Lenin started at a time when the
philistines were respectfully looking up to the Zemstvo leaders,
virtually seeing in them a nucleus of the Constituent Assembly. It was just then that Il'ich was writing about an armed
uprising. I recall that even such a firmly Bolshevik institution
as the Moscow Committee of the party as late as the summer of
1905 treated with some scepticism the armed uprising as a
practical problem. Yet in December barricades were already
being built on the streets of Moscow, and rifles and Mausers
were cracking. And in this regard, with respect to the armed
struggle, Lenin had absorbed the best of what the preceding
revolutionary period had accomplished—and he threw this out

as a slogan which has remained until our days and has material-
ized in our Red Army.

This is what I wanted to say about Lenin in connection
with the Russian revolutionary movement. I repeat: for a long
time many generations of people will honor in him above all
the leader of the world proletariat and will more rarely think
of Lenin as the greatest *Russian* revolutionary. But it would
be unjust to the author of the article "On the National Pride
of the Great Russians" not to place this modest historical
wreath on his grave as well.

XII

Lenin as a Revolutionary Leader

Comrades! . . .

. . . I do not think I will be able to tell you anything new on this matter. I would like to dwell on two questions which, in my opinion, have previously not been touched upon either in articles or in speeches, though to read through all the articles which have appeared on Vladimir Il'ich recently is an absolutely impossible task. There have been many articles on the topic on which I wish to speak. And for this reason, even though Comrade Zinoviev spoke very disapprovingly about the tendency to pursue certain historical parallels (Comrade Zinoviev said in his speech to the Congress of Soviets that "bourgeois scribblers" are trying to find parallels to Lenin in the past),[1] I still regard these parallels as interesting because they depict for us in greater relief the personality and importance of Il'ich. Therefore, allow me to consider these parallels. To speak, however, in general about the importance of Il'ich to such a meeting as yours is completely unnecessary. Old party comrades, you know perfectly well what Lenin means in the history of our party. The first question which I would like to

Originally delivered as a lecture at the training courses for district party secretaries. First published in *Pod znamenem marksizma*, 1924, no. 2, pp. 63–73; reprinted in *Oktiabr'skaia revoliutsiia* (Moscow, 1929), pp. 13–24 (with omissions).

touch upon is: what exactly made Lenin a leader? We Marxists may not consider personality as a creator of history. For us personality is that apparatus through which history acts. Perhaps one day these apparatuses will be created artificially, as we now build electric accumulators artificially. But for the time being this is not so. For the present these apparatuses through which history acts, these accumulators of the social process, are born spontaneously. In this case, then, what qualities make a man suitable for the role of leader? This matter, in my opinion, is brought into relief with exceptional vividness when one considers Lenin and some parallels between Lenin and other political figures.

It seems to me now that the essential quality of Il'ich, when you look back at the past, is his colossal political courage. Political courage—that's not ordinary bravery. Among revolutionaries there are a lot of brave people who do not fear the gallows, or the rope, or hard labor. But these people are afraid to assume the responsibility for great political decisions. The characteristic trait of Il'ich was that he was not afraid to assume the responsibility for political decisions of any size. In this respect he did not retreat in the face of any risk; he took upon himself the responsibility for steps on which hung the fate not only of his own person or of his party, but that of the whole country and to some extent of the world revolution. Because this was such an unusual phenomenon, Il'ich always launched all his actions with a very small group, in as much as there were very few people to be found who were bold enough to follow him. Let me remind you how Lenin campaigned in favor of an armed uprising in 1904–5. This picture seems grandiose to us now when we know what happened later, but to the contemporary philistines it seemed ridiculous. A man in a torn jacket, sitting in the city of Geneva, had declared a fight to the death—against whom?—Russian autocracy, which was governing a land of one hundred and twenty million with a hundred thousand spies and a million bayonets. He threw down the gauntlet. I remember how the bourgeois professors regarded this. For them the word "comrade" was pronounced with nothing less than ridicule. He was an obvious fool. A man who followed Lenin was one of those fools who thought that in Russia it was possible to organize an armed uprising. Lenin was not afraid of this derision and in general did not fear the immensity of this task; he did not even fear that it meant a call for bloodshed and that blood would be shed. Although the first attempt failed, Il'ich did not lose heart. There were many people who became hysterical after December, 1905, saying that there was nothing left for Lenin to do but blow out his brains—but he did not blow out his brains. If the first try did not succeed, the second one would, or the third. February, 1917, justified this tactic of Lenin, the tactic of calling for armed revolt.

This is one aspect, but he had political courage of still another kind. The first revolution failed. The tide fell. We began to quarrel about whether we were facing a small pause in the revolution—such was the view of the overwhelming majority of revolutionaries—or were we facing a long interlude during which it would be necessary to make arrangements of a different kind, to remove our makeup and revolutionary costumes and to dress ourselves for a new part? Il'ich did not decide right away in favor of an interlude, but after nearly a year of reflection he concluded that this was not a pause but a long interlude. It was necessary to reorganize in the conditions of peace. Thus, the man who had sounded the call for armed revolt began to urge us to read the newspaper *Russia* (*Rossiia*), which printed stenographic reports on the sessions of the State Duma. What a hail of ridicule this called forth on Lenin—this time not from the bourgeoisie but from our midst! Who did not jeer at him? Who did not bait him? The man had lost his fire, nothing of a revolutionary was left in him. The faction had to be recalled, the Duma faction liquidated; an armed revolt had to be called for immediately. I will not name names, but I cannot forget how one comrade who now does commendable work in one of the Union Republics, made a speech before the emigrés in Paris on the imminent armed uprising. In his opinion all the elements were present for the uprising. It was true that Mama Revolution had lain down for a little nap, but she would get up very soon and everything would begin to blaze again as before. I will not try to hide that I was one of those who thought this way. I dropped in to see Il'ich and had a prolonged conversation with him for about two hours—perhaps the longest of all those I held with him. I was arguing with him that the course he was taking would lead directly to the reformist and revisionist swamp, that it would drive the Russian workers away from revolution, to Bernsteinism. Il'ich replied that Russian history absolutely guaranteed that the Russian worker would not take such a turn. We have, he said, such a sharp class conflict that you need not worry that the Russian worker will follow the reformists. At the very same time he defended the legal press and the Duma faction. "We will use the Duma," he said.

I did not agree with him and went over to the *Vpered* group, even though I did not share the view of the comrade I mentioned that an armed revolt should be launched right away. Yet, I thought three or four years will pass and again a revolutionary situation will arise. I was thinking about the war which even at that early date was looming on the horizon and would eventually knock the workers' movement off its "peaceful track." Was it worth rebuilding the whole party, was it worth, to use the words of Comrade Bukharin, making an enormous row, a split in the party, in order to reorganize ourselves for a period of three or four years? Such an operation would not pay back the costs. Yet how did it turn out? The faction was used with extraordinary success during the war. The legal press was used even better. You know that *Pravda*, from St. Petersburg, inspired the strikes in Kharkov. The Kharkov printers went on strike after the *Pravda* articles on the strikes in the other factories in the Kharkov Province. In Kharkov, on the spot, they could not get together. All organization was stifled. *Pravda* was able to direct from St. Petersburg and did so with great success. Thus, both the Duma faction and the newspapers were employed legally in the best way and, without doubt, played an enormous role in the proletarian movement that began after Lena[2] and ended in the summer of 1914 in something really resembling a revolution. Had there been no legal press and no Duma faction, none of this would have been achieved. The underground circles would not have been able to achieve this. However, neither did Lenin over-estimate the "opportunities." Someone has recalled in a news-paper how Lenin instructed the Duma faction, how he spoke with Comrade Badaev. Badaev went to ask Il'ich, on behalf of the Duma faction, what position he should take regarding some rather complicated Kadet bill. Il'ich burst out laughing and said something like this: "Why bother listening? Just go out on the rostrum and call the bourgeoisie names. That's ex-actly why you were sent to the Duma, so that the voice of the worker would be heard there, and you leave this matter to the faction's literary group—they will work it all out—don't you rack your brains over it. There is absolutely no point." Il'ich correctly appraised the role of the faction. He valued it as a kind of mouthpiece through which the working class could speak. It would be impossible to manage without this mouth-piece. Nonetheless, in order to make this shift toward "Du-mism," Il'ich needed exceptional political courage—more than was needed to call for an armed uprising. He was called a Menshevik to his face. He was asked: What is the difference now between you and Martov? As you know, however, there was a difference. . . .

Exactly the same story was repeated in connection with the peace of Brest. All the time the Central Committee was officially supporting a revolutionary war. We were being pre-pared for this turn of events. In Brest I happened to have an ex-tremely touching, almost tragic, conversation with our prison-ers of war who were asking me if they would be able to return home soon. I told them: "Comrades, be patient—not soon, not at all, because the Germans are presenting impossible condi-tions. We must not kneel before German imperialism. We shall fight." Imagine, these unfortunate people, who had already been languishing in captivity for a very long time, agreed with me. As they saw me off they cried: "No, no, comrade, don't give up! We shall have to bear it." And so with complete earnest-ness we found ourselves, excuse me for using a Socialist-Revo-lutionary term, in a "sacrificial" mood. We knew that in this revolutionary struggle many of us would perish. We did not know that at this time within the Central Committee Il'ich was already protesting the revolutionary phrasemongering and was saying that there was nothing to fight the war with or for and that the war would lead to nothing but the defeat of Soviet Russia. For this reason, when the Central Committee, upon the initiative of Il'ich, accepted the German ultimatum, it came to us like a crash of thunder out of a clear sky. I remember that I was so exasperated that I lacked the spirit to go up to Lenin in the Catherine Hall of the Tauride Palace and greet him. It seemed to me that something morally horrible beyond the limits of belief had happened. This reaction explains why some broke away to form a group of Left Communists, arguing that since we had been attacked, we ought to repulse the robbers' assault—to do so meant to uphold the slogan which we had in fact proclaimed; having signed and declared in Brest that we were ending war but not concluding peace, we had in fact chosen revolutionary war in the event of a German attack. We used to ask German officers in Brest if it was possible that the Germans would make war on us. I remember one officer's reply: "We are not bandits." It seemed that this criminal attack left us only one course—defense. Suddenly Il'ich was saying: "Surrender, not defense." I repeat—this required a colossal political courage, a colossal conviction that there was no other way out.

In Petrograd there was enormous animation at that time among the workers. Whole factories were coming to enlist in the Red Guard. I arrived in Moscow, began to address workers' meetings there, and became convinced that the mood was only half as strong as that in Petrograd and that even the Moscow proletariat was not in favor of a revolutionary war; as for the peasants, there was no point even in talking about them. It was clear that there was nothing to fight with, even disregarding the question whether Lenin's diplomatic line (subsequently validated by the German revolution) had been correct. But, disregarding that, it was impossible to fight when the masses did not want to fight. In this case Il'ich was right in the most profound way. However, among the party leaders the mood was such that one needed to have enormous political courage to assume the responsibility for saying amidst a general atmosphere of revolutionary war: "No, peace must be concluded whatever the price."

Here you have three examples which in my opinion illustrate this side of Lenin. Try now to compare the leader of the Bolsheviks with the leaders of the other parties. Take the Social Revolutionaries—people who were brave beyond all question. They were tried by us. I served as a prosecutor,[3] and I might say with complete objectivity that they conducted themselves splendidly at the trial, even though they were threatened with a 90 percent chance of execution. They had power in the summer of 1917. On their banners they had written "socialization of the land." And what did they do about socialization of the land? They didn't do anything. They marked time on this issue, alleging that the Constituent Assembly would meet very soon and would give land, but they themselves did not know how to move the Constituent Assembly closer by even an inch and allowed the Kadets to delay it in every possible way. In the end, even before October, they began to disperse the peasant committees which were starting to take land by themselves. What was needed here? Personal courage? The Social Revolutionaries had that to a sufficient degree. Political courage was needed, and much less of it than at the time of the Brest peace. It was a much smaller feat to take away land from the landlords than to call for an armed uprising in 1905. It was enough to say—the landlords' lands are to be seized and handed over to the peasants. Nothing of the kind. Take Maslov's Socialist-Revolutionary project which was issued in October. Its phrasing allowed the landlords to keep all of their land, because enough land was left in each household for the needs of the owner, his family, and all those employed on the estate. Just what was left to take? Nothing was left. Moreover, there were various stipulations: if the estate was developed, if improvements had been carried out, it was not to be touched. Just what was left for the peasants? It turned out that the peasants were to receive the land which they had been leasing—as the Kadets had suggested. This was Maslov's project and it was not implemented. They did not manage to have their way even on this matter. Here is a parallel for you.

Take the leader of the Social Revolutionaries—Chernov. He was a Zimmerwald man, that is, an advocate of peace and an opponent of war. He held power; the whole time he was a minister, the war was going on. And not even once (Kerenskii has maliciously emphasized this in his articles: in our ministry, he has said, there was complete accord), not even once did Chernov vote against the war, against the offensive; he did not vote against capital punishment at the front—he did not vote, though he was a Zimmerwald man, and one, it seems, in good faith. I have no ground to think Chernov was an insincere man, that he was deceiving the public while in fact being a "defensist" at heart. The man was simply not courageous politically, not brave politically, and therefore not fit to be a leader.

That was Il'ich's essential quality as a leader. But, of course, that alone was not enough. Here it is necessary to speak of those of his qualities which supplemented the first, qualities which are known to you and which we will not dwell on for long. First of all, his colossal insight, which towards the end filled me with certain superstitious feelings. I often quarreled with him about practical matters, got into a mess each time, and after this operation was repeated about seven times, I stopped arguing and submitted to Il'ich, even when logic was telling me you must not act that way—but, I thought, he understands better. He sees three *arshin* deep in the ground and I cannot. This amazing insight of his revealed itself repeatedly and most clearly in the fact, known to all of you, of the argument about Article I of the party rules.[4] Today we understand that the direction the party would take was then at stake—would it be a party of the West European parliamentary type, similar to the German Social Democrats, or would it be that completely original combination of the forces of workers and intelligentsia, that completely unique alignment which is called the Bolshevik party and which represents, as experience has proved, the only instrument for actually carrying through the Communist revolution. There is no other way, because the proletariat of the whole world is engaged in the task of organizing such a party. Today it is not hard to understand this. But do you think that many understood in the year 1903 when the hairsplitting between the Mensheviks and Bolsheviks began? Not only the philistines, but even some of us "young" party men were scandalized. Why are they cursing each other: because of the wording of Article I of the rules. The philistine scoffed: how narrow-minded these people are; for the sake of three words, they are throwing dirt at each other. What a disgusting picture! Yet, nonetheless, the entire fate of the party was actually being decided at this point. If, following Martov's prescription, we had overhauled the party with the intelligentsia, all the professors and students whom Martov longed for, then the party would have turned into a friable, flabby organization of the intelligentsia which never would have carried out a revolution of any kind. It's a curious fact that later Martov understood this. This Martov, who had defended his wording of Article I of the rules by arguing that it was necessary to bring in professors and students, after discovering two professors in the Bolshevik delegation to the London Congress of 1907, fell upon them and loudly wailed about how these two professors were destroying the party (the two, by the way, had fully obeyed party discipline). They did not destroy the party, but in any case I cannot refrain from mentioning that one of those professors was Rozhkov, who has now left us. Thus Lenin's judgment on the role of professors was largely proved correct.

That is one example for you of Il'ich's insight—Article I of the rules.

I might also cite for you how he quarreled with Bogdanov, after discovering that a pile of husks, thought to be utterly unrelated to politics, contained a political kernel.[5] One had to have insight to do this. When Il'ich began to quarrel with Bogdanov on the issue of *empiriomonism,* we threw up our hands and decided that simply because of idleness abroad Lenin had gone slightly out of his mind. The moment was critical. The revolution was subsiding. We were confronted by the need for a radical change in our tactics; yet, at that time Il'ich immersed himself in the Bibliothèque Nationale, sitting there for whole days, and wrote a philosophical book as a result. The scoffing was endless. In the end, Il'ich turned out to be right. *The Worker's Truth (Rabochaia pravda)* appeared, and although Bogdanov himself was not connected with it, it had nonetheless been inspired by Bogdanov's ideas. The old platform of the collectivists was written to contain all Bogdanovian ideas, so that even here Il'ich had seen three *arshin* deep and had sensed the future: he reached depths that none of us ever had occasion to reach.

You all know, and it's not worth dwelling on, how at a later time, during the revolution itself, in 1918, Lenin spoke about state capitalism, and had even predicted NEP in his brochure *"Left-Wing" Communism—An Infantile Disorder,* in which a number of pages discusses how the bourgeoisie and capitalism automatically grow out of small-scale production.[6] Everyone more or less remembers this. This second quality, his foresight, was indissoluble from his first quality, the ability to make great decisions. As a matter of fact, Napoleon also had the latter quality and the French newspapers, meaning to flatter Il'ich, have compared Lenin to Napoleon. The eighteenth of Brumaire was, of course, a great decision, and Waterloo was also a great decision. Napoleon had this quality of a political leader, but Napoleon did not have political instinct and that was why he and his whole system fell. He was a magnificent, ideal military organizer, and in this respect he was probably superior to Il'ich. Il'ich would not have been able to do the trick which Napoleon performed in 1815, when he landed empty-handed in a France devoid of an army and war supplies and within three months, in that age before telegraph or railroad, was standing on the border with 200,000 bayonets—and they were such bayonets that they smashed the splendid Prussian army to smithereens and nearly smashed the English. That was a masterstroke in the art of war. Napoleon had great political audacity and talent for organization, but no instinct for politics. He did not understand that he was undertaking a hopeless game and that he would lose it; and he lost it much earlier than he had expected. Thus, this quality alone was not enough. Insight was also needed.

Comrades, it seems to me that with these essential traits— enormous political courage, insight, and powerful instinct— the qualities of Vladimir Il'ich as a leader are basically complete. I will not speak about his immense erudition in theory, because this is not so much the quality of Vladimir Il'ich himself as an indispensable quality of every contemporary leader. It is now impossible to be a leader, particularly of the proletariat, if one has as little education as was displayed by the leaders of the preceding generation. They needed only practical skill. Today you cannot do without theory. Today every editorial in any bourgeois newspaper is a theoretical tract, and sometimes a Marxist tract even though the author is not a Marxist. It's not necessary to talk about this. And so his qualities distinguish Il'ich as a great leader not only from the midst of simple mortals, but they even distinguish him from the midst of leaders. Here I wish to draw the parallels which I spoke about in the beginning. There are only two possible parallels. As regards the ancient world, all those Pericleses, Gracchi, and Caesars, Il'ich was compared to Julius Caesar by the Whites. In one White newspaper the comparison was made (after his first stroke in the spring of 1922) that Lenin's death would now have exactly the same importance as the death of Julius Caesar had had in the year 43 B.C. I will not make this comparison inasmuch as the ancients are known as literary types and not real men. We know virtually nothing authentic about them, because almost no documents have been preserved. A history has survived which in scholarly respects is not much superior to our "History" of Karamzin,[7] and we have to form our opinions on the basis of this more ancient Karamzin. Imagine that for the reign of Ivan the Terrible we had only Karamzin. Would we know much? But there are two leaders of recent times who represent for us genuine historical reality —Cromwell and Robespierre—one instinctively compares Il'ich with them because they were also two great revolutionary leaders.

The comparison with Robespierre is quite exaggerated—in favor of Robespierre. You have heard of Robespierre since you have taken the course on Western history. Robespierre was without doubt a great revolutionary leader who possessed the ability to make great decisions, who to a certain degree possessed foresight. What exactly was it then that destroyed him; what made him fall? You know, of course, that the Thermidorian plot was not directly a conspiracy of the right-wing bourgeoisie; Left Jacobins, for example, Billaud-Varenne and Collot d'Herbois, who were then revolutionaries, participated in it, and the former proved his Jacobinism in a worthy way. Billaud had been exiled to Cayenne. Napoleon I granted him amnesty. He proudly turned it down and refused to become a subject of Napoleon I in order to return to France. What was it that did Robespierre in? The fact that he made a lot of mistakes, by having at first pitilessly destroyed the extreme leftists like Hébert and Chaumette in the spring of 1794, and then by dealing himself the final blow with the ill-fated cult of the Supreme Being, a cult which positively no one needed except Robespierre himself. After his fall not one man in France was interested in the cult of the Supreme Being. On the contrary, this religious reaction had a most negative effect on all the Left Jacobins, the disciples of the Encyclopedists of the eighteenth century. We have quite a few statements made by people from that circle which say: "Look, there is a cult of the Supreme Being here; in Notre Dame the priests are beginning to celebrate the mass. This is a regular reaction." And Robespierre was complacently leading this reaction by introducing the cult of the Supreme Being which no one ever needed. Compare him with Il'ich, who was never forcing any subjective ideas into history, who always keenly followed the direction the historical process was taking, and who always, even with great damage to his personal pride, formulated the issues in accordance with the needs of the historical process at a given moment. Compare Il'ich at the time of the Brest peace—many knew what his personal attitude to this peace was—and compare Robespierre, who was promoting the cult of the Supreme Being without regard to the fact that no one was interested in it, that it was his personal idea which was alienating his allies from him. And if Robespierre's decisiveness was no less than that of Il'ich—and I think that even that was less, because had it been slightly greater, having understood the significance of socialism in its earlier rudimentary forms, he doubtlessly would have carried out the "agrarian law" which he sometimes spoke about, and would have taken more decisive measures to defend the poor about whom he was so fond of expatiating, too—then in foresight Robespierre was immeasurably inferior to Il'ich.

The comparison of Cromwell with Il'ich is the most popular one. This comparison has found expression in literature. A drama by Lunacharskii is steeped in this comparison.[8] What attracted Lunacharskii? Naturally, it was that combination of great statesmanship and unusual external simplicity which equally characterized Cromwell and Il'ich. At meetings I have often spoken about the head of a state of 120 million who was living in two rooms and whose secretaries wore worn-out shoes. That was an amazing picture. Take the secretaries of Poincaré or Coolidge—they probably have never even suspected that shoes with holes exist in the world. This external puritanism was extremely characteristic. It is not an essential or principal point, however. It was a very likeable trait in Il'ich, but it was not what made him a leader, nor did his historical importance rest on it. The resemblance to Cromwell ends precisely here—great statesmanship and enormous external simplicity; a simple man who lives like all people and who, at the very same time, controls the fates of millions. One has to approach this from the political angle, and what exactly was Cromwell from the viewpoint of politics? A soldier and a mystic. What did his principal acts in the English revolution amount to? The most important act of Cromwell in the English revolution amounted to the formation of the parliamentary heavy cavalry, the celebrated "Ironsides." That was the most important kind of armed force in that epoch, equivalent to the artillery of today, which decided the outcome of battles. While this force was well represented in the king's army, composed of nobles, those cavaliers by nature, as it were, the parliamentary army, consisting of journeymen, workers, and peasants, could not immediately create a force of this quality. The enormous organizational achievement of Cromwell consisted in his having created in an army of journeymen, peasants, stewards, and so forth, a heavy cavalry, that is, a force which at that time decided the outcome of battles and seemed to be a particular prerogative of the nobility. That is one aspect. The other—Cromwell was a mystic. Cromwell used to say that although he was a weak, worthless man the Lord was leading him, and so on. This second side, more than anything else, suggests itself as a contrast to our Il'ich. Il'ich was the most progressive thinker of all who have written on this terrestrial globe. You will agree with me that the Marxists represent the most advanced group in the area of social thought. The middle of the seventeenth century, when Cromwell lived, was the age of Galileo, Newton, Hobbes. Such people were working and writing in Cromwell's time. Place Newton's formula and Galileo's telescope alongside Cromwell and his arguments—that Puritans were "saints," that God was leading him, and so on—he was one of the most backward people. English puritanism was not a new trend as were communism and Bolshevism; it was the last splash of that wave which rose in the beginning of the preceding sixteenth century. And, as a matter of fact, if you are really searching for features kindred to those of Il'ich, you might sooner find them not in Cromwell but in the forefather of puritanism and militant Protestantism—in Calvin. Calvin—he was the dogmatist of the early sixteenth century. There was something in him that resembled Il'ich. Admittedly, this was not on the same level as that on which Lunacharskii has discovered a likeness with Cromwell, for Calvin was in essence a narrow, dry, and cruel man, a doctrinaire, a typical theologian-theorist. But some similarity remains all the same. First of all, he created a militant doctrine for the first half of the sixteenth century, a Protestant Leninism of its kind, the militant doctrine of Calvinism. In addition, his political organization is interesting. It resembles very much the structure of our Soviet State. There were two types of institutions. On the one hand, there were civic institutions, but in fact they were subordinated to the church institutions—the *Consistory* and the higher church synod, which legally had no rights at all but in practice directed all institutions. This very much resembles our party system: The Politbureau, on the one hand, and our Soviet system, the Council of People's Commissars and so on, on the other. Thus, certain common features may be found here. But these features are not explained by the personality of Calvin. Calvin was a severe doctrinaire, a professor of theology, and so forth. His personality had nothing in common with that of Il'ich, but the situation, the position did; to the extent that Calvinism inaugurated a struggle, to the extent that it was a nucleus of the militant Protestant organization, it had something in common with Leninism, which is exactly such a nucleus of the Communist revolution. As for Cromwell, well, he was a backward man. By the middle of the seventeenth century his ideas had become obsolete, and of course in this respect he is not suitable for any comparison with Il'ich.

If you place Il'ich next to the most important revolutionary leaders whom we have known up to now, then it must be objectively acknowledged that of these three revolutionary generations of leaders, Lenin is the greatest. This is for me an objective historical fact and not in the least a phrase from an obituary. I am convinced most profoundly that when evaluations are made in two hundred years, they will be made in the following order: in the first place, Lenin; in the second, Cromwell; and in the third, Robespierre. We may be proud that we have been contemporaries and fellow workers of the greatest revolutionary leader of the modern age; the greatest leader altogether whom the world has really known; for, I repeat, we do not know and never will find out about the leaders of the past, of antiquity.

XIII

The Historical Importance
of the October Revolution

We have almost reached the tenth anniversary of our proletarian revolution—the first proletarian revolution in the world which has triumphed. Such an event, the complete and final victory of the working class, has so far taken place only once in history. Until now, every temporary victory of revolution (not counting those cases in which a revolution was defeated before it achieved victory) has invariably been followed by a reaction. Bourgeois historians see this as a law in itself, and they are taking great pains to discover from where, out of which corner, will creep the reaction to the victorious revolution in the U.S.S.R. They have made innumerable predictions, they have been mistaken innumerable times; but to them the "law" seems irrefutable: all the hopes of the bourgeois world have been built and are being built on it; and the bourgeois ideologists are searching endlessly for the reaction they need to make the scheme complete. There is no point in hiding the fact that traces of this outlook may be detected among certain circles in our party, who seem to be seeing and sensing a

First published in *Kommunisticheskaia revoliutsiia,* 1927, no. 20, pp. 3–13. Reprinted with major cuts in *Imperialistskaia voina* (1st ed., Moscow, 1928; 2d ed., Moscow, 1931), and in full in *Izbrannye proizvedeniia,* IV, 92–103.

"reaction" which the blind and thick-skinned majority in power does not see or sense. It is a new and unusual situation—a revolution without reaction. People will probably become accustomed to this phenomenon when the working class wins in a number of countries, just as people became accustomed to flying in the air nose down, although until Pegout's "loop" this maneuver was considered the greatest misfortune of a flyer, signifying inevitable destruction.

As with everything in the world, there must, of course, be an explanation to this unusual fact—a revolution without reaction. There were certain causes which determined precisely that outcome of our revolution in October, 1917. Taken separately these causes have been pointed out more than once and enumerated more than once. For example, among others by Lenin.[1] There is no need to repeat Lenin's characterization: everyone is familiar with it. This makes it unnecessary to give a general answer to the issue under consideration. There are, however, two aspects of the matter which precisely at the present moment are worth singling out and turning particular attention to in connection with our internal and international situation.

Everyone knows the passage from one of Lenin's "Letters from Afar" in which he said that the Russian bourgeoisie was not conducting the war with its own money, and that Russian capitalism was a partner of Anglo-French capitalism.[2] As has so often happened with the descriptions that Lenin used to toss out in passing, the most profound realism of this statement has only now become clear to us after a whole series of long and detailed investigations. These investigations have established without question that Russian large-scale industry and the Russian banks on the eve of the war were regular dependents of foreign capital and that diverse groups of foreign capitalists were engaged in a mutual struggle on Russian territory long before these groups became interlaced in the mortal combat of world war. The gradual displacement from the Russian economy of the German capital which before 1910 had been predominant, or had been confidently moving toward predominance, exactly corresponded to the victory of the pro-Entente forces in Russia. We can watch this struggle in the minutest details—for example, when a factory which under the aegis of a major Anglo-French firm had been producing diverse equipment for torpedo boats halted this work instantly after its shares were acquired by a Berlin bank. The actions taken by banks, though bloodless, very accurately matched the military alignments of the future war.

Toward 1914 the dependence of Russia precisely on Anglo-French Entente capitalism had become quite marked. She no longer had a choice. The extent to which Russian imperialism slavishly obeyed its "elders" was characteristic. Like every imperialism, Russian imperialism eventually was to need an outlet to the ocean, because only when one commanded the ocean routes could one seriously speak of partitioning the world. Everyone knows that the Anglo-German collision above all was a collision of naval interests and naval armaments. Before 1914 Russian imperialism had also set "naval" goals for itself. But why was it attracted by such a "narrow" sea as the one which lies between the Black Sea and the Mediterranean, which could in the end lead Russian imperialism not even to the ocean but to one of the enclosed seas, only several times larger than our Black Sea? Why, the natural question arises, did tsarist Russia not try to establish a direct access to the ocean through Murman, which ultimately had to be used anyway, though only after the war for the Dardanelles had begun? We now know that this was not the vain dream of idle geography lovers, but that in the last prewar decade there existed a definite plan for the exploitation of the Murmansk coast as a Russian naval and merchant-marine base. Yet this project received no "further action," and, as is well known, the Murmansk railroad was constructed only during the war. It is perfectly clear why this happened: in Murman, that is, on the Atlantic Ocean (the so-called Arctic Ocean is really a mere bay of the Atlantic), Russia could not help but collide with England, and the Anglo-French imperialism that was commanding imperialist Russia had absolutely no use for this. However, at the Bosphorus and the Dardanelles Russian imperialists collided with the Germans and their grandiose plan for the Berlin-Baghdad railway. This explains why the "keys to one's own home" had to be sought on the banks of the Golden Horn and not on the banks of the Varanger Fjord. It needs only to be added that the "Murman" project belonged to none other than Witte, of whose pro-German sympathies everyone knows. In this area, too, we can see the victory of Entente capitalism over German capitalism.

During the course of the war dependence on the Entente became a yoke. The English ambassador in St. Petersburg was the second emperor, and when the first emperor failed to obey him, the second took measures to dethrone the first. And if he failed to execute these measures, it was entirely due to "absolutely unforeseen events"—the entry of the working class onto the stage. Later, after the Entente had been freed of the emperor, it began to put ministers in and out of office. The diaries of Buchanan and Paléologue[3] leave no doubt about the fact that Kerenskii had been picked and chosen by the Entente long before his "election" by the Mensheviks and the Social Revolutionaries, who in this case were playing the same role in our country which people of this sort have played and play everywhere in their relations with all imperialists. It is less well known—and for this reason worth mentioning—that even Miliukov was brought down so easily because he did not please the Entente, because he was nagging too much about the Dardanelles, the mention of which always gave England a wry face. It was not the Entente which expelled its tactless servant—the masses drove him out—but it did not defend him, it "offered him as a sacrifice." Four months later, after the Entente also became disappointed in Kerenskii, Kornilov was picked to replace him—Buchanan's diary leaves no doubt about precisely who did this. At the same time American capitalism, which has been more inclined to "economic" pressure than to military plots, put the Social-Revolutionary leaders directly on its payroll; moreover, what is particularly piquant and interesting, on a *private* payroll, at the personal expense of an American millionaire. "Service" can not go further than that.

You should have seen the panic in that camp when the masses, the real masses and not those extras of Kerenskii, came to power. Today we have all the documentary records of that panic. It is nonsense that the Bolsheviks had allegedly concluded peace in spite of a resolute protest by yesterday's "Allies," who were reminding Russia of its "honor and conscience," etc., while the wretched Bolsheviks, needless to say, were paying no attention whatsoever to these protests. In fact, *along with* these official protests the English, Americans, and other Entente elements unofficially kept on whispering to the petty-bourgeois parties whom the October Revolution had overthrown—the content of these whisperings may briefly be put thus: why didn't you fools have the sense to conclude some kind of peace in time? For now with this card the Bolsheviks will trump you until you're finished! And then, after the summer had ended, there began a quest for raspberries. The English ambassador Buchanan, the uncrowned emperor of yesterday, who had become an "undesirable element" under surveillance in Petrograd, cabled his minister that nothing could have been more sensible than "to give Russia back her word"[4] since she did not want to fight. She definitely did not want to; nothing could be done about it. They had forgotten how under Kerenskii soldiers were forcibly being driven back to the battle. Similar thoughts began to stir even in the thick brain of the American ambassador Francis. At the front at this time the Kerenskii men who had lost power were scratching their heads with all five fingers and trying to think up a way to have Chernov—not Lenin—get the job of concluding peace. And finally they hit upon one. Soon afterward the most stupid and base proclamation circulated along the front, contending with an unheard-of shamelessness that it was precisely the Bolsheviks who were the main obstacle to the conclusion of peace:[5] after all, no one had recognized them, so who would negotiate with them? On the other hand, if one placed a government "of all socialist parties" at the head of the state, with Victor Mikhailovich Chernov as its leader, then the story would be quite different. Everyone would take it for an honor to have talks with this esteemed gentleman and his esteemed colleagues, and the peace for which "the country has been waiting impatiently for three years" (as if the rule of Kerenskii with its endeavors to keep Russia in the war was not included in these three years) would be concluded in two seconds. Moreover, General Dukhonin, who refused to conduct negotiations with the Germans as ordered by the Council of People's Commissars, used to declare in private conversations that he was not at all against peace and did not mind conducting negotiations with anybody as long as it was not on behalf of the Bolsheviks, of course. The foreign military representatives who had at first reacted with a terrible outburst to the order of the Council of People's Commissars on negotiations later suddenly relented and began to say that they were, in fact, not against peace but against *disorder;* in other words, still against the Bolsheviks. Quite from their hearts (but all the same with the help of the telegraph) they declared that they and their governments were advising the conclusion of peace as soon as possible. Of course, when it turned out that of the whole front only two companies of shock troops and three squadrons of Polish uhlans were still under the command of General Dukhonin and his aides and that the commander in chief of the Western Front felt himself safe to any degree only in the quarters of the Polish general Dowbor-Muśnicki, the telegram was declared a forgery.[6]

Meanwhile "tempters" began to come to Smol'nyi Palace. These people without an official status, whose names the official diplomats tried even not to mention, were unofficially connected with the top leaders of the Entente coalition and were promising the Bolsheviks miracles, provided the Bolsheviks gave up the trump card which no one was able to beat —that is, provided they gave up the conclusion of peace. Among these "tempters" there were people of all sorts: there was the naïve French "defensist" Sadoul, who later became a Communist; there was also that extremely dubious American Robins, who combined in himself the most diverse qualities— of a miner, a colonel, and a clergyman; there was also the Englishman Lockhart, a downright spy; and the French monarchist Count de Lubersac, who looked at Lenin with "an evil eye," but who granted that the wisest thing to do was to conclude peace right away. We talked with this motley crowd, hoping to squeeze out of them those things which the newly created workers' republic frantically needed for the future, the immediate future, to carry on the desperate struggle with the entire bourgeois world: locomotives and airplanes, shells and machine guns, food and military technicians. Some of these people even remained convinced that if that particular telegram had arrived a week earlier, then, assuredly, Russia would have rejoined the war on the side of the Entente. But Lenin was squinting his eyes cunningly and preparing war not against any particular imperialism, but against imperialism in general.

All these Entente intrigues regarding a peace with Germany remind us once again how important and necessary peace was at that moment not for the Bolsheviks, as the corrupt bourgeois press was shouting, but for the *country,* the whole country, all Russia. At this moment a reaction in Russia would have expressed itself in a return to the war; that is, above all, why a reaction was impossible. In this respect the Russia of 1917–18 and the Germany of the following winter were in diametrically opposite situations. The German bourgeoisie turned out to be a bit more clever than Kerenskii & Co., and concluded peace on its own, not waiting for a victorious proletarian government to conclude it. This cut the roots out of the German revolutionary movement: not only did the revolution fail to give peace, but, on the contrary, it even threatened immediate intervention on the part of the victorious Entente. We had an intervention too, but in our country it was at the height of the last fight between two contending imperialists, the English and the German, and it could not take on any serious dimension. The Entente armies were "busy," whereas the German revolution was faced by a "relieved" Entente.

The fact that the proletarian revolution meant that Russia would withdraw from the war, however, continued to have an effect even long after peace was concluded; in a certain sense it continues to operate even to this day. For what was important in the Brest peace, which not everyone grasped at the time, was not so much the *peace* with the Germans as the *rupture* with the Entente. The bourgeoisie wailed that the peace was "indecent" and "despicable," but in fact the peace was leading Russia out of the most despicable condition that one can imagine for any country at all, in which a foreign ambassador becomes the uncrowned emperor of a country. An end was put to the Entente's yoke upon Russia, and this was most clearly expressed not so much by the fact that we concluded peace as by the fact that we refused to *pay all,* war and prewar, *debts.* We ceased to be "accomplices," or partners in capitalism and imperialism of whatever kind, and no one shall drive us again into that servile condition. If reaction meant war in 1917, reaction now means that a tribute in the hundred millions would be imposed on the workers and peasants of the Soviet Union. It is significant that the intelligent White-Guardists perceived long ago that the most difficult aspect of a "restoration" was precisely the question of debts. If only the Russian bourgeois could come home with a document wherein all foreign capitalists have magnanimously released the successors of the late Russian Empire from all and sundry promissory notes signed at any time by the latter! A bourgeois, however, is bourgeois for the very reason that he never absolves anyone from a single penny of debt. And as long as reaction will mean a tribute, to that day there can be no reaction, except following an armed invasion from without.

Such were the international conditions which determined that our revolution, as distinct from all its predecessors, would be a revolution without a reaction. There also occurred, however, closely related to these international conditions, an internal purification of the revolution in general and of our party in particular from the influence of those elements that in all previous revolutions had been preparing the ground for reaction.

All past revolutions, even those in which the insurgent masses were essentially proletarian, such as the Paris Commune of 1871, took place under the leadership of the *petty bourgeoisie.* The petty bourgeoisie, the urban middle class, was nowhere the *army* of the revolution, contrary to what has been sometimes said with great oversimplification; with the exception of the Russian Revolution, however, it has always been the revolutionary *staff*. The petty-bourgeois ideology prevailed even in purely bourgeois revolutions. The slogans of liberty and equality, advanced by the French Revolution at the end of the eighteenth century, were not at all the slogans of industrial capitalism for which the revolution was paving the way. The bourgeois factory does not know and can not know either liberty or equality. The masses who work in it are subordinated to the iron dictatorship of capital and are managed hierarchically. Liberty and equality—this is an ideal of the world of small producers, small artisans, each of whom works in his own corner and for this reason is "free," or imagines himself such, and each of whom strives to have his own work of an isolated artisan placed under absolutely the same conditions as the work of every other artisan. For this reason everyone should be free and equal. Such an isolated man is extremely useful to large capital: he can easily be put under control; such methods are much more convenient than to have dealings with people who are united or organized in any sort of way. The model of all revolutions, the French Revolution, after having proclaimed the rights of man and citizen, forbade the strike. Nor is the slogan of the "defense of the fatherland" a slogan of large capital, inasmuch as capital has no fatherland or, more exactly, its fatherland is wherever it can extract surplus value. "Defense of the fatherland"—this is again a typical slogan of the world of small producers for whom an "enemy invasion" means a burned-out house, a ruined farm, a stolen cow, and a raped wife. Every small producer is by nature a "defensist." Large capital takes advantage of this too; an invasion does not threaten it directly because the invaders do not usually burn stocks and bonds (in the Franco-Prussian War we have an example of how immediately after peace was concluded shares went up higher than before the war); not to mention those profits which the bourgeoisie makes on war supplies and all sorts of profiteering that goes with war. What capital needs is the defense of the market from its competitors, and not the defense of the fatherland from an enemy attack. It is easy to substitute one for the other, however; and nowhere and never have slogans of the "defense of the father-land" been so abused as in capitalist countries during the imperialist war.[7]

All modern revolutions which have taken place anywhere in the world before 1917, I repeat, were soaked to the brim with petty-bourgeois ideology, and there was a strong petty-bourgeois tinge to our first revolution of 1905–7. We should not close our eyes to the fact that this ideology commanded the allegiance of a fairly broad segment of the workers in addition to the petty-bourgeois masses that were directly participating in the revolutionary struggle. Whole industries, the printers, for example, followed the Mensheviks; and in the election to the Second Duma (1906) some of the major factories in St. Petersburg proved to be so much in the hands of the Social Revolutionaries that the latter totaled up to 40 percent of all votes in the workers' curia. The complete emancipation of the proletariat from this petty-bourgeois slag, which took place mainly before and during the war, was the main indicator of the rise of the working masses. However, the degree to which the rank and file of workers was still easily susceptible to petty-bourgeois influence is demonstrated by the "honest defensism" and the petty-bourgeois composition first of the St. Petersburg Soviet and then also of the first All-Russian Executive Committee. In the course of the revolution of 1917 conscious workers remained for a long time in the minority, and the bourgeois, mainly the urban bourgeois, prevailed over the worker.

An enormous danger lay in this. The petty bourgeoisie, with its habits and ways, is the disintegrative element in every revolution. The petty bourgeois is an individualist—and we have seen why. This means, however, that it is very difficult to organize the petty bourgeois for mass actions of any kind, it is exceptionally difficult to subordinate him to a single mood, to place him within the frame of a single plan—which the proletariat does so easily. There is always something and somebody for the petty bourgeois to oppose. He always finds it below his dignity to agree with others. Under all circumstances he must have "his own opinion." Moreover, he conceives of dictatorship only in a personal form and there are, of course, always several candidates available for the dictator. Consequently, all petty-bourgeois parties have split and still are splitting into an infinite number of small factions (the Robespierrists, Dantonists, and Hébertists in the French Revolution; the Broussists, Guesdists, Allemanists, and Jaurèsists in the French Socialist party, that typically petty-bourgeois party at the end of the nineteenth century).[8] But what is worst of all, the petty bourgeois treats even the masses in an individualist manner. He sees the mass as an individual man, driven by personal opinions, moods, and passions: petty-bourgeois historians have written an infinite number of volumes about "passions" as the motive principle of the masses. It is for this reason, incidentally, that the petty bourgeois so reluctantly accepts the theory of class struggle. It appears to him preposterous and inconceivable that there can exist objective conditions that make the hostility between the proletarian and the bourgeois irreconcilable. Why *irreconcilable?* One can always persuade, work out an agreement, arrange a deal. And so the petty bourgeois "arranges," usually at the expense of the worker, of course.

Hence, as a rule, the petty bourgeois is a typical *conciliator.* And precisely because he has the soul of a conciliator, he is "intransigent" and "does not make any compromises" in the moment of upsurge. As if in a trance, he demands immediate and decisive actions, he tolerates no halfway measures: either all or nothing. He likes least of all to subordinate his own part to the general plan of the revolutionary struggle. Simultaneously he very much likes sweeping theoretical plans. The more grandiose they are, the better. But he does not have a clear view of what will emerge from these plans. Overestimation of one's own strength and capacities, underestimation of obstacles along the way—such is one of the basic traits of the petty bourgeois.

The October Revolution had to deal with both these manifestations of the petty-bourgeois outlook. From the first, petty-bourgeois conciliationism was a roadblock for the revolution. After the petty-bourgeois parties of the Mensheviks and Social Revolutionaries found themselves in a minority at the Second Congress of the Soviets,[9] it nonetheless seemed to many people that the revolution would be unable to hold its own unless an agreement was reached with these parties which were defeated by the revolution, and that only a government composed of representatives of "all socialist parties" was capable of retaining power. It was odd to see how the generals from the Ministry of War, who were outsitting the Bolsheviks, liked this slogan—"government of the representatives of all socialist parties." While refusing to obey orders of the Council of People's Commissars, these generals were saying with serious expressions on their faces: "How can we obey one socialist party? What sort of government is one which lacks representatives from the other democratic parties?" The old man Engels was right when he said that in the moment of the victory of the socialist revolution the blackest reactionaries would be hiding behind the flag of "pure democracy."

When we now read the telephone conversations between the headquarters of different fronts and between those and the Committee for the Salvation of the Fatherland and the Revolution,[10] we see to whom the slogan "ministry of the representatives of all socialist parties" really belonged. Since the whole front had quickly gone over to the Bolshevik side, no time was left to make this experiment; and the first roadblock, the petty-bourgeois tendency to compromise, was easily and quickly removed from the path of the revolution. It was barely removed, however, when another roadblock appeared. Compromising attitudes dissolved in the light of the plain facts, but in their place petty-bourgeois "intransigence" rose up to its full height. Peace must not be concluded with the imperialists because no peace between socialism and imperialism is possible (a rather exact repetition of the phrase of Archpriest Avvakum: "there is no peace between the Lord God and Belial"). Lenin had to work hard to defeat this formulation of petty-bourgeois feelings: it took a whole month and a half, from the beginning of January to the end of February [1918], for the truly proletarian point of view on the party's tasks in the face of advancing imperialism to gain ascendancy, and this was achieved at the cost of enormous tensions in the party and enormous objective losses to the revolution.

It goes without saying that not every carrier of petty-bourgeois ideology is necessarily a petty bourgeois himself; we have seen earlier that in the past this ideology used to have the allegiance of a broad segment of the most authentic proletarians. This is why the petty-bourgeois disease has not always been unconditionally fatal to everyone. Many have cured themselves of it. The fact that even now there are people in our ranks who suffer from this disease shows how chronic the disease has become and how difficult it is to get rid of it. The petty-bourgeois outlook continues even to the present as a disintegrative force in the party, although, it should be said, the spread of this epidemic shares the fate of all recent epidemics: cholera, typhus, Spanish flu, etc.; all these epidemics are subsiding rapidly and instead of millions, as was the case in Western Europe, instead of hundreds of thousands, as was the case in this country early in 1917, now only individuals are "ill."

Thus it is enormously important that the October Revolution in purely *objective* terms dealt a most severe blow to the petty-bourgeois Weltanschauung. After concluding peace, the revolution shattered the bourgeois illusion of a "national war," a war "for the defense of the homeland." A bourgeois was capable of giving up the Dardanelles, but he was incapable of giving up the province of Grodno. The way in which the bourgeois representatives of the Central Powers at Brest were interpreting the Russian delegation's struggle against the expansionism of Austro-German imperialism shows how difficult it is for the bourgeois of any rank to give up the geographic delimitations of his "fatherland." General Hoffmann assures us that our delegates "cried with anger" when they spoke about "Russia's" loss of eighteen "Russian" provinces.[11] Czernin attributes to Trotsky the regret that "Russia" was losing about 150,000 square *verst*. It is not necessary to add that our delegates at Brest were sufficiently literate to know that the province of Grodno is not Russia and that "one hundred and fifty thousand *verst*" had to be saved not from the German yoke but from the yoke of *imperialism*. But the German bourgeois—for that is what Hoffmann was, despite his general's uniform, and Czernin, despite his title of count—were incapable of understanding even the *language* spoken by the representatives of the workers' revolution.

The proletariat was not about to shed its own blood for the defense of a geographical "fatherland," that true product of feudal conquests sanctified by antiquity. It announced loudly and clearly to all that the defense of its class interests, the defense of the achievements of its revolution mattered more to it than any nationalistic geography. Thereby it put an end once and for all to one of the pillars of the petty-bourgeois Weltanschauung. After this, it dealt a severe blow to the other petty-bourgeois fetish, a democracy based on "liberty and equality" which did not prevent nine hundred and ninety-nine out of every one thousand people from being enslaved by the remaining one. By dispersing the Constituent Assembly (at least half of which was elected by the same "votes of the befooled petty bourgeois" as the Second Duma, which Lenin had characterized in these words, had been), the proletarian dictatorship has put an end once and for all to the faith in the absolute rightness of an unorganized, atomized arithmetical majority, on which capitalist exploitation has rested and continues to rest most firmly.

The October Revolution removed the objective foundation of petty-bourgeois illusions and thereby made a revival of petty-bourgeois illusions in whatever form unusually difficult. This *fact* has exerted a stronger effect on the entire petty-bourgeois masses than thousands of the most persuasive speeches and articles ever could. That is why the bourgeois intelligentsia, the advanced and most conscious detachment of the petty bourgeoisie, is going over to the Marxist viewpoint in ever increasing numbers. One material fact is worth ten theories. And this is why a reaction in our country has been made so difficult: to leap back to the time before the Brest peace and the dispersal of the Constituent Assembly, to restore the illusions of petty-bourgeois democracy and the nationalistic fatherland is a task that cannot be performed. Petty-bourgeois sentiments, which ten years ago manifested themselves here in such a large and dangerous form, in the present day are able to rally only quite insignificant cliques which no longer represent a serious threat to the revolutionary cause, but are merely an additional reminder of the greater danger that was hanging over the party ten years ago.

Notes

INTRODUCTION

1. O. D. Sokolov, "Revoliutsioner, uchenyi, gosudarstvennyi deiatel'," *Voprosy istorii KPSS*, 1964, no. 5, p. 82.

2. M. N. Pokrovskii, "Po povodu stat'i tov. Rubinshteina," *Pod znamenem marksizma*, 1924, no. 10–11, pp. 210–11.

3. Speech at the meeting in honor of Pokrovskii's sixtieth anniversary, October 25, 1928, reprinted in *Istoricheskaia nauka i bor'ba klassov* (2 vols., Moscow-Leningrad, 1933), II, 297–98.

4. Quoted by O. D. Sokolov, "Revoliutsioner...," *op. cit.*, p. 81.

5. P. G. Vinogradov, ed., *Kniga dlia chteniia po istorii srednikh vekov* (4 vols., Moscow, 1896–99).

6. The chapter in the home-study volume and the two symposia essays were respectively: "Otrazhenie ekonomicheskogo byta v 'Russkoi pravde'," in V. N. Storozhev, ed., *Russkaia istoriia s drevneishikh vremen do Smutnogo vremeni* (Moscow, 1898), I, 518–28; "Mestnoe samoupravlenie v drevnei Rusi," in P. D. Dolgorukov and D. I. Shakhovskoi, eds., *Melkaia zemskaia edinitsa* (1st ed., St. Petersburg, 1903), pp. 186–239; "Zemskii sobor i parliament," in I. V. Gessen and A. I. Kaminka, eds., *Konstitutsionnoe gosudarstvo* (1st ed., St. Petersburg, 1905), pp. 313–41.

7. *Istoricheskaia nauka*, II, 299.

8. M. N. Pokrovskii, "Vozhd'," in N. L. Meshcheriakov, ed., *O Lenine. Vospominaniia* (Moscow, 1925), II, 18.

9. M. N. Pokrovskii, in collaboration with N. M. Nikolskii and V. N. Storozhev, *Russkaia istoriia s drevneishikh vremen* (5 vols., Moscow, 1910–13). A. I. Gukovskii, "Kak sozdavalas' 'Russkaia istoriia s drevneishikh vremen' M. N. Pokrovskogo," *Voprosy istorii*,

1968, no. 8, pp. 122–32, and no. 9, pp. 130–42, gives a valuable account of Pokrovskii's work on the book and a history of its publication, based on Pokrovskii's correspondence with the publishers.

10. "Neskol'ko dokumentov iz tsarskikh arkhivov o M. N. Pokrovskom," *Krasnyi arkhiv*, LXII (1932), 28–29.

11. "Po povodu . . . ," *Pod znamenem marksizma*, 1924, no. 10–11, p. 210.

12. M. N. Pokrovskii, "Lenin kak tip revoliutsionnogo vozhdia," *Pod znamenem marksizma*, 1924, no. 2, p. 65. (See "Lenin as a Revolutionary Leader," this volume, chap. XII.) "Bernsteinism" in the socialist parlance of the time stood for the policy of gradual democratic reforms as opposed to violent revolutionary action.

13. V. I. Lenin, *Polnoe sobranie sochinenii* (Moscow, 1959–67), XLVIII, 19. See also V. I. Lenin, *op. cit.*, XLVII, 173–74, 211.

14. Pokrovskii, "Lenin kak tip revoliutsionnogo vozhdia," *Pod znamenem marksizma*, 1924, no. 2, pp. 66–68. Cf. this volume, chap. XII.

15. V. I. Lenin, *Sochineniia* (4th ed., Moscow, 1950), XXXII, 102–3.

16. A. L. Sidorov, "Nekotorye razmyshleniia o trude i opyte istorika," *Istoriia SSSR*, 1964, no. 3, pp. 122, 125.

17. Otto Hoetzsch, "M. N. Pokrovskij," *Zeitschrift für Osteuropäische Geschichte*, VI (II) (1932), 540.

18. Bernadotte E. Schmitt, "Russia and the War," *Foreign Affairs*, XIII (1934), 133.

19. Many of those articles were printed posthumously (and with important deletions) in Pokrovskii, *Istoricheskaia nauka i bor'ba klassov* (2 vols., Moscow-Leningrad, 1933).

20. V. I. Lenin, *Polnoe sobranie sochinenii*, LXII, 90, 374.

21. "Obshchestvennye nauki v SSSR za 10 let," *Vestnik Kommunisticheskoi Akademii*, 1928, no. 26, p. 15.

22. Konstantin F. Shteppa, *Russian Historians and the Soviet State* (New Brunswick, N.J., 1962), pp. 97, 107.

23. O. D. Sokolov, "Ob istoricheskikh vzgliadakh M. N. Pokrovskogo," *Kommunist*, 1962, no. 4, pp. 76–78.

24. "Po povodu nekotoroi putanitsy," *Istorik-marksist*, 1932, no. 1–2, pp. 23–24.

25. *Istorik-marksist*, 1927, no. 4, p. 196, quoted by D. Dorotich, "History in the Soviet School, 1917–1937" (Ph.D. diss., McGill University, 1964), p. 47.

26. *Istorik-marksist*, 1927, no. 3, p. 167, and Dorotich, *op. cit.*, p. 53.

27. M. N. Pokrovsky, *Brief History of Russia*, trans. D. S. Mirsky (2 vols., New York, 1933), I, 119 (hereafter cited: *Brief History*).

28. *Ibid.*

29. Pokrovskii, *Istoricheskaia nauka*, II, 272–74, 262.
30. The preceding account is based on *op. cit.*, I, 121; II, 55, 109, 216–17, 298, 392–93, 303–4.
31. *Ocherki po istorii revoliutsionnogo dvizheniia v Rossii XIX-XX vv.* (Moscow-Leningrad, 1924), pp. 81–82.
32. The first two volumes are available in an English translation (approved, and with a special introduction, by the author). See M. N. Pokrovsky, *History of Russia from the Earliest Times to the Rise of Commercial Capitalism,* translated by J. D. Clarkson and M. R. M. Griffiths (New York, 1931; reprint ed., Bloomington, Ind., 1966).
33. See M. N. Pokrovskii, "Vneshniaia politika Rossii v kontse XIX veka," *Istoriia Rossii v XIX veke* (Moscow, 1907–10), IX, 164–236.
34. M. N. Pokrovskii, "Svoeobrazie russkogo istoricheskogo protsessa i pervaia bukva marksizma," *Pravda,* July 5, 1922, and *Istoricheskaia nauka i bor'ba klassov,* I, 151, 146–47. Trotsky replied that he always regarded Russia to have been "insufficiently primitive" to become a colony, yet "sufficiently backward" to require a "monstrous straining of the people's economic forces" for the rise of the state. See "Parokhod—ne parokhod, a barzha," *Pravda,* July 7, 1922, and *1905* (1st ed., Moscow, 1922), p. 18.
35. Karl Marx, *Capital,* trans. S. Moore and E. Aveling (New York, 1967), I, 751. (Pokrovskii's italics.) Pokrovskii quoted from a Russian translation by Stepanov. See Pokrovskii, *Istoricheskaia nauka,* I, 144.
36. Pokrovskii, *Istoricheskaia nauka,* I, 145.
37. *Brief History of Russia* consists in fact of two books. Parts I and II, which cover the material to the end of the nineteenth century, are that "briefest outline" which Pokrovskii presented in his lectures and then published. Part III was written later and is a popular history of early twentieth-century Russia.
His earlier history of Russia had been a theoretical work, designed for students and teachers of history. The reader of the later book, on the other hand, was not expected to possess any previous knowledge of history. This was addressed to that reader for whom the *ABC of Communism* by 'Comrade Bukharin' had been written. "It is necessary for the [class] conscious worker to know not only what is Communism, but also what is Russia." *Russkaia istoriia v samom szhatom ocherke* (1st ed., Moscow, 1920), p. 3; "*K* istorii SSSR (Predislovie k cheshskomu perevodu 'Russkoi istorii. . . .')," *Istorik-marksist,* XVII (1930), 17–20.
38. *Russkaia istoriia v samom szhatom ocherke* (1st ed., Moscow, 1920), p. 3.
39. *Brief History,* I, 115–16, 91, 99, 101. (Pokrovskii's italics.)
40. *Ibid.,* II, 296, 289–290.

41. M. N. Pokrovskii, *Ocherki po istorii revoliutsionnogo dvizheniia v Rossii XIX i XX vv.* (Moscow, 1924), pp. 141–42.

42. *Russkaia istoriia s drevneishikh vremen* (3d ed., Moscow, 1920), IV, 373–77, 370, 407, 418.

43. *Ocherki po istorii revoliutsionnogo dvizheniia*, pp. 7, 9, 11, and *Brief History*, I, 143.

44. It seems to me that Pokrovskii contradicted himself when he said (chap. V of this anthology) that "industrial capital" stood on the side of the "Manchesterist nobles": the "Manchesterist noble" according to Pokrovskii opposed high import tariffs (because they prevented him from buying cheap foreign farm machinery) while tariffs were indispensable for Russian industrial capital. Pokrovskii must have meant under "industrial capital" not the actual industrial interests in Russia but the principle of legal equality and liberty, as opposed to "merchant capital" which stood for inequality ("extra-economic coercion").

45. "Istoriia povtoriaetsia," *Narodnoe prosveshchenie*, no. 32, April 26, 1919, pp. 2–3.

46. *Ibid.*, pp. 3–5.

47. "Marks kak istorik," *Vestnik Sotsialisticheskoi Akademii*, 1923, no. 4, pp. 381–83.

48. "Korni bol'shevizma v russkoi pochve," *Pravda*, March 14, 1923.

49. This is a necessarily brief summary of Pokrovskii's reflections on this subject. For a fuller account see R. Szporluk, "Pokrovskii's View of the Russian Revolution," *Slavic Review*, XXVI, no. 1 (March, 1967), 70–84.

50. See Anatole G. Mazour, *Modern Russian Historiography* (2d ed., Princeton, N.J., 1958), pp. 197–98, and *The Slavonic and East European Review*, XIII (1934), 204–5, for English translations of the decree of May 16, 1934. The original is available among others in *Na fronte istoricheskoi nauki (Sbornik materialov)* (Leningrad, 1937), pp. 3–4.

51. Cf. A. Pankratova, "Za bol'shevistskoe preobrazovanie istorii," *Bol'shevik*, 1934, no. 23, pp. 35–51.

52. "V Sovnarkome Soiuza SSSR i TsK VKP(b)," *Izvestiia*, January 27, 1936, and *Na fronte*, p. 5.

53. See for example, N. Bukharin, "Nuzhna-li nam istoricheskaia nauka?," *Izvestiia*, January 27, 1936, as reprinted in *Na fronte*, pp. 86–89; M. Kammari, "Teoreticheskie korni oshibochnykh vzgliadov Pokrovskogo," *Pod znamenem marksizma*, 1936, no. 4, pp. 5–7; A. Shcheglov, "Metodologicheskie istoki oshibok M. N. Pokrovskogo," *ibid.*, 1936, no. 5, pp. 66–69; "Istoricheskaia nauka i leninism," *Bol'shevik*, 1936, no. 3, as reprinted in *Na fronte*, p. 23; "Prepoda-

vanie istorii v shkole," *Pravda*, January 27, 1936, as reprinted in *Na fronte*, p. 17.

54. B. Grekov, *et al.*, eds., *Protiv istoricheskoi kontseptsii M. N. Pokrovskogo* (Moscow-Leningrad, 1939), I; *Protiv antimarksistskoi kontseptsii M. N. Pokrovskogo* (Moscow-Leningrad, 1940), II.

55. A. Pankratova, "Razvitie istoricheskikh vzgliadov M. N. Pokrovskogo," *Protiv . . . Pokrovskogo*, I, 5. Cf. also Em. Iaroslavskii, "Antimarksistskie izvrashcheniia 'shkoly' M. N. Pokrovskogo," *ibid.*, II, 17, 20–21. See Konstantin F. Shteppa, *Russian Historians and the Soviet State* (New Brunswick, N.J., 1962), pp. 107–20, for a discussion of the symposium and its significance in the history of Soviet historiography.

56. V. P. Volgin, E. V. Tarle, and A. M. Pankratova, eds., *Dvadtsat' piat' let istoricheskoi nauki v SSSR* (Moscow-Leningrad, 1942), pp. 7–8, 9, 78.

57. E. V. Tarle, "Soviet Historical Research," *Science and Society*, VII (1943), 230.

58. N. L. Rubinshtein, *Russkaia istoriografiia* (Moscow, 1941), p. 577.

59. *Bol'shaia sovetskaia entsiklopediia* (2d ed., Moscow, 1955), XXXIII, 492–93.

60. D. Dorotich, "Disgrace and Rehabilitation of M. N. Pokrovsky," *Canadian Slavonic Papers*, VIII (1966), 167–81.

61. Kommunisticheskaia partiia Sovetskogo Soiuza, *XXII S'ezd: Stenograficheskii otchet* (Moscow, 1962), II, 185.

62. See George M. Enteen, "Soviet Historians Review Their Past: The Rehabilitation of M. N. Pokrovskii," *Soviet Studies*, XX, no. 3 (January, 1969), 306–20, for a discussion of Pokrovskii's rehabilitation. See also Kurt Marko, *Sowjethistoriker zwischen Ideologie und Wissenschaft* (Cologne, 1964).

63. M. E. Naidenov, "Velikaia Oktiabrskaia sotsialisticheskaia revoliutsiia v sovetskoi istoriografii," *Voprosy istorii*, 1957, no. 10, p. 171; Naidenov, "Problemy periodizatsii sovetskoi istoricheskoi nauki," *Istoriia SSSR*, 1961, no. 1, pp. 87, 89–90; Naidenov, "M. N. Pokrovskii i ego mesto v sovetskoi istoriografii," *Istoriia SSSR*, 1962, no. 3, pp. 65, 68, 70–71. In 1957 Naidenov presented the 1930's as a time of a great triumph for the Leninist interpretation of the Russian revolution and Stalin's *Short Course* as a crowning achievement of the Leninist school. See "Velikaia Oktiabr'skaia sotsialisticheskaia revoliutsiia v osveshchenii sovetskoi (russkoi) literatury," *Iz istorii Velikoi Oktiabrskoi sotsialisticheskoi revoliutsii. Sbornik statei* (Moscow, 1957), pp. 313, 307–8.

64. See M. V. Nechkina, "K itogam diskussii o periodizatsii," *Istoriia SSSR*, 1962, no. 2, pp. 63–69, 59, and M. V. Nechkina, I. A.

Poliakov, L. V. Cherepnin, "O proidennom puti," in N. M. Druzhinin *et al.*, eds., *Sovetskaia istoricheskaia nauka ot XX k XXII s'ezdu KPSS, Istoriia SSSR* (Moscow, 1962), p. 15.

65. S. M. Dubrovskii, "Akademik M. N. Pokrovskii i ego rol' v razvitii sovetskoi istoricheskoi nauki," *Voprosy istorii*, 1962, no. 3, pp. 24, 27–29. See also S. M. Dubrovskii, "M. N. Pokrovskii i ego rol' v marksistskoi razrabotke istorii Rossii," in M. V. Nechkina *et al.*, eds., *Ocherki istorii istoricheskoi nauki v SSSR* (Moscow, 1963), III, 225, and L. V. Cherepnin, "M. N. Pokrovskii i ego rol' v razvitii sovetskoi istoricheskoi nauki," M. V. Nechkina *et al.*, eds., *Ocherki istorii istoricheskoi nauki v SSSR* (Moscow, 1966), IV, 187, 198.

66. E. A. Lutskii, "Razvitie istoricheskoi kontseptsii M. N. Pokrovskogo," in M. Nechkina, ed., *Istoriia i istoriki* (Moscow, 1965), pp. 336–37.

67. P. Fedoseev and I. Frantsev, "Istoriia i sotsiologiia," *Kommunist*, 1964, no. 2, p. 63, and *Istoriia i sotsiologiia*, pp. 45–46.

68. M. N. Pokrovskii, *Izbrannye proizvedeniia v chetyrekh knigakh* (Moscow, 1965–67). Volumes I–II contain *Russkaia istoriia s drevneishikh vremen*, volume III is *Russkaia istoriia v samom szhatom ocherke*, and volume IV puts together articles, reviews, speeches, etc. (all previously published), grouped under the following headings: Lenin; History of the Revolutionary Movement; Historiography; Popular Education and the Higher School; Archives. Although Sokolov's introduction to volume I promised that volume IV would include also previously unpublished works, the promise has not been kept.

69. *Izbrannye proizvedeniia*, I, 71, 42–47.

70. "All historians—indeed, all involved in any kind of cultural or ideological work—were threatened," according to Jonathan Frankel, "Party Genealogy and the Soviet Historians," *Slavic Review*, XXV, no. 4 (December, 1966), 596. Stalin's intervention in historical studies is analyzed in Cyril E. Black, ed., *Rewriting Russian History* (2d ed., New York, 1962). For the text of Stalin's letter see Marin Pundeff, comp. and ed., *History in the USSR, Selected Readings* (San Francisco, 1967), pp. 91–95. (This volume contains other important documents in full or in long excerpts.) Erwin Oberländer, *Sowjetpatriotismus und Geschichte* (Cologne, 1967), provides a detailed documentation of the change in Soviet historiography.

71. *Vsesoiuznoe soveshchanie o merakh uluchsheniia podgotovki nauchno-pedagogicheskikh kadrov po istoricheskim naukam, 18–21 dekabria 1962 g.* (Moscow, 1964), p. 270.

72. *Ibid.*, p. 75.

73. *Istoriia i sotsiologiia* (Moscow, 1964), pp. 230–31.

74. A. L. Sidorov, "Nekotorye razmyshleniia o trude i opyte istorika," *Istoriia SSSR*, 1964, no. 3, p. 132.

75. "Izuchenie otechestvennoi istorii za 50 let Sovetskoi vlasti," *Voprosy istorii,* 1967, no. 11, pp. 6–7, 9–12, 17–18. Cf. Enteen, *loc. cit.,* pp. 319–20 n. If some areas of study continue to be subject to strict ideological controls, there are others where the situation is different. For a fuller picture see the essays by A. P. Mendel, D. M. Shapiro, and John Erickson in *Contemporary History in Europe: Problems and Perspectives,* ed. Donald C. Watt (New York-Washington, 1969), and John Keep, ed., *Contemporary History in the Soviet Mirror* (New York-London, 1964).

76. See Rushton Coulborn, ed., *Feudalism in History* (Princeton, N.J., 1956), pp. 415–16, for M. Szeftel's comments on the Stalinist periodization of Russian history, and D. P. Makovskii, *Razvitie tovarno-denezhnykh otnoshenii v sel'skom khoziaistve Russkogo gosudarstva v XVI veke* (Smolensk, 1963), who argues that capitalism began to rise in Russia in the sixteenth century and then was halted by unfavorable political developments. Cf. Richard Hellie, "The Foundations of Russian Capitalism," *Slavic Review,* XXVI, no. 1 (March, 1967), 152.

77. See, for example, Isaac Deutscher, *Stalin* (London, 1961), pp. 342–43, and George Lichtheim, *Marxism: An Historical and Critical Study* (New York, 1963), pp. 157–58.

78. See J. V. Stalin, *Works* (Moscow, 1955), XII, 63, for a reference to the "Bukharin, Rykov, and Tomsky platform" accusing Stalin of a "military feudal exploitation of the peasantry." See also Konstantin F. Shteppa, *Russian Historiography and The Soviet State* (New Brunswick, N.J., 1962), especially pp. 62, 73, 78–79, 86–87, Isaac Deutscher's biography of Trotsky, and Max Shachtman, *The Bureaucratic Revolution: The Rise of the Stalinist State* (New York, 1962).

79. *Literaturna Ukraina* (Kiev), June 25, 1963, p. 3. (Speech by A. Skaba, secretary of the C.C., C.P. of the Ukraine, at the plenary session of the Central Committee, C.P.S.U., Moscow, June, 1963.) The fullest account of the nationality problem in Soviet historiography is in Lowell Tillett, *The Great Friendship: Soviet Historians on the Non-Russian Nationalities* (Chapel Hill, N.C., 1969).

80. M. V. Nechkina, "K itogam diskussii o 'voskhodiashchei' i 'niskhodiashchei' stadiiam feodalizma," *Voprosy istorii,* 1963, no. 12, pp. 51, 46. To note this does not imply that Soviet historians have neglected to study the history of other countries.

CHAPTER I

1. Karl Marx, *Capital* (New York, 1967), I, 751.

CHAPTER II

1. V. I. Lenin, *The State and Revolution* (New York, 1932), p. 97.
2. See Loyd D. Easton and Kurt H. Guddat, eds. and trans., *Writings of the Young Marx on Philosophy and Society* (Garden City, N.Y., 1967), p. 185: "The spirit of bureaucracy is thoroughly Jesuitical and theological. The bureaucrats are the state's Jesuits and theologians. Bureaucracy is the priest's republic."
3. G. R. Noyes, ed., *Masterpieces of the Russian Drama* (New York, 1933), p. 93.
4. V. I. Semevskii (1848–1910), author of books on Russian peasants in the eighteenth and nineteenth centuries, and on Russian political thought and revolutionary movements.
5. E. Meyer, *Geschichte des alten Aegyptens* (Berlin, 1887).
6. See Karl Marx and V. I. Lenin, *The Civil War in France: The Paris Commune* (New York, 1968), pp. 54–55.
7. Vasilii Osipovich Kliuchevskii (1841–1911), author of studies on the political institutions and social classes in old Russia and of a *History of Russia* in 5 vols. (available in English).
8. *Polnoe sobranie zakonov Rossiiskoi Imperii* (1st series, St. Petersburg, 1830), IV, 436, decree of December 18, 1708 (hereafter cited as *PSZ*).
9. *PSZ*, IV, 721, decree of July 28, 1711. For the emperor's own highly unorthodox spelling cf. *Pis'ma i bumagi Imperatora Petra Velikogo,* vol. XI, pt. 2 (Moscow, 1964), p. 51.
10. *PSZ*, IV, 778, decree of January 16, 1712 (in the original "June," not "July" as quoted by Pokrovskii).
11. *PSZ*, VI, 662–63, decree of April 27, 1722.
12. *PSZ*, IV, 636, decree of March 5, 1711.
13. *PSZ*, IV, 635, decree of March 2, 1711. Excerpts quoted in English translation in B. Dmytryshyn, ed., *Imperial Russia, A Source Book 1700–1917* (New York, 1967), p. 15.
14. *PSZ*, VI, 291, decree of January 16, 1721. This document was titled "Reglament ili Ustav Glavnogo Magistrata," and included, in chapter X, the passage quoted by Pokrovskii.
15. See Dmytryshyn, *op. cit.*, pp. 19–21, for the "Table of Ranks" established by Peter the Great.
16. Marx and Lenin, *op. cit.*, pp. 54–55.
17. V. I. Lenin, *State and Revolution* (New York, 1932), pp. 91–92.

CHAPTER III

1. S. M. Solov'ev (1820–79), author of *History of Russia from the Earliest Times* in 29 volumes. Pokrovskii regarded Solov'ev as the most brilliant of Russian historians.

2. "Zavolochye"—area northeast of Novgorod, toward the Dvina River.

3. Ivan the Terrible (1533–84) divided his realm into two parts: the *Oprichnina*, which was under the tsar's direct rule, and *Zemshchina*, which was administered by him indirectly, retaining the *boyar* administration.

4. "The Godunovs": tsar Boris Godunov, 1598–1605, tsar Fedor Godunov, the former's son was killed shortly after his father's death; "Pseudo-Dmitrii," ruled 1605–6 (claimed to be the son of Ivan the Terrible who had been killed in 1591); Vasilii Shuiskii, tsar (1606–10) who succeeded Dmitrii and was then overthrown and succeeded by Vladislav (Wladyslaw), son of Zygmunt III of Poland (Sigismund Vasa), who was placed on the Moscow throne under the Polish pressure (1610–12).

The period between 1605 and 1613 (when Michael Romanov became tsar) is known in Russian history as *Smuta* or "The Time of Troubles."

5. See Dmytryshyn, *op. cit.*, pp. 34–40, for excerpts from Ivan Pososhkov's (1652–1726) "Book on Poverty and Wealth."

6. Pugachev rebellion (1773–74), peasant revolt in the Urals and Volga areas under Pugachev who pretended to be "Peter III" (killed in 1762), husband of Catherine II (1762–96).

7. "The "possessionary peasants" were permanently attached to certain industrial enterprises.

8. "Decembrists"—members of a conspiracy who participated in the unsuccessful uprising of December 25, 1825. They were mainly army officers of the noble class.

"Zemstvo"—provincial and county self-government, established during the Great Reforms of 1860's.

"Zemstvo movement"—moderate opposition and reform programs put forth by those active in the Zemstvo bodies.

9. V. I. Lenin, "K otsenke russkoi revoliutsii" (1908), in *Polnoe sobranie sochinenii*, XVII, 44.

10. *Osvobozhdenie* (Liberation)—opposition newspaper published by P. B. Struve in Stuttgart and Paris (1902–5). "The Union of Liberation" was a political organization advocating democratic reforms. Its members included *Zemstvo* leaders and radical intellectuals, among them Struve.

11. "Kadets"—from *konstitutsionnye demokraty* ("Constitu-

tional Democrats"), colloquial name of the Party of People's Freedom. Established in October, 1905, with leaders P. N. Miliukov and I. I. Petrunkevich. Included former members of the Union of Liberation.

12. "Octobrists," "Union of 17th October" from the date (17th October [30th October, New Style], 1905) when Nicholas II issued his Constitutional Manifesto creating an elected legislature (*Duma*) in Russia and proclaiming citizen's rights.

13. "Union of Zemstvos" and "Union of Towns" were established after the outbreak of World War I to assist the war effort (food and medical supplies). Merged in 1915 to form Union of Zemstvos and Towns (*Zemgor*). "War Industries Committees," "Special Council for Defense" (and similar councils for food supply, transport, refugees, etc.) were created in 1915, and included government officials and representatives of *zemstvo*, business, and labor organizations.

14. "Progressive Bloc"—included Duma deputies of the Kadet, Octobrist and Progressive parties, formed August, 1915, and provided the leaders of the Provisional Government after the fall of tsarism (March, 1917).

15. "Mensheviks"—the democratic and moderate of the two factions into which the Russian Social-Democratic Labor party split in 1903; expected that socialism would have to be preceded in Russia by a long period of "bourgeois democracy"; opposed to "Bolsheviks" led by Lenin.

"Social Revolutionaries," established in 1902 and led by Victor Chernov, were advocating the abolition of private ownership of land. Supported by the peasant masses, this party won a majority in the Constituent Assembly (elected November, 1917, and disbanded after one session in January, 1918). After the October coup, the left wing of the party collaborated with the Bolsheviks but broke off after the peace of Brest Litovsk.

CHAPTER IV

1. Pokrovskii is referring here to the peasant uprisings during the "Time of Troubles," 1605–13. (See also chapter III, note 4.)

CHAPTER V

1. K. D. Kavelin (1818–1885), *Mysli i zametki po russkoi istorii* (Moscow, 1866), argued that the history of Western Europe and that of Russia had been profoundly different, "had nothing in common."
2. Some of the tribes that eventually formed Kievan Rus'.
3. Pokrovskii apparently referred to N. P. Semenov, *Osvobozhdenie krestian v tsarstvovanie imperatora Aleksandra II* (3 vols. in 4 pts., St. Petersburg, 1889–92), published by M. E. Komarov. Scholars generally think that Nicholas I died a natural death.
4. Emancipation of Labor Group—the first Russian Marxist organization established in Geneva by G. V. Plekhanov (1883).

CHAPTER VI

All notes for Chapter 6 are from Pokrovskii's 1967 Soviet edition.

1. S. I. Witte, *Vospominaniia* (Moscow, 1960), III, 273–74. Cf. *The Memoirs of Count Witte,* trans. and ed. Abraham Yarmolinsky (Garden City, N.Y., and Toronto, 1921), p. 265.
2. A. A. Bibikov, *Zapiski o zhizni i sluzhbe Aleksandra Il'icha Bibikova synom ego senatorom Bibikovym* (St. Petersburg, 1817), pp. 283–84.
3. N. Dubrovin, *Istoriia voiny i vladichestva russkikh na Kavkaze,* V (St. Petersburg, 1887), 411–12; *ibid.,* VI (St. Petersburg, 1888), 302 (the bracketed words are Pokrovskii's—Soviet ed., 1967).
4. Umalat Laudaev, "Chechenskoe plemiia (s primechaniiami)," *Sbornik svedenii o kavkazskikh gortsakh,* no. 6 (Tiflis, 1872), p. 70.
5. Evg. Markov, *Rossiia v Srednei Azii. Ocherki puteshestviia po Zakavkaziiu, Turkmenii, Bukhare, Samarkandskoi, Tashkentskoi i Ferganskoi oblastiam, Kaspiiskomu mor'iu i Volge* (St. Petersburg, 1901), I, 530, 378–79, 524.
6. [V. I. Lenin, *Collected Works* (Moscow, 1960), III, 594n ("The Development of Capitalism in Russia").] V. I. Lenin, *Sobranie sochinenii,* 2d ed., III, 465n, and *Polnoe sobranie sochinenii,* III, 596n.

CHAPTER VII

1. Otto Liman von Sanders (1885–1929)—German general appointed commander of the Constantinople military district in 1913; this action caused protests by Russia, France, and Britain. The crisis was resolved when Liman was elevated to the rank of "field marshal" (which required him to give up the area command) in January, 1914.

2. *Novoe Vremia*, a conservative daily newspaper (St. Petersburg, 1868–1917).

3. Reference to the burning of Moscow in 1812, when the city was occupied by the French.

4. "Keys of Bethlehem Church": a dispute over the respective rights of Catholic and Orthodox Christians in the Holy Places was an ostensible cause of the "Crimean War" between Russia on the one side and Turkey, Britain, France, and Sardinia on the other (1854–56). Russia's defeat in the war was followed by "the age of reforms" under Alexander II (1855–81).

5. V. I. Steingel', "Zapiski," *Obshchestvennoe dvizhenie v Rossii v pervuiu polovinu XIX veka*, ed. V. I. Semevskii and P. E. Shchegolev (St. Petersburg, 1905), I, 321–475.

CHAPTER VIII

1. Pokrovskii was alluding to a widely held view that Emperor Paul I (1796–1801) had not in fact been a son of his legal father, Peter III, but rather of one of Catherine II's lovers, Saltykov. Accordingly, Paul and his descendants, including Nicholas II, were "Pseudo-Romanovs."

2. In November, 1912, the Greek army liberated the Mt. Athos monasteries from the Turkish rule. The status of Mt. Athos was determined by the London Conference of 1913 whereby the monasteries received self-government under the protection of Greece (i.e., an Orthodox power).

3. Count Bobrinskii was Russia's leading producer of sugar beet and sugar.

4. W. A. Graham Clark, *Cotton Textile Trade in Turkish Empire, Greece, and Italy* (Washington, D.C., 1908).

CHAPTER IX

1. P. G. Vinogradov, "Politicheskie pis'ma," *Russkie Vedomosti,* August 5, 14, and 19, 1905. See M. V. Nechkina *et al.,* eds., *Ocherki istorii istoricheskoi nauki v SSSR* (Moscow, 1955–), III (1963), 103–4 for a quotation from Vinogradov's article, and for Lenin's polemic with Vinogradov.

2. A. Mathiez, *La Révolution française* (3 vols., Paris, 1922–24); *Autour de Robespierre* (Paris, 1925). (Note by Soviet ed., 1967.)

3. In the Soviet edition (1967) there is an editorial note stating that Pokrovskii's view of the annexation of various peoples, and in particular of the Ukraine, by Russia was "erroneous." See *Izbrannye proizvedeniia,* IV, 64.

4. *Le Temps,* April 4, 1906, as quoted in M. N. Pokrovskii, "The 1905 Revolution and Bourgeois Europe," *Communist International,* no. 18–19, 1925, p. 57: "Without enumerating all the differences which distinguish one country from the other [France in 1789 from Russia in 1906], we must refer to one of the most essential: In Russia, i.e., with the Russian people, there is no political understanding in the exact sense of the word."

5. *Volost'*—administrative subdivision of the county (*uezd*), comprising several villages.

6. The first Constitution of the RSFSR was adopted on June 10, 1918. Pokrovskii had been a member of the Constitutional Commission appointed earlier. Article 65 deprived nonworking classes of suffrage. *Zamoskvorechie*—district of the city beyond the Moscow River.

7. Pokrovskii was elected a deputy in the Smolensk electoral district. See *Vserossiiskoe uchreditel'noe sobranie* (Moscow-Leningrad, 1930), p. 129.

8. See note 6 above.

9. The full radical program of 1905 (republic, constituent assembly, abolition of great landed property) was referred to in the controlled press, following the defeat of the revolution, as "uncut slogans."

CHAPTER X

1. Pokrovskii appears to have had in mind Woodrow Wilson's "Note to the Belligerent Governments" of December 18, 1916 (signed by Robert Lansing, secretary of state). See *The New Democracy,*

Presidential Messages . . . by Woodrow Wilson, ed. R. A. Baker and Wm. E. Dodd (2 vols., New York and London, 1926), II, 402–6.

2. G. V. Plekhanov, *Sochineniia* (Moscow, 1923–27), IV, 54. Plekhanov said at the first Congress of the Second International (Paris, 1889): "The revolutionary movement in Russia can triumph only as a revolutionary movement of the workers. No other course exists or is possible!" See also Samuel H. Baron, *Plekhanov: The Father of Russian Marxism* (Stanford, Calif., 1963).

3. "Dnevnik Nikolaia Romanova," *Krasnyi arkhiv,* 1927, I (XX), 138. (Pokrovskii's italics.)

4. Miliukov, *Istoriia vtoroi russkoi revoliutsii,* I, 20 [Pokrovskii's note]. See also P. N. Milukow [sic], *Geschichte der zweiten Russischen Revolution,* trans. Alexander Rabinowitsch (Vienna, Berlin, Leipzig, New York, n.d.), p. 42.

5. See Robert P. Browder and Alexander F. Kerensky, eds., *The Russian Provisional Government 1917* (3 vols., Stanford, Calif., 1961), I, 130–31 for Miliukov's speech.

6. *Ibid.,* pp. 132–33.

7. See the principal documents on the abdication of Nicholas II and the refusal of Grand Duke Michael to accept the throne in Browder and Kerensky, *op. cit.,* 83–116.

8. "Dnevnik Nikolaia Romanova," *op. cit.,* 1927, I (XX), 136–37. (Pokrovskii's italics.) Pokrovskii did not cite the entry for March 2 in its entirety. It continued: "At one o'clock A.M. I left Pskov with a heavy feeling about what I had experienced. There is treason and cowardice and deception around!" The text of General Ruzskii's conversation with Duma President Rodzianko is in *Krasnyi arkhiv,* 1927, II (XXII), 55–59; an abridged English version, in Browder and Kerensky, *op. cit.,* I, pp. 92–93.

9. N. N. Sukhanov, *The Russian Revolution 1917,* ed., abr., and trans. Joel Carmichael (London, New York, Toronto, 1955), pp. 48–49. (Original Russian: N. Sukhanov, *Zapiski o revoliutsii,* vol. I.)

10. *Ibid.,* pp. 6–7.

11. *Ibid.,* p. 11.

12. Cf. Alexander Kerensky, *Russia and History's Turning Point* (New York, 1965), pp. 421–22: "Toward the end of September [1917] I sent a letter to Lloyd George informing him that our army was now undergoing reorganization and would be reduced in size. I emphasized, however, that an all-out military offensive by the Western Allies in 1918 would be given all necessary support on the Russian Front, but that Russia could not undertake a major offensive. The letter was sent on to London by the British Ambassador, and to this day it lies unpublished in some British Government archive." See also George Buchanan, *My Mission to Russia* (2 vols., Boston, 1923), II, 193–94.

13. Sukhanov, *The Russian Revolution 1917*, p. 68. "Zimmerwaldians"—supporters of the peace program of internationalist socialists who met in Zimmerwald, Switzerland, in 1915.

CHAPTER XI

1. V. I. Lenin, *Collected Works* (Moscow, 1966), XXXI, 284, 287.
2. Emperor Alexander II was assassinated on March 1, 1881. Andrei Zheliabov and Sofia Perovskaia and three other conspirators were hanged on April 3, 1881.
3. Speech at the Second Congress of Soviets, January 26, 1924, reprinted in N. K. Krupskaia, *O Lenine: sbornik statei i vystuplenii* (Moscow, 1965), pp. 19–21.
4. See "N. Lenin (Vladimir Il'ich Ul'ianov). Ocherki zhizni i deiatel'nosti," in G. Zinoviev, *Sochineniia* (Leningrad, 1924), XV, 7–8, and G. Zinovieff, *Nicolai Lenin. His Life and Work* (London, n.d. [1918?]), pp. 5–6.
5. V. I. Lenin, *Collected Works* (Moscow, 1961), V, 474. (The words in square brackets added by Editor of this volume.)
6. *Ibid.*, pp. 474–75.
7. Lenin, *Collected Works* (Moscow, 1964), XXI, 103.
8. S. I. Mitskevich, "Russkie iakobintsy," *Proletarskaia revoliutsiia*, 1927, nos. 6–7, pp. 18–19. Cf. Jonathan Frankel, ed., *Vladimir Akimov on the Dilemmas of Russian Marxism 1895–1903* (Cambridge, England, 1969), pp. 4–7.
9. Quoted from Franco Venturi, *Roots of Revolution* (New York, 1966), p. 295. See *ibid.*, chapter 11 ("Young Russia") for a detailed discussion of P. G. Zaichnevskii's (1842–96) proclamation of 1862.
10. P. N. Tkachev (1844–86) published from 1875 to 1881 (irregularly) in Geneva, *Nabat* ("Alarm" or "Tocsin"). See Venturi, *op. cit.*, chapter 16 ("Petr Nikitich Tkachev"), for his biography and program. "Trial of the Fifty" took place in Moscow, March, 1877.
11. V. I. Lenin, *Collected Works* (Moscow, 1961), V, 475–76.
12. S. G. Nechaev (1847–82), coauthor (with Bakunin) of *Revolutionary Catechism*, believed that any means were admissible in the revolutionary war against autocracy; M. A. Natanson (1850–1919), who was one of the leading members of the so-called Chaikovskii Circle and of the Land and Freedom organization, favored long-term policies and did not share Nechaev's preoccupation with direct action. (See Venturi, *op. cit.*, pp. 356–57 and *passim*.)

13. S. N. Khalturin (1856–82), leader of the Northern Union of Russian Workers (created in 1878), who was engaged in Populist propaganda among the workers of St. Petersburg and organized an unsuccessful plot to kill Alexander II (explosion in the Winter Palace). Executed in 1882.

14. See "Farewell Letter to the Swiss Workers," in V. I. Lenin, *Collected Works*, XXIII, 371, and "The Tasks of the Proletariat in the Present Revolution," *op. cit.*, XXIV, 21–26.

15. Pokrovskii was misquoting the title of Lenin's "celebrated" work. Lenin wrote *Materialism and Empirio-Criticism*, published in English as vol. 14 of *Collected Works* (Moscow, 1962), and it was Bogdanov who was the author of *Empiriomonism* (St. Petersburg, 1906).

16. In Bogdanov's novel, "etheronef" was the ship used by the Martians for travel in space.

17. F. Dan and B. I. Nikolaevskii, eds., *Pis'ma P. B. Aksel'roda i Iu. O. Martova* (Berlin, 1924; reprint ed., The Hague, 1967), pp. 176–77. These passages in Martov's letter and postscript (not the next letter) slightly differ from Pokrovskii's quotation. Martov wrote: "Lenin, as usual, left first," and "[Dan] also 'escaped' to Helsingfors."

CHAPTER XII

1. "Nash Vozhd'" (speech at the second Congress of Soviets, January 26, 1924), in G. Zinoviev, *Sochineniia*, XV, 126.

2. In April, 1912, the workers in the Lena gold mines (Siberia) went on strike. The police opened fire at a protest march which followed the arrest of some of the strike leaders, killing 270 and wounding about 250 workers. The "Lena Massacre" was followed by a wave of demonstrations and strikes all over Russia.

3. See *Protsess P.S.-R. Rechi gosudarstvennykh obvinitelei: Lunacharskogo, Pokrovskogo, Krylenko . . .* (Moscow, 1922).

4. At the Second Party Congress held in Brussels (1903), Lenin proposed that Article I of the party rules define a party member as one "who recognizes the Party's program and supports it by material means *and by personal participation in one of the party organizations.*" Martov did not require "personal participation" and proposed instead "regular personal assistance under the direction of one of the party organizations." Lenin wanted to narrow down party membership to those who were active revolutionists, while Martov favored a broader, less restricted membership. See Bertram D. Wolfe, *Three*

Who Made a Revolution (Boston, 1960), pp. 240 ff. See also Leopold H. Haimson, *The Russian Marxists and the Origins of Bolshevism* (Boston, 1966), pp. 165–97.

5. For Bogdanov's controversy with Lenin, see Bertram D. Wolfe, *Three Who Made a Revolution* (Boston 1960), pp. 496–517. See also S. V. Utechin, "Philosophy and Society: Alexander Bogdanov," in Leopold Labedz, ed., *Revisionism* (New York, 1962), pp. 117–25, and Dietrich Grille, *Lenins Rivale: Bogdanov und seine Philosophie* (Cologne, 1966).

6. Lenin wrote in " 'Left-Wing' Communism—An Infantile Disorder": "Unfortunately, small-scale production is still widespread in the world, and small-scale production *engenders* capitalism and the bourgeoisie continuously, daily, hourly, spontaneously, and on a mass scale." See V. I. Lenin, *Selected Works* (3 vols., New York, 1967), III, 339.

7. Nikolai Mikhailovich Karamzin (1766–1826), author of *History of the Russian State* in 12 vols. Karamzin's Foreword to his work is available in English in M. Raeff, *Russian Intellectual History: An Anthology* (New York, 1966), pp. 117–24. See also Richard Pipes, *Karamzin's Memoir on Ancient and Modern Russia* (Cambridge, Mass., 1959).

8. "Oliver Kromvel' [Oliver Cromwell]," in A. V. Lunacharskii, *Dramatischeskie proizvdeniia* (2 vols., Moscow, n.d. [1923]), I, 481–564.

CHAPTER XIII

1. Pokrovskii was presumably referring to the "specific conditions," that, according to Lenin, had facilitated the Bolshevik victory: the ending of the war by the Bolsheviks; their taking advantage of the continuing "mortal conflict" between the imperialist powers; the large size of the country and the poor means of communications which enabled the Bolsheviks to endure a long civil war; and utilization of peasant radicalism. See " 'Left-Wing' Communism—An Infantile Disorder," in V. I. Lenin, *Selected Works* (3 vols., New York, 1967), III, 374. See also *op. cit.*, II, 543, 573–79.

2. V. I. Lenin, "Letters from Afar," in *Collected Works* (Moscow, 1964), XXIII, 335: "Russia is waging this war with foreign money. Russian capital is a *partner* of Anglo-French capital."

3. George Buchanan, *My Mission to Russia* (2 vols., Boston, 1923), Maurice Paléologue, *An Ambassador's Memoirs* (3 vols., New York, n.d. [1927?]).

4. George Buchanan, *My Mission to Russia*, II, 225.

5. "Nakanune peremiriia," *Krasnyi arkhiv*, 1927, IV (XXIII), 196, and M. N. Pokrovskii, "Bol'sheviki i front v oktiabre-noiabre 1917 goda," *Krasnaia nov'*, 1927, no. 11, pp. 165, 169 (Note by Soviet ed., 1967).

6. *Krasnyi arkhiv*, 1927, IV (XXIII), 239–241; *Krasnaia nov'*, 1927, no. 11, pp. 169–70 (Note by Soviet ed., 1967).

7. The editors of the Soviet edition (1967) of this work appended a footnote here, declaring that the concepts of "fatherland" and "defense of fatherland" were historically justified. Thus, Lenin spoke of a "socialist fatherland" after 1917, and he also approved of "defense of fatherland" in "wars for national liberation."

8. Maximilien de Robespierre (1758–94), Georges Jacques Danton (1759–94), Jacques Hébert (1757–94); Paul Broussé (1844–1912), Jules Guesde (1845–1922), Jean Allemane (1843–1935), Jean Jauès (1859–1914).

9. The Second All-Russian Congress of the Soviets of Workers and Soldiers Deputies, October 25–26 (November 7–8), 1917, met in the night following the Bolshevik take-over in Petrograd. To be distinguished from the Second *All-Union* Congress of Soviets (1924) at which Zinoviev and Krupskaia made speeches referred to in chapters XII and XI, respectively.

10. " . . . a counterrevolutionary organization formed in Petrograd in the night preceding October 26 (November 8), 1917, for the struggle against the October revolution. The Committee led the Junker armed mutiny of October 29 (November 11). After the suppression of the mutiny the Soviet power liquidated the Committee" (Soviet ed., 1967).

11. See Max Hoffmann, *War Diaries and Other Papers* (2 vols., London, 1929), II, 203: "Pokrovsky said, with tears in his eyes, it was impossible to speak of a peace without annexations when about eighteen governments [provinces] were torn from the Russian Empire." See also Ottokar Czernin, *In the World War* (New York and London, 1920), pp. 276–77. Grodno is a town in Belorussia, i.e., not in Russia.

Index